# THE *SOLARO STUDY GUIDE*

The *SOLARO Study Guide* is designed to help students achieve success in school and to provide teachers with a road map to understanding the concepts of the Common Core State Standards. The content in each study guide is 100% curriculum aligned and serves as an excellent source of material for review and practice. The *SOLARO Study Guide* introduces students to a process that incorporates the building blocks upon which strong academic performance is based. To create this resource, teachers, curriculum specialists, and assessment experts have worked closely to develop instructional pieces that explain key concepts. Every exercise question comes with a detailed solution that offers problem-solving methods, highlights concepts that are likely to be tested, and points out potential sources of errors.

The *SOLARO Study Guide* is intended to be used for reviewing and understanding course content, to prepare for assessments, and to assist each student in achieving their best performance in school.

The *SOLARO Study Guide* consists of the following sections:

## TABLE OF CORRELATIONS

The Table of Correlations is a critical component of the *SOLARO Study Guide*.

Castle Rock Research has designed the *SOLARO Study Guide* by correlating each question and its solution to Common Core State Standards. Each unit begins with a Table of Correlations, which lists the standards and questions that correspond to those standards.

For students, the Table of Correlations provides information about how each question fits into a particular course and the standards to which each question is tied. Students can quickly access all relevant content associated with a particular standard.

For teachers, the Table of Correlations provides a road map for each standard, outlining the most granular and measurable concepts that are included in each standard. It assists teachers in understanding all the components involved in each standard and where students are excelling or require improvement. The Table of Correlations indicates the instructional focus for each content strand, serves as a standards checklist, and focuses on the standards and concepts that are most important in the unit and the particular course of study.

Some concepts may have a complete lesson aligned to them but cannot be assessed using a paper-and-pencil format. These concepts typically require ongoing classroom assessment through various other methods.

## LESSONS

Following the Table of Correlations for each unit are lessons aligned to each concept within a standard. The lessons explain key concepts that students are expected to learn according to Common Core State Standards.

As each lesson is tied to state standards, students and teachers are assured that the information will be relevant to what is being covered in class.

## EXERCISE QUESTIONS

Each set of lessons is followed by two sets of exercise questions that assess students on their understanding of the content. These exercise questions can be used by students to give them an idea of the type of questions they are likely to face in the future in terms of format, difficulty, and content coverage.

## DETAILED SOLUTIONS

Some study guides only provide an answer key, which will identify the correct response but may not be helpful in determining what led to the incorrect answer. Every exercise question in the *SOLARO Study Guide* is accompanied by a detailed solution. Access to complete solutions greatly enhances a student's ability to work independently, and these solutions also serve as useful instructional tools for teachers. The level of information in each detailed solution is intended to help students better prepare for the future by learning from their mistakes and to help teachers discern individual areas of strengths and weaknesses.

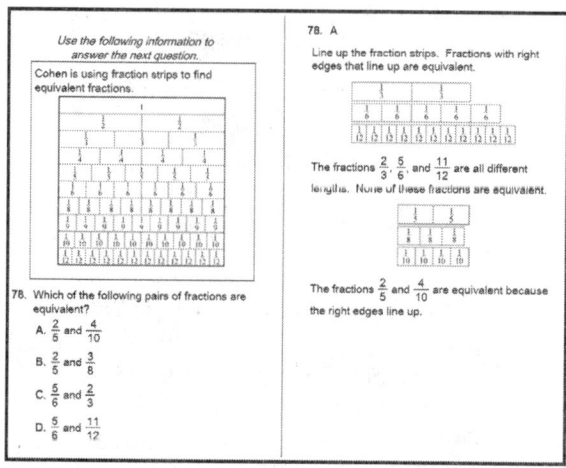

For the complete curriculum document, visit www.corestandards.org/the-standards.

**SOLARO Study Guide**s are available for many courses. Check www.solaro.com/orders for a complete listing of books available for your area.

For more enhanced online resources, please visit www.SOLARO.com.

*Student-Oriented Learning, Assessment, and Reporting Online*

SOLARO is an online resource that provides students with regionally and age-appropriate lessons and practice questions. Students can be confident that SOLARO has the right materials to help them when they are having difficulties in class. SOLARO is 100% compliant with each region's core standards. Teachers can use SOLARO in the classroom as a supplemental resource to provide remediation and enrichment. Student performance is reported to the teacher through various reports, which provide insight into strengths and weaknesses.

# SOLARO
### STUDY GUIDE

## Mathematics 4

**SOLARO Study Guide** is designed to help students achieve success in school. The content in each study guide is 100% curriculum aligned and serves as an excellent source of material for review and practice. To create this book, teachers, curriculum specialists, and assessment experts have worked closely to develop the instructional pieces that explain each of the key concepts for the course. The practice questions and sample tests have detailed solutions that show problem-solving methods, highlight concepts that are likely to be tested, and point out potential sources of errors. **SOLARO Study Guide** is a complete guide to be used by students throughout the school year for reviewing and understanding course content, and to prepare for assessments.

FARMINGDALE PUBLIC LIBRARY
116 MERRITTS ROAD
FARMINGDALE, NY 11735

Copyright © 2013 Castle Rock Research Corporation

All rights reserved. No part of this book covered by the copyright hereon may be reproduced or used in any form or by any means graphic, electronic, or mechanical, including photocopying, recording, taping, or information storage and retrieval systems without the express permission of the publisher.

Rao, Gautam, 1961 –
**SOLARO STUDY GUIDE –** Mathematics 4 (2013 Edition) Common Core State Standards

1. Mathematics – Juvenile Literature. I. Title

Castle Rock Research Corporation
2410 Manulife Place
10180 – 101 Street
Edmonton, AB T5J 3S4

1  2  3  MP  15  14  13

Printed in Canada

**Publisher**
Gautam Rao

*Dedicated to the memory of Dr. V. S. Rao*

# TABLE OF CONTENTS

**KEY TIPS FOR BEING SUCCESSFUL AT SCHOOL** ............................................................ 1
    Key Factors Contributing to School Success ............................................................ 2
    How to Find Your Learning Style ............................................................................... 3
    Scheduling Study Time .............................................................................................. 4
    Creating Study Notes ................................................................................................ 5
    Memorization Techniques ......................................................................................... 7
    Key Strategies for Reviewing .................................................................................... 7
    Key Strategies for Success: A Checklist ................................................................... 8

## CLASS FOCUS

**OPERATIONS AND ALGEBRAIC THINKING** ........................................................................ 9
    **Table of Correlations** ............................................................................................. 10
    **Concepts** ................................................................................................................ 11
        Using Multiplication to Make Comparisons
        Multiplication and Division Word Problems
        Interpreting Remainders and Estimating
        Prime and Composite Numbers
        Creating Number and Geometric Patterns
    **Exercise #1—Operations and Algebraic Thinking** ................................................. 28
    **Exercise #1—Operations and Algebraic Thinking Answers and Solutions** .......... 31
    **Exercise #2—Operations and Algebraic Thinking** ................................................. 35
    **Exercise #2—Operations and Algebraic Thinking Answers and Solutions** .......... 38

**NUMBER AND OPERATIONS IN BASE TEN** ...................................................................... 43
    **Table of Correlations** ............................................................................................. 44
    **Concepts** ................................................................................................................ 46
        Place Value
        Reading, Writing, and Comparing Whole Numbers
        Rounding Whole Numbers
        Adding and Subtracting Three- and Four-Digit Numbers
        Multiplying Two-, Three-, and Four-Digit Numbers
        Dividing Up to Four-Digit Numbers
    **Exercise #1—Number and Operations in Base Ten** ............................................... 75
    **Exercise #1—Number and Operations in Base Ten Answers and Solutions** ...... 78
    **Exercise #2—Number and Operations in Base Ten** ............................................... 87
    **Exercise #2—Number and Operations in Base Ten Answers and Solutions** ...... 91

**NUMBER AND OPERATIONS—FRACTIONS** ..................................................................... 99
    **Table of Correlations** ............................................................................................. 100
    **Concepts** ................................................................................................................ 102
        Equivalent Fractions
        Comparing Like and Unlike Denominators
        Adding and Subtracting Fractions with Like Denominators

Understanding Fractions and Mixed Numbers
Adding and Subtracting Mixed Numbers with Like Denominators
Word Problems that Use Fractions with Like Denominators
Multiplying Fractions
Solving Problems Involving Multiplying Whole Numbers by Fractions
Writing Fractions
Relating Decimals to Fractions
Ordering Decimals

Exercise #1—Number and Fractions ..................................................................................136
Exercise #1—Number and Fractions Answers and Solutions ...........................................144
Exercise #2—Number and Fractions ..................................................................................152
Exercise #2—Number and Fractions Answers and Solutions ...........................................160

## MEASUREMENT AND DATA ..................................................................................169
Table of Correlations ..........................................................................................................170
Concepts ...............................................................................................................................172

Units of Measurement
Solving Word Problems Involving Measurement
Finding Area and Perimeter
Using Line Plots
Measuring Angles
Constructing Angles
Estimating the Size of Angles
Finding Unknown Angles

Exercise #1—Measurement and Data .................................................................................207
Exercise #1—Measurement and Data Answers and Solutions ..........................................215
Exercise #2—Measurement and Data .................................................................................221
Exercise #2—Measurement and Data Answers and Solutions ..........................................230

## GEOMETRY ..............................................................................................................237
Table of Correlations ..........................................................................................................238
Concepts ...............................................................................................................................239

Identifying Lines, Rays, and Angles
Identifying Triangles and Quadrilaterals
Symmetry

Exercise #1—Geometry .......................................................................................................260
Exercise #1—Geometry Answers and Solutions ................................................................265
Exercise #2—Geometry .......................................................................................................269
Exercise #2—Geometry Answers and Solutions ................................................................274

**CREDITS**

Every effort has been made to provide proper acknowledgement of the original source and to comply with copyright law. However, some attempts to establish original copyright ownership may have been unsuccessful. If copyright ownership can be identified, please notify Castle Rock Research Corp so that appropriate corrective action can be taken. Some images in this document may be from www.clipart.com, copyright © 2013 Clipart.com, a division of Getty Images. Some images in this document may be from www.nasa.com. Some images may be from National Atmospheric and Oceanic Administration http://www.noaa.gov/. Some images may be from www.usgs.gov/.

# Key Tips for Being Successful at School

# KEY TIPS FOR BEING SUCCESSFUL AT SCHOOL

## Key Factors Contributing to School Success

In addition to learning the content of your courses, there are some other things that you can do to help you do your best at school. You can try some of the following strategies:

- **Keep a positive attitude:** Always reflect on what you can already do and what you already know.
- **Be prepared to learn:** Have the necessary pencils, pens, notebooks, and other required materials for participating in class ready.

- **Complete all of your assignments:** Do your best to finish all of your assignments. Even if you know the material well, practice will reinforce your knowledge. If an assignment or question is difficult for you, work through it as far as you can so that your teacher can see exactly where you are having difficulty.
- **Set small goals for yourself when you are learning new material:** For example, when learning the parts of speech, do not try to learn everything in one night. Work on only one part or section each study session. When you have memorized one particular part of speech and understand it, move on to another one. Continue this process until you have memorized and learned all the parts of speech.
- **Review your classroom work regularly at home:** Review to make sure you understand the material you learned in class.
- **Ask your teacher for help:** Your teacher will help you if you do not understand something or if you are having a difficult time completing your assignments.

- **Get plenty of rest and exercise:** Concentrating in class is hard work. It is important to be well-rested and have time to relax and socialize with your friends. This helps you keep a positive attitude about your schoolwork.
- **Eat healthy meals:** A balanced diet keeps you healthy and gives you the energy you need for studying at school and at home.

## HOW TO FIND YOUR LEARNING STYLE

Every student learns differently. The manner in which you learn best is called your learning style. By knowing your learning style, you can increase your success at school. Most students use a combination of learning styles. Do you know what type of learner you are? Read the following descriptions. Which of these common learning styles do you use most often?

- **Linguistic Learner:** You may learn best by saying, hearing, and seeing words. You are probably really good at memorizing things such as dates, places, names, and facts. You may need to write down the steps in a process, a formula, or the actions that lead up to a significant event, and then say them out loud.

- **Spatial Learner:** You may learn best by looking at and working with pictures. You are probably really good at puzzles, imagining things, and reading maps and charts. You may need to use strategies like mind mapping and webbing to organize your information and study notes.

- **Kinesthetic Learner:** You may learn best by touching, moving, and figuring things out using manipulatives. You are probably really good at physical activities and learning through movement. You may need to draw your finger over a diagram to remember it, tap out the steps needed to solve a problem, or feel yourself writing or typing a formula.

## SCHEDULING STUDY TIME

You should review your class notes regularly to ensure that you have a clear understanding of all the new material you learned. Reviewing your lessons on a regular basis helps you to learn and remember ideas and concepts. It also reduces the quantity of material that you need to study prior to a test. Establishing a study schedule will help you to make the best use of your time.

Regardless of the type of study schedule you use, you may want to consider the following suggestions to maximize your study time and effort:

- Organize your work so that you begin with the most challenging material first.
- Divide the subject's content into small, manageable chunks.
- Alternate regularly between your different subjects and types of study activities in order to maintain your interest and motivation.
- Make a daily list with headings like "Must Do," "Should Do," and "Could Do."
- Begin each study session by quickly reviewing what you studied the day before.
- Maintain your usual routine of eating, sleeping, and exercising to help you concentrate better for extended periods of time.

# CREATING STUDY NOTES

## MIND-MAPPING OR WEBBING

Use the key words, ideas, or concepts from your reading or class notes to create a mind map or web (a diagram or visual representation of the given information). A mind map or web is sometimes referred to as a knowledge map. Use the following steps to create a mind map or web:

1. Write the key word, concept, theory, or formula in the centre of your page.

2. Write down related facts, ideas, events, and information, and link them to the central concept with lines.

3. Use coloured markers, underlining, or symbols to emphasize things such as relationships, timelines, and important information.

The following examples of a Frayer Model illustrate how this technique can be used to study vocabulary.

| Definition | Notes |
|---|---|
| • Perimeter is the distance around the outside of a polygon. | • Perimeter is measured in linear units (e.g., metres, centimetres, and so on). |

**Perimeter**

| Examples | Non-Examples |
|---|---|
| • The length of a fence around a yard<br>• The distance around a circle (circumference) | • The area of grass covering a lawn<br>• The size of a rug lying on a floor |

| Definition | Notes |
|---|---|
| • A cube is a solid 3-D object with six faces. | • A cube is different from other shapes because it has six equally-sized square faces, eight vertices, and twelve equal edges. |

**Cube**

| Examples | Non-Examples |
|---|---|
| (dice, block with B) | (pyramid, cylinder, rectangular prism) |

## INDEX CARDS

To use index cards while studying, follow these steps:

1. Write a key word or question on one side of an index card.
2. On the reverse side, write the definition of the word, answer to the question, or any other important information that you want to remember.

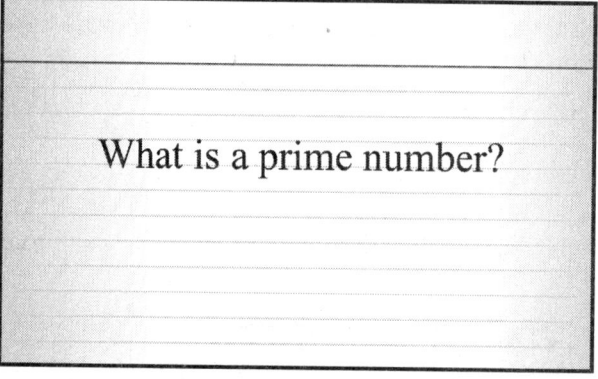

## SYMBOLS AND STICKY NOTES—IDENTIFYING IMPORTANT INFORMATION

Use symbols to mark your class notes. The following are some examples:

- An exclamation mark (!) might be used to point out something that must be learned well because it is a very important idea.
- A question mark (?) may highlight something you are not certain about
- A diamond (◊) or asterisk (*) could highlight interesting information that you want to remember.

Sticky notes are useful in the following situations:

- Use sticky notes when you are not allowed to put marks in books.
- Use sticky notes to mark a page in a book that contains an important diagram, formula, explanation, or other information.
- Use sticky notes to mark important facts in research books.

## MEMORIZATION TECHNIQUES

- **Association** relates new learning to something you already know. For example, to remember the spelling difference between dessert and desert, recall that the word *sand* has only one *s*. So, because there is sand in a desert, the word *desert* has only one *s*.

- **Mnemonic** devices are sentences that you create to remember a list or group of items. For example, the first letter of each word in the phrase "Every Good Boy Deserves Fudge" helps you to remember the names of the lines on the treble-clef staff (E, G, B, D, and F) in music.

- **Acronyms** are words that are formed from the first letters or parts of the words in a group. For example, RADAR is actually an acronym for Radio Detecting and Ranging, and MASH is an acronym for Mobile Army Surgical Hospital. HOMES helps you to remember the names of the five Great Lakes (Huron, Ontario, Michigan, Erie, and Superior).

- **Visualizing** requires you to use your mind's eye to "see" a chart, list, map, diagram, or sentence as it is in your textbook or notes, on the chalkboard or computer screen, or in a display.

- **Initialisms** are abbreviations that are formed from the first letters or parts of the words in a group. Unlike acronyms, an initialism cannot be pronounced as a word itself. For example, GCF is an initialism for **G**reatest **C**ommon **F**actor.

## KEY STRATEGIES FOR REVIEWING

Reviewing textbook material, class notes, and handouts should be an ongoing activity. Spending time reviewing becomes more critical when you are preparing for a test. You may find some of the following review strategies useful when studying during your scheduled study time:

- Before reading a selection, preview it by noting the headings, charts, graphs, and chapter questions.

- Before reviewing a unit, note the headings, charts, graphs, and chapter questions.

- Highlight key concepts, vocabulary, definitions, and formulas.

- Skim the paragraph, and note the key words, phrases, and information.

- Carefully read over each step in a procedure.

- Draw a picture or diagram to help make the concept clearer.

# KEY STRATEGIES FOR SUCCESS: A CHECKLIST

Reviewing is a huge part of doing well at school and preparing for tests. Here is a checklist for you to keep track of how many suggested strategies for success you are using. Read each question, and put a check mark (✓) in the correct column. Look at the questions where you have checked the "No" column. Think about how you might try using some of these strategies to help you do your best at school.

| **Key Strategies for Success** | Yes | No |
|---|---|---|
| Do you attend school regularly? | | |
| Do you know your personal learning style—how you learn best? | | |
| Do you spend 15 to 30 minutes a day reviewing your notes? | | |
| Do you study in a quiet place at home? | | |
| Do you clearly mark the most important ideas in your study notes? | | |
| Do you use sticky notes to mark texts and research books? | | |
| Do you practise answering multiple-choice and written-response questions? | | |
| Do you ask your teacher for help when you need it? | | |
| Are you maintaining a healthy diet and sleep routine? | | |
| Are you participating in regular physical activity? | | |

# Algebraic Thinking

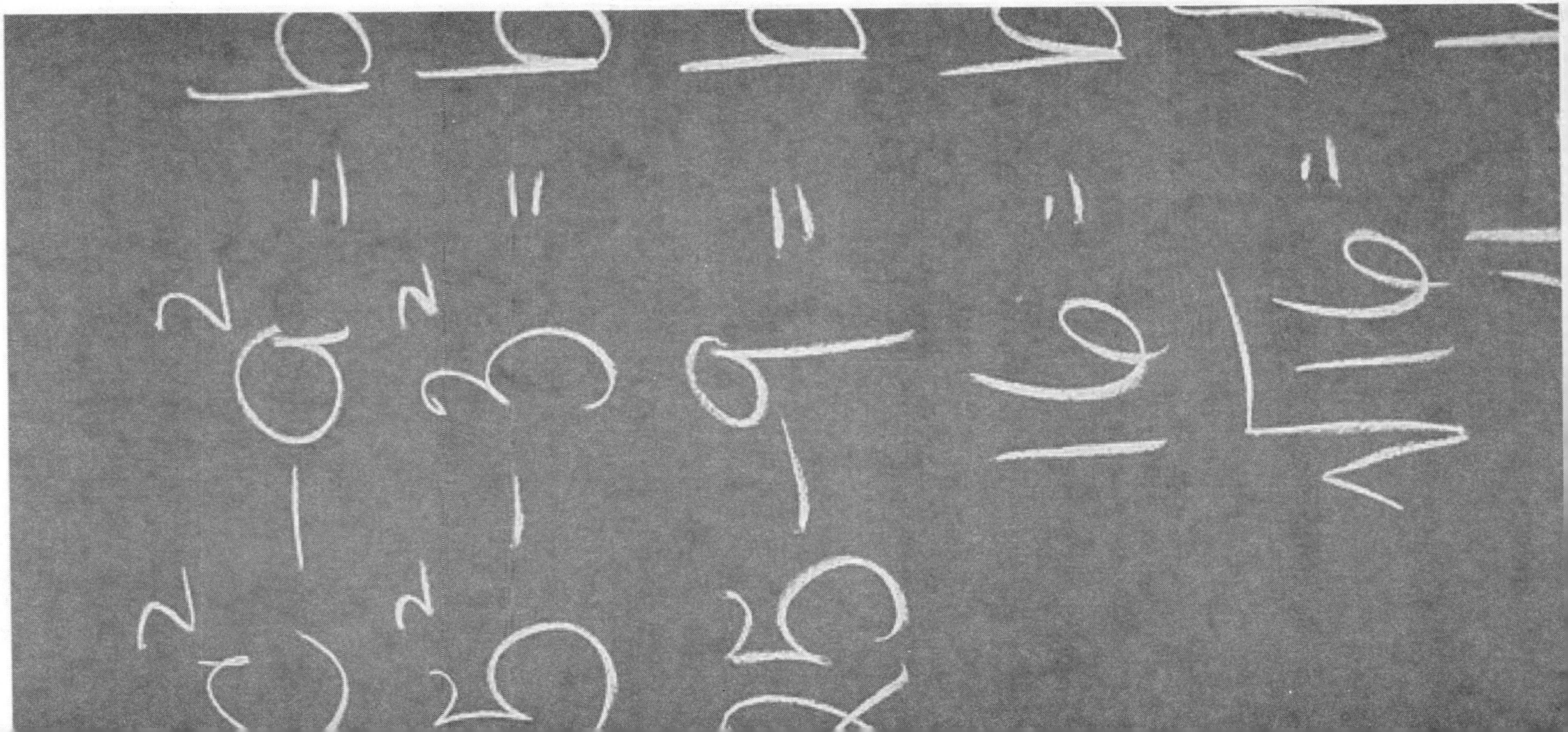

$$c^2 - a^2 = b$$
$$5^2 - 3^2 = b$$
$$25 - 9 = b$$
$$16 = b$$
$$\sqrt{16} =$$

# OPERATIONS AND ALGEBRAIC THINKING

## Table of Correlations

| Standard | | Concepts | Exercise #1 | Exercise #2 |
|---|---|---|---|---|
| 4.OA | | Operations and Algebraic Thinking | | |
| 4.OA.1 | Interpret a multiplication equation as a comparison. | Using Multiplication to Make Comparisons | 1 | 15 |
| 4.OA.2 | Multiply or divide to solve word problems involving multiplicative comparison. | Using Multiplication to Make Comparisons | 1 | 15 |
| | | Solving One-Digit by Two-Digit Multiplication Problems | 2 | 16 |
| | | Solving Two-Digit by Two-Digit Multiplication Problems | 3 | 17 |
| | | Solving Two-Digit by One-Digit Division Problems | 4 | 18 |
| | | Solving Three-Digit by One-Digit Division Problems | 5 | 19 |
| 4.OA.3 | Solve multistep word problems posed with whole numbers and having whole-number answers using the four operations, including problems in which remainders must be interpreted. Represent these problems using equations with a letter standing for the unknown quantity. Assess the reasonableness of answers using mental computation and estimation strategies including rounding. | Solving One-Digit by Two-Digit Multiplication Problems | 2 | 16 |
| | | Solving Two-Digit by Two-Digit Multiplication Problems | 3 | 17 |
| | | Solving Two-Digit by One-Digit Division Problems | 4 | 18 |
| | | Solving Three-Digit by One-Digit Division Problems | 5 | 19 |
| | | Using Symbols for Unknowns | | |
| | | Interpreting Remainders When Solving Problems | 6 | 20 |
| | | Estimating Sums of Whole Numbers up to 1,000 | 7 | 21 |
| | | Estimating Differences of Whole Numbers up to 1,000 | 10 | 22 |
| | | Solving Two-Step Problems | 8 | 23 |
| | | Estimating with Compatible Numbers to Solve Division Problems | 9 | 24 |
| 4.OA.4 | Find all factor pairs for a whole number in the range 1–100. Recognize that a whole number is a multiple of each of its factors. Determine whether a given whole number in the range 1–100 is a multiple of a given one-digit number. Determine whether a given whole number in the range 1–100 is prime or composite. | Identifying Prime Numbers | 11 | 25 |
| | | Identify Composite Numbers | 12 | 26 |
| | | Finding Multiples | 13 | 27 |
| 4.OA.5 | Generate a number or shape pattern that follows a given rule. Identify apparent features of the pattern that were not explicit in the rule itself. | Creating Number and Geometric Patterns | 14 | 28 |

*4.OA.2  Multiply or divide to solve word problems involving multiplicative comparison.*

## Using Multiplication to Make Comparisons

When you multiply, you are comparing the quantities of two amounts. For example, in the equation 3 × 5 = 15, you know that 15 is equal to 3 sets of 5 or 5 sets of 3.

To describe these relationships in words, use comparative language and say "five times more than" or "three times as many as." So, instead of saying that 15 is equal to 3 sets of 5, you will say that 15 is 3 times as many as 5 or 3 times more than 5.

*Example*
In this picture, there are 3 gumballs on the left and 18 gumballs on the right.

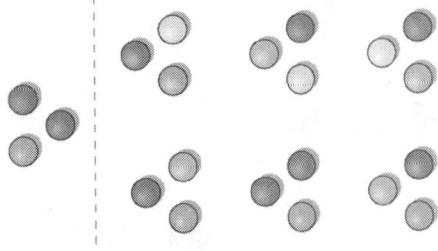

You can see that there are 6 times as many gumballs in the picture on the right. Therefore, you have identified the comparative relationship in the picture: 18 is 6 times as many as 3.
3 × 6 = 18

*Example*
   Don is 9 years old, and his uncle Clint is 27 years old.
   In words, describe the given comparative relationship by telling how many times older Clint is than Don.

*Solution*
   Because 9 × 3 = 27, Clint is 3 times older than Don.

## Solving One-Digit by Two-Digit Multiplication Problems

Many multiplication problems contain one-digit and two-digit numbers. It is important to know how to multiply two-digit numbers.

Use the following steps to solve number problems:

1. Determine what the problem is asking.
2. Identify the important information.
3. Apply the strategy or operation.
4. Check your answer.

For a multiplication problem with a two-digit number, use the following steps when you apply the operation:

1. Line up the numbers based on their place value.
2. Multiply the one-digit number by the digit in the ones place of the two-digit number. Regroup if necessary.
3. Multiply the one-digit number by the digit in the tens place of the two-digit number. Regroup if necessary.

*Example*

Tyra has 7 books, and each book has 25 pages.

Find the total number of pages in all the books.

*Solution*

**Step 1**

Determine what the problem is asking.

The problem is asking how many pages there are in all the books together.

**Step 2**

Identify the important information.

Tyra has 7 books. Each book has 25 pages.

**Step 3**

Apply the operation.

Line up the numbers based on their place value.

```
  25
×  7
```

Multiply the one-digit number by the digit in the ones place of the two-digit number.
$7 \times 5 = 35$

Regroup the 35 into 3 tens and 5 ones. Carry the 3 tens over to the tens place.

```
  ³
  25
×  7
   5
```

Multiply the one-digit number by the digit in the tens place of the two-digit number.
$7 \times 2 = 14$

Add the 3 tens that were carried over.
$14 + 3 = 17$

You have 17 tens. This is regrouped as 7 tens and 1 hundred.

```
  ³
  25
×  7
 175
```

**Step 4**

Check your answer.

Check multiplication problems using division.
$175 \div 25 = 7$

There are 175 pages in total.

## SOLVING TWO-DIGIT BY TWO-DIGIT MULTIPLICATION PROBLEMS

Multiplication problems often involve two-digit numbers. To solve a problem in which a two-digit whole number is multiplied by a two-digit whole number, use the following steps:

1. Determine what the problem is asking by identifying the important information.
2. Multiply the first two-digit number by the ones of the second number. Regroup if necessary.
3. Multiply the first two-digit number by the tens of the second number. Regroup if necessary.
4. Add the two products.

*Example*

There are 29 students in Brianne's class. Each student bakes 12 cookies for a bake sale.

In total, how many cookies will Brianne's class bake for the bake sale?

*Solution*

**Step 1**

Determine what the problem is asking by identifying the important information:

- There are 29 students.
- Each student bakes 12 cookies.
- The question asks how many cookies the class will bake in total.

The word *total* means addition or multiplication.
The number 12 could be added 29 times, but this would take a long time.
The operation needed is multiplication.

**Step 2**

Multiply 29 by the ones of the number 12, and regroup.

```
  1
  29
×  2
  58
```

**Step 3**

Multiply 29 by the tens of the number 12.

```
   29
× 10
  290
```

**Step 4**

Add the two products.

```
290
+58
348
```

Brianne's class will bake 348 cookies for the bake sale.

## SOLVING TWO-DIGIT BY ONE-DIGIT DIVISION PROBLEMS

Whenever you have a word problem, you need to decide if you will add, subtract, multiply, or divide. You need to use division if you have a problem with something being split up into smaller groups. Here are some situations when you would divide:

- You know how many things are in each group, and you want to know how many groups there are.
- You know how many groups there are, and you want to know how many things are in each group.

*Example*

Mila is making a scrapbook of her family vacation. She has 75 pictures. She can paste five pictures onto each page.

How many pages will there be in the scrapbook?

*Solution*

Decide which operation to use.

Mila has 75 pictures. She will split them up into groups of five. The operation to use is division.

**Method 1**

Use long division.

$$\begin{array}{r} 15 \\ 5\overline{)75} \\ \underline{5\downarrow} \\ 25 \\ \underline{25} \\ 0 \end{array}$$

Mila will use 15 pages.

**Method 2**

Use short division.

$$5\overline{)7^25}\phantom{0}^{1\phantom{0}5}$$

Mila will use 15 pages.

**Method 3**

Use repeated subtraction.

$$\begin{array}{r} 75 \\ -50 \\ -25 \\ 0 \end{array} \begin{array}{l} 5 \times 10 \\ 5 \times 5 \end{array} \quad 10 + 5 = 15$$

Mila will use 15 pages.

---

*Example*

Max has 84 marbles. He wants to organize them by sorting them into seven small bags.

How many marbles will go in each bag?

*Solution*

Decide which operation to use.

Max has 84 marbles. He will split them up into seven equal groups. The operation to use is division.

**Method 1**

Use long division.

$$\begin{array}{r} 12 \\ 7\overline{)84} \\ \underline{7\downarrow} \\ 14 \\ \underline{14} \\ 0 \end{array}$$

Max will put 12 marbles into each bag.

### Method 2
Use short division.

$$7\overline{)8^14}$$
  $\phantom{7)}1\ 2$

Max will put 12 marbles into each bag.

### Method 3
Use repeated subtraction.

$$\begin{array}{r} 84 \\ -70 \\ -14 \\ \hline 0 \end{array}\ \begin{array}{l} 7\times 10 \\ 7\times 2 \end{array}\ 10 + 2 = 12$$

Max will put 12 marbles into each bag.

---

## SOLVING THREE-DIGIT BY ONE-DIGIT DIVISION PROBLEMS

To solve a division problem, you need to break the whole number into smaller parts.

Use the following steps when solving a division problem:

1. Determine what the problem is asking.
2. Write the equation.
3. Carry out the operation.
4. Determine if the solution is reasonable.

*Example*

Simon makes $960 per month at his part-time job. He wants to save a week's worth of pay so he can buy a new TV.

How much money will Simon save in 1 week?

*Solution*

### Step 1
Determine what the problem is asking.
The problem is asking how much money Simon will save in 1 week from his part-time job.

### Step 2
Write the equation.
To set up the division equation, use the formula

$$\text{divisor}\overline{)\text{dividend}}^{\,\text{quotient}} = 4\overline{)960}$$

### Step 3
Carry out the operation.
Determine whether the first number in the dividend is large enough to be divided by the divisor to produce a whole number.
The number 9 is large enough. The number 4 goes into 9 twice.
Write the number 2 in the quotient portion.

```
    2
4)960
    8
    1
```

Bring down the 6, and divide 16 by 4.

```
   24
4)960
   8↓
   16
   16
    0
```

Bring down the 0, and divide 0 by 4. Even though the answer is 0, place a 0 in the quotient to hold the place value.

```
   240
4)960
   8 ↓
   16 ↓
   16 ↓
    0 0
```

### Step 4
Determine if the solution is reasonable.
Use multiplication to check if your answer is reasonable.
240 × 4 = 960
The answer is reasonable. Simon will be able to save $240 in 1 week.

---

*4.OA.3* *Solve multistep word problems posed with whole numbers and having whole–number answers using the four operations, including problems in which remainders must be interpreted. Represent these problems using equations with a letter standing for the unknown quantity. Assess the reasonableness of answers using mental computation and estimation strategies including rounding.*

## USING SYMBOLS FOR UNKNOWNS

In a problem, there is always an unknown. An **unknown** is what you are trying to find out by performing some type of operation (the solution to the problem).

A problem can be written in equation form with the unknown expressed as a symbol, such as a letter, question mark, or shape. The unknown can come anywhere in the equation.

These are some examples of ways to represent a problem using a symbol:

- Write 2 plus 3 equals a number as 2 + 3 = $N$.
- Write 2 plus a number equals 5 as 2 + ? = 5.
- Write a number plus 3 equals 5 as □ + 3 = 5.

*Example*

If Ruby has 17 pencils and then gives some away, she will have $17 - p$ pencils. In this example, $p$ is the number of pencils that she gave away. The number of pencils that she has left depends on how big $p$ is:

- If she gave away 4 pencils, then she has 13 left because $17 - 4 = 13$.
- If she gave away 15 pencils, then she has 2 left because $17 - 15 = 2$.

The letter $p$ in $17 - p$ is called a **variable**. You use a variable to show that there is a number that you do not know. The variable can represent any number.

---

*Example*

Lily picked some apples from the apple tree in her backyard. After she gave her neighbor 14 apples, she had 9 apples left. Lily's sister wants to know how many apples Lily picked.

To solve this problem, you can let the letter $A$ represent the unknown, which is the number of apples that Lily picked. Two equations that you can write to express this problem are as follows:
$A - 14 = 9$
$A = 14 + 9$

The letter $A$ is the variable in this question. It has to represent 23 because $\underline{23} - 14 = 9$ and $\underline{23} = 14 + 9$. If $A$ is any other number, it will make the equation false.

---

## INTERPRETING REMAINDERS WHEN SOLVING PROBLEMS

Many division problems result in a remainder. How the remainder is handled often depends on the context of the problem. Certain problems may involve situations requiring three different methods of interpreting remainders:

- Ignoring the remainder
- Rounding up the quotient
- Keeping the remainder as the answer

## IGNORING THE REMAINDER

These problems usually involve situations that require making teams with equal numbers or sharing items in equal groups. Breaking the remainder into bits and pieces for equal sharing does not make sense or is impossible, so the remainder is ignored.

*Example*

Mr. Kairns was organizing teams to practice running relay races during recess. As the students arrived for the practice, he made teams by placing 5 students on each team. There were 102 students that showed up.

Calculate the number of 5-student teams that could be made, and explain your answer.

*Solution*

**Step 1**
Calculate the number of teams.
Divide 102 by 5.
There can be 20 teams of 5 students with 2 students left over.

**Step 2**
Explain your answer.
There are not enough students to make another group of 5, so the 2 students left over cannot be part of a team.
Since the remainder cannot be part of the answer, it needs to be ignored.

## ROUNDING UP THE QUOTIENT

These problems usually involve situations that require purchasing items sold in packs or making accommodations for a designated number of people. Since you cannot break up the packs and need to keep the designated number of people together, it makes sense to round up the quotient.

*Example*
   Mrs. Muchler wants to buy a Halloween pencil for each one of the 127 students attending Grade 1 in her school. The local store sells Halloween pencils in packages of 8.
   Calculate how many packages Mrs. Muchler needs to buy so every Grade 1 student receives a pencil.

*Solution*
   **Step 1**
   Divide 127 by 8.
   There are 15 equal groups of 8 pencils with 7 pencils left over.
   **Step 2**
   Determine the number of packages needed.
   If Mrs. Muchler bought 15 packages (the quotient), 7 students (the remainder) would not get pencils. Therefore, the quotient needs to be rounded up to 16 so that there will be enough pencils for each student.
   Mrs. Muchler needs to buy 16 packages of pencils.

## KEEPING THE REMAINDER AS THE ANSWER

These problems usually involve questions where the remainder, not the quotient, is the answer to the problem.

*Example*
   Jonathan puts 249 hockey cards into his new card binder. Each page in the binder has 8 pockets.
   If Jonathan starts with the first page and puts one card in each pocket, how many cards will he put on the last page?

*Solution*
   **Step 1**
   Divide 249 by 8.
   Since each page holds 8 cards, Jonathan can make 31 equal groups of 8 with 1 card left over.
   **Step 2**
   Determine the number of cards on the last page.
   There will be 31 pages (the quotient) with 8 cards on each page and a remainder of 1. The remainder of 1 represents the card that will need to be placed on the last page.
   Jonathan will place 1 card on the last page of his binder.

# Estimating Sums of Whole Numbers up to 1,000

An estimate does not give an exact answer to a problem. An estimate gives an answer that is close to the correct answer.

To determine whether your estimate is reasonable, calculate the actual answer and compare it to your estimate. If the two numbers are close together, then your estimate is reasonable. If the two numbers are far apart, then your estimate is not reasonable.

There are two different strategies you can use to estimate:

1. Front-end estimation
2. Rounding

## Front-End Estimation

To estimate using front-end estimation, use only the first digit in each number and change the rest of the digits to zeros. To determine the sum, add the two estimated numbers together.

*Example*
  Estimate the sum of 342 + 534 using front-end estimation.

*Solution*

**Step 1**
Rewrite the numbers using front-end estimation. The first number remains the same, and all the other numbers are turned into zeros.
342 → 300
534 → 500

**Step 2**
Add the estimated numbers.
500 + 300 = 800
The estimated sum is 800.

**Step 3**
Check your estimate.
342 + 534 = 876
The numbers 800 and 876 are close together. This means that 800 is a good estimate.

# ROUNDING

When rounding a whole number, look at the digit to the right of the value you are rounding to. If that digit is greater than or equal to 5, round up. If the digit is less than 5, leave the number the same. All the digits after the rounded number are changed to zeros. To determine the sum, add the two estimated numbers together.

*Example*

Estimate the sum of 213 + 454 by rounding.

*Solution*

**Step 1**
Round each number to the nearest hundred.
Begin with 213. Look at the digit to the right of the value you are rounding to. The place value to the right of the hundreds is the tens. The digit in the tens is a 1. Since 1 is less than 5, the digit in the hundreds place value remains the same. All the other digits are changed to zeros.
213 → 200
Next, round 454. The digit in the tens place is a 5. Since 5 is equal to 5, the digit in the hundreds place value is rounded up. Round 4 up to 5. All the other digits are changed to zeros.
454 → 500

**Step 2**
Add the estimated numbers.
200 + 500 = 700
The estimated sum is 700.

**Step 3**
Check your estimate.
213 + 454 = 667
The numbers 700 and 667 are close together. This means that 700 is a good estimate.

---

# ESTIMATING DIFFERENCES OF WHOLE NUMBERS UP TO 1,000

An estimate does not give an exact answer to a problem. An estimate gives an answer that is close to the correct answer.

To determine if your estimate is reasonable, calculate the actual answer, and compare it to your estimate. If the two numbers are close together, then your estimate is reasonable. However, if the two numbers are far apart, then your estimate is not reasonable.

There are two different strategies you can use to estimate:

1. Front-end estimation
2. Rounding

# FRONT-END ESTIMATION

To estimate by using front-end estimation, use only the first digit in each number, and change the rest of the digits to zeros. To determine the difference, subtract the two estimated numbers.

*Example*
   Estimate the difference of 534 – 312 by using front-end estimation.

*Solution*

**Step 1**
Rewrite the numbers by using front-end estimation.
312 → 300
534 → 500

**Step 2**
Subtract the estimated numbers.
500 – 300 = 200
The estimated difference is 200.

**Step 3**
Check if your estimate is reasonable.
534 – 312 = 222
Because 200 and 222 are close together, your estimate is reasonable.

---

# ROUNDING

When you round a whole number, use the single digit to the right of the place value you are rounding to. If that digit is greater than or equal to 5, round up. If the digit is less than 5, leave the number the same. All the other digits are changed to zeros. To determine the difference, subtract the two estimated numbers.

*Example*
   Estimate the difference of 455 – 213 by rounding to the nearest hundred.

*Solution*

**Step 1**
Round each number to the nearest hundred.

For the number 213, look at the place value to the right of the place value you are rounding to. The place value to the right is the tens, and the single digit in the tens is a 1. Since 1 is less than 5, the digit in the hundreds place remains the same, and all the other digits become zeros.
213 → 200

For the number 455, look at the place value to the right of the place value you are rounding to. The place value to the right is the tens. Since the single digit in the tens is a 5, increase the digit in the hundreds place by 1, and make all the other digits zeros.
455 → 500

**Step 2**
Subtract the estimated numbers.
500 – 200 = 300
The estimated sum is 300.

Step 3
Check if your estimate is reasonable.
455 − 213 = 242
Because 300 and 242 are close together, your estimate is reasonable.

## SOLVING TWO-STEP PROBLEMS

Solving two-step problems is similar to solving regular problems. The difference is that you have to do one operation first to get a number you will need to solve the rest of the question.

To solve two-step problems follow these steps:

1. Determine what the problem is asking.
2. Identify the important information.
3. Choose the operations to use.
4. Carry out the first operation.
5. Carry out the second operation.

The following keywords tell you when to use the different operations:

- Addition: sum, total, equal, greater than, plus
- Subtraction: difference, less than, reduced, minus
- Multiplication: times, multiply, product
- Division: groups, quotient, each, divide

*Example*

Mikala bought six mechanical pencils at a stationary store. The price of each pencil was $2.00. She paid for the pencils with a $20 bill.

How much change did Mikala get back?

*Solution*

Step 1
Determine what the problem is asking.
The problem is asking how much change Mikala got back from her $20 bill after she bought the pencils.

Step 2
Identify the important information. The following information is important:

- Mikala bought six pencils.
- Each pencil cost $2.00.
- She paid with a $20 bill.

Step 3
Choose the operations to use.
To find out how much change Mikala got back, you first need to find out how much she paid altogether. To find this, use multiplication.
The difference between the total cost of the pencils and Mikala's $20 bill will be the amount of change she got back. To find this, use subtraction.

Step 4
Carry out the first operation.
6 × 2 = 12
The pencils cost Mikala $12.

Algebraic Thinking

**Step 5**
Carry out the second operation.
20 − 12 = 8
Mikala got $8 back in change.

## ESTIMATING WITH COMPATIBLE NUMBERS TO SOLVE DIVISION PROBLEMS

When you estimate using compatible numbers, you are looking for numbers that you can work with easily. Compatible numbers are often related to each other in some way. For example, compatible numbers could be factors or multiples. The numbers 36 and 6 are compatible numbers because 36 can be divided evenly by 6.

*Example*

Shayla is making treat bags to give out on Halloween. She has 395 candies to put into the treat bags. She plans to put five candies into each bag. The packages of treat bags come in groups of 25. Shayla estimates the number of bags she will need and then buys four packages of bags.

Use the estimation strategy of compatible numbers to judge the reasonableness of Shayla's decision to buy four packages of bags.

*Solution*

**Step 1**
Determine the operation needed to solve this problem.
Since you need to determine the number of groups (bags needed), you need to divide.

**Step 2**
Think of a number close to 395 that can be easily divided by 5.
395 → 400
Since 400 can be easily divided by 5, 400 and 5 are compatible numbers.

**Step 3**
Divide 400 by 5.
400 ÷ 5 = 80
Shayla will need about 80 bags.

**Step 4**
Determine the number of packages of bags needed.
Since there are 25 bags in a package, Shayla will need four packages: 25, 50, 75, 100.
Shayla made a reasonable estimate when she decided to buy four packages of treat bags for the 395 candies.

*4.OA.4  Find all factor pairs for a whole number in the range 1–100. Recognize that a whole number is a multiple of each of its factors. Determine whether a given whole number in the range 1–100 is a multiple of a given one–digit number. Determine whether a given whole number in the range 1–100 is prime or composite.*

## IDENTIFYING PRIME NUMBERS

A prime number is a natural number that has exactly two factors: one and itself.

An example of a prime number is 5 because it has exactly two factors: 1 and 5.
5 → 1 × 5

The factors are 1 and 5.

*Example*

Use a hundreds chart to find how many prime numbers there are between 1 and 100.

*Solution*

On a hundreds chart, circle the prime numbers and shade the composite numbers.

**Step 1**
Cross out the number 1 because it is neither prime nor composite.

**Step 2**
Circle the number 2 because it is prime, and shade all the numbers divisible by 2 because they are composite.

Algebraic Thinking — Castle Rock Research

**Step 3**
Circle the number 3 because it is prime, and shade all the numbers divisible by 3 because they are also composite.

Continue circling the prime numbers and shading the numbers that are divisible by the prime numbers circled.

There are 25 prime numbers on the hundreds chart.

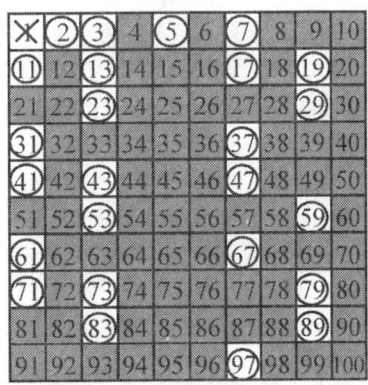

## IDENTIFY COMPOSITE NUMBERS

A **composite number** is a natural number that has three or more factors.
An example of a composite number is 4 because it has three factors: 1, 2, and 4.
$4 \to 1 \times 4$
$4 \to 2 \times 2$
The factors are 1, 2, and 4.

To identify if a number is a composite number, find the number of factors it has by breaking the number down into prime factors.

*Example*
Identify if the number 12 is a prime or composite number.

Decompose the composite factors into prime factors.

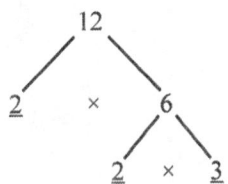

OR

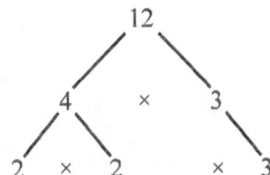

The number 12 is a composite number because it has more than two factors.

# Finding Multiples

**Multiple** is another word for product. For example, a multiple of 2 is the product of 2 and any other number. This means that 12 is a multiple of 2 because you can multiply 6 by 2 to get 12. Multiplication is one way of finding the multiples of a number.

*Example*

Find the first five multiples of 3.

*Solution*

Multiply 3 by 1, 2, 3, 4, and 5. The products will be the first five multiples.
$3 \times 1 = 3$
$3 \times 2 = 6$
$3 \times 3 = 9$
$3 \times 4 = 12$
$3 \times 5 = 15$

The first five multiples of 3 are 3, 6, 9, 12, and 15.

---

Another way to find multiples is by skip counting. If you wanted to determine the first five multiples of 3, you would need to skip count by 3 five times. The first five multiples of 3 are 3, 6, 9, 12, and 15.

By looking at the multiples of 3, you can see that they all divide evenly by 3. This means that you can identify a multiple by using division.

*Example*

Find if 56 is a multiple of 8.

*Solution*

**Method 1**
Use skip counting.
Skip count forward from 8 to see if you reach 56.
8, 16, 24, 32, 40, 48, 56
This means that 56 is a multiple of 8.

**Method 2**
Use division.
If 56 divides evenly by 8, then it is a multiple of 8.
$56 \div 8 = 7$
This means that 56 is a multiple of 8.

*4.OA.5  Generate a number or shape pattern that follows a given rule. Identify apparent features of the pattern that were not explicit in the rule itself.*

## CREATING NUMBER AND GEOMETRIC PATTERNS

To create a pattern, start with a pattern rule and then follow that rule. A pattern rule explains how the pattern is made.

*Example*

Create a geometric pattern that uses big squares and little squares.

The pattern rule could be 2 big squares, 3 little squares, repeat.

This is what the pattern will look like:

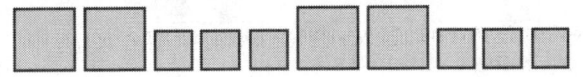

*Example*

Start at 45 and make a pattern of numbers for five counts. Show your pattern of numbers in the chart below. Explain the pattern rule you used.

| 1st | 2nd | 3rd | 4th | 5th | 6th |
|---|---|---|---|---|---|
| 45 | | | | | |

*Solution*

Example pattern

| 1st | 2nd | 3rd | 4th | 5th | 6th |
|---|---|---|---|---|---|
| 45 | 38 | 31 | 24 | 17 | 10 |

Example explanation

The pattern rule I used to make this pattern of numbers is subtract 7 from each number to get the next number.

# EXERCISE #1—OPERATIONS AND ALGEBRAIC THINKING

1. Which of the following statements describes the comparative relationship in the equation 5 × 7 = 35?
   A. Five is 7 times more than 35.
   B. Seven is 5 times as many as 35.
   C. Thirty-five is 7 times more than 5.
   D. Thirty-five is 5 times as many as 5.

*Use the following information to answer the next question.*

In a school cafeteria, there are 15 tables. Each table has 4 chairs.

2. What is the total number of chairs in the cafeteria?
   A. 50
   B. 55
   C. 60
   D. 65

*Use the following information to answer the next question.*

Mrs. Jefferson's class held a raffle to win a bicycle. There were 31 students in the class, and they bought 12 tickets each.

3. How many tickets were sold in total? _____

*Use the following information to answer the next question.*

There are 72 fence posts along a highway. Every sixth post has a bird feeder on it.

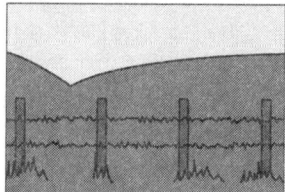

4. How many bird feeders are there?
   A. 11
   B. 12
   C. 13
   D. 14

*Use the following information to answer the next question.*

> Bobby has 124 stamps in his stamp collection. He has filled four albums with an equal number of stamps.
>
>

5. How many stamps are in each album?
   A. 30
   B. 31
   C. 32
   D. 33

*Use the following information to answer the next question.*

> Janelle is making a scrapbook of her family. She has chosen 175 pictures to put in it. Each page of the scrapbook has room for 4 pictures.

6. If Janelle starts with the first page and puts 4 pictures on each page, how many pictures will she put on the last page? _____

7. Which of the following numbers is the **best** estimate for the sum of 651 + 378?
   A. 700
   B. 800
   C. 1,000
   D. 1,100

*Use the following information to answer the next question.*

> Rahid and Jasmine are collecting rocks for a class project. Rahid collects 23 rocks, and Jasmine collects 31 rocks. They need to collect 100 rocks for the project.

8. How many more rocks do they need to collect for their project? _____

*Use the following information to answer the next question.*

> Jessa is making treat bags for her birthday party. She has 280 candies to divide among 23 bags.

9. About how many pieces of candy will go in each treat bag?
   A. 11
   B. 15
   C. 21
   D. 25

*Use the following information to answer the next question.*

> Beth solves the following math problem:
> 85 − 16 = 69
> She rounds each number to the nearest ten to check if her answer is reasonable.

10. Which estimate should Beth use?
    A. 80 − 10 =
    B. 80 − 20 =
    C. 90 − 10 =
    D. 90 − 20 =

11. Which of the following lists of numbers contains four prime numbers?
    A. 3, 5, 7, 19
    B. 4, 5, 11, 19
    C. 5, 7, 19, 21
    D. 17, 18, 19, 23

*Use the following information to answer the next question.*

A list of numbers is shown.
21, 22, 23, 24

12. Which of the given numbers are composite numbers?
    A. 21, 22, 24
    B. 21, 22, 23
    C. 21, 23, 24
    D. 22, 23, 24

13. Which of the following numbers is **not** a multiple of 9?
    A. 18
    B. 36
    C. 69
    D. 72

*Use the following information to answer the next question.*

Alexander's teacher asked him to draw a geometric pattern that followed the pattern rule "add two to each figure to get the next figure."

14. Which of the following patterns did Alexander draw?

    A.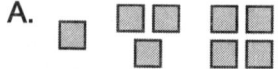

    B.

    C.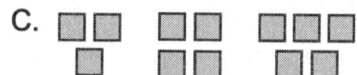

    D.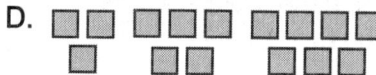

Not for Reproduction

# EXERCISE #1—OPERATIONS AND ALGEBRAIC THINKING
## ANSWERS AND SOLUTIONS

| 1. C    | 5. B  | 9. A   | 13. C |
| 2. C    | 6. 3  | 10. D  | 14. D |
| 3. 372  | 7. D  | 11. A  |       |
| 4. B    | 8. 46 | 12. A  |       |

### 1. C

The equation 5 × 7 = 35 means that there are 5 sets of 7 or 7 sets of 5 in 35.

Another way to describe this relationship is to say that 35 is 7 times more than 5 or 5 times more than 7.

The statement that 35 is 7 times more than 5 is the only given statement that describes the equation.

### 2. C

**Step 1**
Organize the information.

- Number of tables in the school cafeteria = 15
- Number of chairs at each table = 4
- Total number of chairs = 15 × 4

**Step 2**
Perform the operation.

```
  2
  15
×  4
  60
```

There are 60 chairs in the cafeteria.

### 3. 372

**Step 1**
Determine the equation.
There are 31 students who each bought 12 tickets for the fund-raiser.
To find the total number of tickets sold, multiply 31 by 12.

```
  31
× 12
```

**Step 2**
Multiply 31 by the ones.
Multiply 31 by 2.

```
  31
×  2
  62
```

**Step 3**
Multiply 31 by the tens.
Multiply 31 by 10.

```
   31
×  10
  310
```

**Step 4**
Add the two products together.

```
 310
 +62
 372
```

A total of 372 tickets were sold to the 31 students.

### 4. B

**Step 1**
Determine the equation.
There are 72 posts, with a bird feeder every 6 posts.
6)72

SOLARO Study Guide – Mathematics 4    31    Algebraic Thinking

**Step 2**
The first digit of the dividend is larger than 6, so it can be divided by 6 to produce a whole number.
The number 7 contains 1 set of 6, so write the number 1 above the 7 in the division bracket.

$$\begin{array}{r}1\phantom{0}\\6\overline{)72}\end{array}$$

Multiply the 6 by the 1, and write the product (6) below the 7 in the dividend.
Draw a line under the product (6), and subtract 6 from 7.
Bring down the 2. The number 12 will be left.

$$\begin{array}{r}12\\6\overline{)72}\\-6\phantom{0}\\\hline 12\end{array}$$

How many 6s fit into the number 12?
The number 6 fits 2 times.
Write 2 above the division bracket to the right of the 1.
Multiply the 6 by the 2, and write the product (12) below the 12.
Subtract the two numbers to see if there is a remainder.

$$\begin{array}{r}12\\6\overline{)72}\\-6\phantom{0}\\\hline 12\\-12\\\hline 0\end{array}$$

There is no remainder, so the solution is 12.
There are 12 bird feeders.

5. **B**

**Step 1**
Write out the equation.
There are 124 stamps in four albums.
$4\overline{)124}$

**Step 2**
The first number of the dividend (1) is not big enough for 4 to fit into it.
In this case, start with the number in the tens position (12). The number 4 fits into 12 three times.

$$\begin{array}{r}3\phantom{00}\\4\overline{)124}\end{array}$$

Multiply the 4 by the 3, and write the product below the 12 of the dividend. Draw a line under the new 12, and subtract it from 12. Bring down the ones (4).

$$\begin{array}{r}3\phantom{00}\\4\overline{)124}\\-12\phantom{0}\\\hline 4\end{array}$$

**Step 3**
How many 4s fit into the number 4? Write 1 above the division bracket to the right of the 3.
Multiply the 4 by the 1, and write the product below the 4.
Subtract the two numbers to see if there is a remainder.
There is no remainder because 4 – 4 = 0.

$$\begin{array}{r}31\\4\overline{)124}\\-12\phantom{0}\\\hline 4\\-4\\\hline 0\end{array}$$

Each album Bobby filled has 31 stamps in it.

6. **3**

**Step 1**
Divide 175 by 4.

$$\begin{array}{r}43\phantom{0}\\4\overline{)175}\\-16\downarrow\\\hline 15\\-12\\\hline R3\end{array}$$

**Step 2**
Determine the number of pictures on the last page.
There will be 43 pages (the quotient) that will have four pictures on each page.
The remainder of 3 represents the pictures that will be placed on the 44th page.
Every page will have 4 pictures except the last page, which will have 3 pictures.

7. **D**

   **Step 1**
   Round 651 to the nearest hundred.
   651 → 700

   **Step 2**
   Round 378 to the nearest hundred.
   378 → 400

   **Step 3**
   Add the rounded numbers together.
   700 + 400 = 1,100

8. **46**

   **Step 1**
   Determine what the problem is asking.
   The problem is asking how many more rocks Rahid and Jasmine need to collect.

   **Step 2**
   Identify the important information.
   Rahid collected 23 rocks, and Jasmine collected 31 rocks. They need to collect 100 rocks in total.

   **Step 3**
   Determine which operations to use.
   To find out the total number of rocks, add the number of rocks each person collected. Then, to find out how many more rocks they need to collect, subtract the number of rocks they have from 100.

   **Step 4**
   Carry out the first operation.
   23 + 31 = 54
   They collected 54 rocks.

   **Step 5**
   Carry out the second operation.
   100 − 54 = 46
   They have to collect 46 more rocks.

9. **A**

   **Step 1**
   Think of numbers close to 280 and 23 that are compatible and can be easily divided.
   280 → 275
   23 → 25
   Since 275 and 25 are easy to divide, they are compatible numbers.

   **Step 2**
   Divide 275 by 25.

   $$25\overline{)275}$$

   About 11 candies will go in each treat bag.

10. **D**

    DBeth should use the estimate 90 − 20 = to check her answer.

    When estimating, round each number to the nearest ten.

    The number 85 is rounded to 90. There are 8 tens in <u>8</u>5. The number of ones (5) is 5 or greater, so the 8 tens become 9 tens, and the 5 ones become 0.

    The number 16 is rounded to 20. There is 1 ten in <u>1</u>6. The number of ones (6) is 5 or greater, so the 1 ten becomes 2 tens, and the 6 ones become 0.
    90 − 20 = 70

11. **A**

    **Step 1**
    Rule out the incorrect choices.
    All even numbers except 2 are not prime numbers. This means that 4 and 18 are not prime numbers.
    The list that contains 4 is incorrect. The list that contains 18 is also incorrect.

    **Step 2**
    Identify the non-prime numbers in the remaining options.
    The factors of the number 21 are 1, 3, 7, and 21. The number 21 is therefore not a prime number. The list that contains 21 is incorrect.
    The numbers 3, 5, 7, and 19 are prime numbers.

12. **A**

    **Step 1**
    Determine the factors of 21. A factor is a natural number that divides evenly into another natural number.
    The factors of 21 are 1, 3, 7, and 21. Therefore, 21 is a composite number because it has more than two factors.

**Step 2**

Determine the factors of 22.

The factors of 22 are 1, 2, 11, and 22. Therefore, 22 is a composite number because it has more than two factors.

**Step 3**

Determine the factors of 23.

The factors of 23 are 1 and 23. Therefore, 23 is not a composite number because it has only two factors.

**Step 4**

Determine the factors of 24.

The factors of 24 are 1, 2, 3, 4, 6, 8, 12, and 24. Therefore, 24 is a composite number because it has more than two factors.

**13. C**

Determine the multiples of 9 by skip counting forward by 9.

The multiples of 9 are 9, 18, 27, 36, 45, 54, 63, 72, 81, …

The number 69 is not listed as one of the multiples. This means that 69 is not a multiple of 9.

**14. D**

The pattern rule Alexander was given was "add two to each figure to get the next figure." The following pattern follows this pattern rule. There are three squares in the first figure, five squares in the next figure, and seven squares in the last figure.

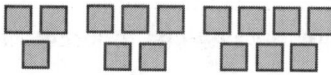

# EXERCISE #2—OPERATIONS AND ALGEBRAIC THINKING

15. Which of the following statements describes the comparative relationship in the equation 8 × 6 = 48?
    A. The number 6 is 8 times as many as 48.
    B. The number 48 is 6 times as many as 8.
    C. The number 48 is 8 times more than 8.
    D. The number 8 is 6 times more than 48.

*Use the following information to answer the next question.*

> At a rodeo, Jim sees that it takes four horses to pull a wagon. There are 12 wagons at the rodeo.

16. How many horses in total will be needed to pull the 12 wagons?
    A. 12
    B. 24
    C. 48
    D. 72

*Use the following information to answer the next question.*

> The fourth grade students at Glenmore Elementary are having a bake sale. There are 42 students in fourth grade. Each student brings in 24 baked items for the sale.

17. How many baked items are there in total? _____

*Use the following information to answer the next question.*

> For a snack, 4 children equally shared a box of mini pretzels.

18. If there were 96 pretzels in the box, how many pretzels did each child get?
    A. 26
    B. 24
    C. 22
    D. 20

*Use the following information to answer the next question.*

> Melissa has collected 592 books. She has a large bookcase with 4 shelves to store them. She wants to put an equal number of books on each shelf.

19. How many books will go on each shelf?
    A. 108
    B. 124
    C. 136
    D. 148

*Use the following information to answer the next question.*

One summer day, 245 students participated in a school-wide race. Miss Hay wanted to buy each student a participation ribbon for their efforts. Each pack of ribbons at the store had 9 ribbons.

20. How many packages of ribbons did Miss Hay need to buy so every student who raced received one ribbon?
    A. 27
    B. 28
    C. 30
    D. 31

21. Neza estimates the sum of 419 + 850 by rounding to the nearest hundred and then adding. Which of the following equations shows Neza's answer?
    A. 400 + 800 = 1,200
    B. 400 + 900 = 1,300
    C. 500 + 800 = 1,300
    D. 500 + 900 = 1,400

*Use the following information to answer the next question.*

Mrs. Barker used 482 stickers this year. Last year, she used 628 stickers. She asked her students to help her find about how many fewer stickers she used this year than last year.

22. Which estimate is **most** helpful to Mrs. Barker?
    A. 490 + 630 =
    B. 480 + 620 =
    C. 630 − 490 =
    D. 630 − 480 =

*Use the following information to answer the next question.*

Three students bought food and plants for their class fish. The food cost $5, and the plants cost $7. The students shared the total cost equally.

23. How much did each student have to pay for the food and plants? $_____

*Use the following information to answer the next question.*

Anne paid $316 for 8 tickets to a concert.

24. Using the compatible numbers strategy, which of the following totals is the **best** estimate for the cost of each ticket?
    A. $20
    B. $30
    C. $40
    D. $50

*Use the following information to answer the next question.*

The year that Adela was born is a prime number. The day of the month on which she was born is also a prime number. In the year 2000, her age was a prime number.

25. Which of the following dates could be Adela's birthday?
    A. April 29, 1995
    B. May 13, 1987
    C. August 21, 1973
    D. September 19, 1999

26. How many numbers from 30 to 50 are composite numbers?
   A. 5
   B. 8
   C. 16
   D. 18

27. Which of the following values is a multiple of 12?
   A. 28
   B. 34
   C. 60
   D. 70

*Use the following information to answer the next question.*

Leon makes a repeating pattern that starts with the numbers 10, 20, and 30.

28. Which of the following patterns did Leon make?
   A. 10, 20, 30, 40, 50, 60, 70, 80, 90
   B. 10, 20, 30, 10, 20, 30, 10, 20, 30
   C. 10, 20, 30, 20, 30, 40, 30, 40, 50
   D. 10, 20, 30, 20, 40, 60, 40, 60, 90

# EXERCISE #2—OPERATIONS AND ALGEBRAIC THINKING ANSWERS AND SOLUTIONS

| 15. B | 19. D | 23. 4 | 27. C |
| 16. C | 20. B | 24. C | 28. B |
| 17. 1008 | 21. B | 25. B | |
| 18. B | 22. D | 26. C | |

**15. B**

The equation 8 × 6 = 48 means that in 48 there are 8 sets of 6 or 6 sets of 8.

Another way to describe this relationship is to say that the number 48 is 6 times as many as 8 or 8 times as many as 6.

The statement that the number 48 is 6 times as many as 8 is the only statement that describes the comparative relationship in the equation 8 × 6 = 48.

**16. C**

**Step 1**
Determine what the problem is asking.
The problem is asking for the total number of horses that are needed to pull 12 wagons.

**Step 2**
Determine how many horses in total are needed.
Four horses are needed to pull 1 wagon, and the total number of wagons is 12. The easiest way to find the total number of horses needed to pull 12 wagons would be to multiply 12 by 4.
12 × 4 = 48
The total number of horses needed to pull 12 wagons is 48.

**17. 1008**

**Step 1**
Determine the equation.
There are 42 students, and each student brings 24 baked items.
To find the total number of baked items, multiply 42 by 24.
```
  42
× 24
```

**Step 2**
Multiply 42 by the ones.
Multiply 42 by 4.
```
  42
×  4
 168
```

**Step 3**
Multiply 42 by the tens.
Multiply 42 by 20.
```
  42
× 20
 840
```

**Step 4**
Add the two products together.
```
  168
+ 840
1,008
```
There are 1,008 baked items in total.

**18. B**

Decide which operation to use.

The 4 children split a box of 96 pretzels. The operation to use is division.

**Method 1**
Use long division.
```
    24
 4)96
   -8
    16
   -16
     0
```
Each child got 24 pretzels.

**Method 2**
Use short division.
```
    2 4
 4)9¹6
```
Each child got 24 pretzels.

**Method 3**
Use repeated subtraction.
```
  96
- 80    4 × 20
  16           20 + 4 = 24
- 16    4 × 4
   0
```
Each child got 24 pretzels.

19. **D**

**Step 1**
Write out the equation.
There are 592 books to store on 4 shelves.
4)592

**Step 2**
Divide the first digit of the dividend by the divisor.
The first digit of the dividend is larger than 4, so it can be divided by 4 to produce a whole number. Since 4 can fit into 5 one time, write the number 1 above the 5 in the division bracket.
```
   1
4)592
```
Multiply the 4 by the 1, and write the product below the 5 of the dividend.
Draw a line under the new 4, and subtract it from 5.
Bring down the tens (9).
You will now have the number 19 left.
```
   1
4)592
 - 4
   19
```

**Step 3**
Divide the number you have left by the divisor.
How many times does 4 fit into the number 19? Since 4 goes into 19 four times, write 4 above the division bracket to the right of the 1.
Multiply the 4 by the 4, and write the product below the 19.
Subtract 16 from 19. You are now left with 3.
Bring down the ones (2). You will now have the number 32 left.
```
    14
4)592
 - 4
   19
 - 16
    32
```

**Step 4**
Divide the number you have left by the divisor.
How many times does 4 fit into the number 32? Since 4 goes into 32 eight times, write 8 above the division bracket to the right of the 4.
Multiply the 4 by the 8, and write the product below the 32.
Subtract the two numbers to see if there is a remainder.
```
   148
4)592
 - 4
   19
 - 16
    32
  - 32
     0
```
There is no remainder. Therefore, 148 books will go on each shelf of Melissa's bookcase.

20. **B**

**Step 1**
Divide 245 by 9.
```
    27
9)245
 - 18 ↓
    65
  - 63
    R2
```

**Step 2**
Determine the number of packages needed.
If Miss Hay bought 27 packs (the quotient), the remainder of 2 means that 2 students would not get a ribbon. The quotient must be rounded up to 28 so every racing student receives one ribbon.
Miss Hay must buy 28 packs.

21. **B**

**Step 1**
Round 419 to the nearest hundred.
419 → 400

**Step 2**
Round 850 to the nearest hundred.
850 → 900

**Step 3**
Add the rounded numbers together.
400 + 900 = 1,300

**22. D**

Choice D is correct. The best estimate for 628 − 482 is 630 − 480 = .

To find how many fewer stickers were used, you need to subtract 628 − 482.

To estimate, round the numbers to the nearest ten.

The number 6<u>2</u>8 is rounded to 630.

The number 4<u>8</u>2 is rounded to 480.

**23. 4**

**Step 1**
Determine what the problem is asking.
The problem is to find how much money each student paid.

**Step 2**
Identify the important information.
There are 3 students. The food cost $5, and the plants cost $7.

**Step 3**
Determine the operations to use.
Use addition to find out the total cost of the food and plants. To find out how much each student had to pay, divide the total cost by the number of students.

**Step 4**
Carry out the first operation.
5 + 7 = 12
The total cost was $12.

**Step 5**
Carry out the second operation.
$12 ÷ 3 = $4
Each student had to pay $4.

**24. C**

Since the total of $316 is divided between 8 tickets, use division to solve the problem.

**Step 1**
Think of a number close to 316 that can be easily divided by 8.
316 → 320

**Step 2**
Divide 320 by 8.

$$8 \overline{)320} \quad \begin{array}{r} 40 \\ -32 \\ \hline 0 \end{array}$$

The cost of each ticket is about $40.

**25. B**

The year 1995 is divisible by 5. Since a prime number is only divisible by 1 and itself, 1995 is not prime. Therefore, A is incorrect.

The date 21 is divisible by 3. Since a prime number is only divisible by 1 and itself, 21 is not prime. Therefore, C is incorrect.

For B and D, find Adela's age in the year 2000.

| Year of birth | Date of birth | Adela's age in the year 2000 |
|---|---|---|
| 1987 | 13 | 13 |
| 1999 | 19 | 1 |

The number 1 is neither prime nor composite. Therefore, D is also incorrect.

By a process of elimination, the correct answer is B The year 1987 is a prime number and the day 13 is a prime number. In the year 2000, Adela would be 13 years old, which is also a prime number.

**26. C**

**Step 1**
Start by making a chart with the numbers 30, 31, 32, …48, 49, 50 written in order in the squares.

| 30 | 31 | 32 | 33 | 34 | 35 |
|---|---|---|---|---|---|
| 36 | 37 | 38 | 39 | 40 | 41 |
| 42 | 43 | 44 | 45 | 46 | 47 |
| 48 | 49 | 50 | | | |

**Step 2**
Cross out all the numbers that can only be divided by 1 and themselves. These are the prime numbers.

| 30 | ✗ | 32 | 33 | 34 | 35 |
|---|---|---|---|---|---|
| 36 | ✗ | 38 | 39 | 40 | ✗ |
| 42 | ✗ | 44 | 45 | 46 | ✗ |
| 48 | 49 | 50 | | | |

**Step 3**
The numbers that are not crossed out are composite numbers because they have more than two factors.

The composite numbers are 30, 32, 33, 34, 35, 36, 38, 39, 40, 42, 44, 45, 46, 48, 49, and 50.

There are 16 composite numbers from 30 to 50.

**27. C**

Determine the multiples of 12 by skip counting forward by 12.

Multiples of 12 are 12, 24, 36, 48, 60, and 72.

The number 60 is a multiple of 12.

**28. B**

In a repeating pattern, the numbers continue to repeat over and over.

The number pattern 10, 20, 30, 10, 20, 3010, 20, 30 is the only pattern that repeats the numbers 10, 20, and 30 over and over.

# NOTES

# Number and Base Ten

# NUMBER AND OPERATIONS IN BASE TEN

## Table of Correlations

| Standard | | Concepts | Exercise #1 | Exercise #2 |
|---|---|---|---|---|
| 4.NBT | Number and Operations in Base Ten | | | |
| 4.NBT.1 | Recognize that in a multi-digit whole number, a digit in one place represents ten times what it represents in the place to its right. | Representing Whole Numbers to 1,000,000 | 29 | 53 |
| | | Understanding Place Value to a Million | 30 | 54 |
| 4.NBT.2 | Read and write multi-digit whole numbers using base-ten numerals, number names, and expanded form. Compare two multi-digit numbers based on meanings of the digits in each place, using >, =, and < symbols to record the results of comparisons. | Reading Number Words to One Million | 31 | 55 |
| | | Compare Whole Numbers < 1,000,000 | 32 | 56 |
| | | Writing Numbers in Words to a Million | 33 | 57 |
| 4.NBT.3 | Use place value understanding to round multi-digit whole numbers to any place. | Round Whole Numbers (in the millions) to the Nearest Ten Thousand | 34 | 58 |
| | | Round Whole Numbers in the Millions to the Nearest Hundred | 35 | 59 |
| | | Round Whole Numbers in Millions to the Nearest Thousand | 36 | 60 |
| | | Round Whole Numbers in the Millions to the Nearest Hundred Thousand | 37 | 61 |
| 4.NBT.4 | Fluently add and subtract multi-digit whole numbers using the standard algorithm. | Adding Three- and Four-Digit Numbers | 38 | 62 |
| | | Subtracting Three- and Four-Digit Numbers | 39 | 63 |
| 4.NBT.5 | Multiply a whole number of up to four digits by a one-digit whole number, and multiply two two-digit numbers, using strategies based on place value and the properties of operations. Illustrate and explain the calculation by using equations, rectangular arrays, and/or area models. | Multiplying a Two-Digit Number by Another Two-Digit Number | 40 | 64 |
| | | Dropping and Then Adding Zero | 41 | 65 |
| | | Using Mental Math Strategies to Multiply Whole Numbers by 10, 100, and 1,000 | 42 | 66 |
| | | Representing Multiplication Using an Area Model | 48 | 70 |
| | | Multiplying a One-Digit Number by a Two-Digit Number with Regrouping | 43 | 71 |
| | | Multiplying Two Digits by One Digit without Regrouping | 44 | 72 |
| | | Multiplying a Four-Digit Number by a One-Digit Number | 45 | 69 |
| | | Representing the Distributive Property by Using an Area Model | 46 | 68 |
| | | Multiplying a Three-Digit Number by a One-Digit Number | 47 | 67 |

| 4.NBT.6 | Find whole-number quotients and remainders with up to four-digit dividends and one-digit divisors, using strategies based on place value, the properties of operations, and/or the relationship between multiplication and division. Illustrate and explain the calculation by using equations, rectangular arrays, and/or area models. | Dividing 3-Digit by 1-Digit Whole Numbers | 49 | 73 |
|---|---|---|---|---|
| | | Representing Division Using an Area Model | 50 | 74 |
| | | Dividing Multi-Digit Numbers by One-Digit Numbers | 51 | 75 |
| | | Dividing Two-Digit Numbers by One-Digit Numbers | 52 | 76 |

*4.NBT.1 Recognize that in a multi-digit whole number, a digit in one place represents ten times what it represents in the place to its right.*

## REPRESENTING WHOLE NUMBERS TO 1,000,000

Whole numbers are digits like 0, 1, 2, 3, 4, 5, 6, 7, 8, 9 and any combination of these digits.

Whole numbers are used to count things, but not parts of things. Decimals, fractions and negative numbers are not whole numbers.

You can use place value charts and expanded notation to represent numbers.

## BASE TEN BLOCKS

When dealing with large whole numbers, such as millions, base ten blocks can show place value to help you understand the large numbers.

Numerals are organized into groups of three digits from right to left. These groups are called **periods**.

- Ones period (hundreds, tens, ones)
- Thousands period (hundreds, tens, ones)
- Millions period (hundreds, tens, ones)

*Example*

| Thousands | | | Ones | | |
|---|---|---|---|---|---|
| Hundreds | Tens | Ones | Hundreds | Tens | Ones |
| ▦ | ▯ | □ | ▦ | ▯ | □ |
| 100 000 | 10 000 | 1 000 | 100 | 10 | 1 |

× 10   × 10   × 10   × 10   × 10   × 10

In the given chart, base ten blocks are used to show place value.

The small cube can represent 1 in the ones period, and it can also represent 1,000 in the thousands period.

The ten rod can represent 10 in the ones period and 10,000 in the thousands period.

The hundred flat can represent 100 in the ones period and 100,000 in the thousands period.

---

## PLACE VALUE CHART

You can also organize numbers into a place value chart using periods.

*Example*

| Thousands | | | Ones | | |
|---|---|---|---|---|---|
| H | T | O | H | T | O |
| 9 | 5 | 0 | 0 | 0 | 0 |

What whole number is represented in the given place value chart?

*Solution*

Determine the value of each digit in the chart from left to right.

There is a 9 in the hundred thousand position, so it represents 900,000.

There is a 5 in the ten thousand position, so it represents 50,000.

There are 0's in the rest of the positions, so the values from thousands to ones is 0.

Therefore, 950,000 is represented in the place value chart.

---

## EXPANDED NOTATION

*Example*

Represent the number 875,411 in expanded form.

*Solution*

**Step 1**
Start at the left and write the value of each digit in the number.

- 8 has a value of 800,000 (8 × 100,000)
- 7 has a value of 70,000 (7 × 10,000)
- 5 has a value of 5,000 (5 × 1,000)
- 4 has a value of 400 (4 × 100)
- 1 has a value of 10 (1 × 10)
- 1 has a value of 1 (1 × 1)

**Step 2**
Write the expanded notation by showing each digit being multiplied by its place value position.
(8 × 100,000)+(7 × 10,000)+(5 × 1,000)+(4 × 100)+(1 × 10)+(1 × 1)

---

## UNDERSTANDING PLACE VALUE TO A MILLION

Understanding place values and period names will help you find the value of a large whole number.

Large numbers are broken up into groups with three digits each. Each group is called a **period**. From right to left, the first period is the ones period, followed by the thousands period. Each period is then broken down into three place values: ones, tens, and hundreds.

To determine the value of a digit in a given place value, use the following steps:

1. Place the number into a place value chart.
2. Identify the value of the digit.

*Example*

Determine the value of the digit 8 in the number 678234.

*Solution*

Place the number in a place value chart.

| Thousands | | | Ones | | |
|---|---|---|---|---|---|
| H | T | O | H | T | O |
| 6 | 7 | 8 | 2 | 3 | 4 |

The digit 8 is in the ones position of the thousands period.

Therefore, the digit 8 has a value of 8,000.

---

*4.NBT.2 Read and write multi–digit whole numbers using base-ten numerals, number names, and expanded form. Compare two multi–digit numbers based on meanings of the digits in each place, using >, =, and < symbols to record the results of comparisons.*

## READING NUMBER WORDS TO ONE MILLION

When you read a number written in words, begin on the left and read to the right. Identify the place value for each number word as you read.

*Example*

When you read the number four thousand one hundred fifty-five, start at the left and read to the right.

The first term, four thousand, tells you the digit 4 is in the thousands place.

The second term, one hundred, tells you the digit 1 is in the hundreds place.

The third term, fifty-five, has a hyphen (-). The first digit 5 is in the tens place. The second digit 5 is in the ones place.

The number four thousand one hundred fifty-five is written as the numeral 4,155.

---

A place value chart can help you see the relationship between the place value of each digit and the written words that represent that digit.

To deal with larger numbers, some place value charts are broken down into periods. Each period has hundreds, tens, and ones.

The following chart shows the number nine hundred ninety-nine thousand nine hundred ninety-nine in a place value chart.

| Thousands | | | Ones | | |
|---|---|---|---|---|---|
| H | T | O | H | T | O |
| 9 | 9 | 9 | 9 | 9 | 9 |

*Example*

Rebecca reads that there are six hundred fifty-six thousand five hundred sixty-two people living in Austin.

Write the population of Austin in numerals.

*Solution*

**Step 1**

Break the number words into their periods.

Six hundred fifty-six thousand is in the thousands period.

Five hundred sixty-two is in the ones period.

| Thousands | | | Ones | | |
| --- | --- | --- | --- | --- | --- |
| H | T | O | H | T | O |
| 6 | 5 | 6 | 5 | 6 | 2 |

**Step 2**

Write the number as a numeral.

In numerals, the population of Austin is 656,562.

## COMPARE WHOLE NUMBERS < 1,000,000

Numbers can be **compared** to see which number has the **greatest** value, the **least** value, or if they have an **equal** (same) value.

When comparing numbers, **words** or **symbols** can be used. When using symbols, compare the first number on the **left** to the number that is on its **right**.

**Greater than** can be shown by the symbol > . For example, 6 is greater than 5 or 6 > 5

**Less than** can be shown by the symbol < . For example, 1 is less than 3 or 1 < 3.

**Equal to** can be shown by the symbol = . For example, 8 is equal to 8 or 8 = 8.

When comparing numbers, start at the left and compare the digits in each place value position.

*Example*

Compare the numbers 78,605 and 78,593. Which number is greater?

*Solution*

| | 78,605 | 78,593 |
| --- | --- | --- |
| Start at the left. Compare the digits in the ten thousands place. Both numbers have a 7 in the ten thousands place. | <u>78</u> 605 | <u>78</u> 593 |
| Move to the right. Compare the digits in the thousands place. Both numbers have an 8 in the thousands place. | 7<u>8</u> 605 | 7<u>8</u> 593 |
| Move to the right again. Compare the numbers in the hundreds place. Since 6 is greater than 5, 78,605 is greater than 78,593. | 78 <u>6</u>05 | 78 <u>5</u>93 |
| You do not need to compare the digits in the tens place or ones place because you already know that 78,605 is greater than 78,593. | | |

78,605 is greater than 78,953
78,605 > 78,593.

## WRITING NUMBERS IN WORDS TO A MILLION

When you write numbers in words up to one million, it is important to know the place value of each digit.

Place values for large numbers are arranged in groups of three. Each group of three is called a **period**. Each period includes hundreds, tens, and ones.

When you write whole numbers in words, write each period from left to right.

*Example*
Express the number 345,622 in words.

*Solution*

### Step 1
Place the number in a place value chart.

| Thousands | | | Ones | | |
| --- | --- | --- | --- | --- | --- |
| H | T | O | H | T | O |
| 3 | 4 | 5 | 6 | 2 | 2 |

### Step 2
To write a number in words, start from the left and work your way to the right.
The number in the thousands period is 345. It is written as three hundred forty-five thousand.
The number in the ones period is 622. It is written as six hundred twenty-two.

### Step 3
Put the two written forms together.
The number 345,622 is written as three hundred forty-five thousand six hundred twenty-two.

---

*4.NBT.3 Use place value understanding to round multi-digit whole numbers to any place.*

## ROUND WHOLE NUMBERS (IN THE MILLIONS) TO THE NEAREST TEN THOUSAND

Numbers can be rounded to the nearest 10, 100, 1,000, 10,000, and even 100,000. The same rule of rounding is used regardless of the place value that you are rounding to.

Rounding numbers requires knowledge of place value. When rounding a number in the ten thousands, look at the number in the thousands.

| Millions | | | Thousands | | | Ones | | |
| --- | --- | --- | --- | --- | --- | --- | --- | --- |
| H | T | O | H | T | O | H | T | O |
| 0 | 0 | 0 | 0 | 1 | 0 | 0 | 0 | 0 |

- If the digit to the right has a value of 0 to 4, the digit you are rounding to stays the same. All other digits to the right are replaced with zeros.
- If the digit to the right has a value of 5 to 9, the digit you are rounding to is rounded up by one. All other digits to the right are replaced with zeros.

Not for Reproduction

*Example*
Round the number 4,000,563 to the nearest ten thousand.

*Solution*
**Step 1**
Look at the number to the right of the place value you are rounding to.
Look at the number of thousands. Since 0 is less than 5, the 0 ten thousands will stay the same.
**Step 2**
Replace all other digits to the right with zeros.
The 5, 6 and 3 will then be replaced with zeros.
Rounded to the nearest ten thousand, 4,000,563 becomes 4,000,000.

---

## ROUND WHOLE NUMBERS IN THE MILLIONS TO THE NEAREST HUNDRED

Numbers can be rounded to the nearest 10, 100, 1,000, 10,000, and even 100,000. The same rule of rounding is used regardless of the place value that you are rounding to.

Rounding numbers requires knowledge of place value. When rounding a number to the nearest hundred, look at the number in the tens.

| Millions | | | Thousands | | | Ones | | |
| --- | --- | --- | --- | --- | --- | --- | --- | --- |
| H | T | O | H | T | O | H | T | O |
| 0 | 0 | 0 | 0 | 0 | 0 | 1 | 0 | 0 |

- If the digit to the right has a value of 0 to 4, the digit you are rounding to stays the same. All other digits to the right are replaced with zeros.
- If the digit to the right has a value of 5 to 9, the digit you are rounding to is rounded up by one. All other digits to the right are replaced with zeros.

*Example*
Round the number 4,000,563 to the nearest hundred.

*Solution*
**Step 1**
Look at the number to the right of the place value you are rounding to.
Look at the number of tens. Since 6 is greater than 5, the 5 hundreds will round up to 6 hundreds.
**Step 2**
Replace all other digits to the right with zeros.
The 6 and 3 will then be replaced with zeros.
Rounded to the nearest hundred, 4,000,563 becomes 4,000,600.

# ROUND WHOLE NUMBERS IN MILLIONS TO THE NEAREST THOUSAND

Numbers can be rounded to the nearest 10, 100, 1,000, 10,000, and even 100,000. The same rule of rounding is used regardless of the place value that you are rounding to.

Rounding numbers requires knowledge of place value. When rounding a number to the nearest thousand, look at the number in the hundreds.

| Millions | | | Thousands | | | Ones | | |
|---|---|---|---|---|---|---|---|---|
| H | T | O | H | T | O | H | T | O |
| 0 | 0 | 0 | 0 | 0 | 1 | 0 | 0 | 0 |

- If the digit to the right has a value of 0 to 4, the digit you are rounding to stays the same. All other digits to the right are replaced with zeros.
- If the digit to the right has a value of 5 to 9, the digit you are rounding to is rounded up by one. All other digits to the right are replaced with zeros.

*Example*
  Round 4,000,563 to the nearest thousand.

*Solution*
  **Step 1**
  Look at the number to the right of the place value you are rounding to.
  Look at the number of hundreds, since 5 is equal to 5, the thousands will round up to 1 thousands.
  **Step 2**
  Replace all numbers to the right with zeros.
  The 5, 6, and 3 will be replaced with zeros.
  Rounded to the nearest thousand, 4,000,563 becomes 4,001,000.

---

# ROUND WHOLE NUMBERS IN THE MILLIONS TO THE NEAREST HUNDRED THOUSAND

Numbers can be rounded to the nearest 10, 100, 1,000, 10,000, and even 100,000. The same rule of rounding is used regardless of the place value that you are rounding to.

Rounding numbers requires knowledge of place value. When rounding a number in the hundred thousands, look at the number in the ten thousands.

| Millions | | | Thousands | | | Ones | | |
|---|---|---|---|---|---|---|---|---|
| H | T | O | H | T | O | H | T | O |
| 0 | 0 | 0 | 1 | 0 | 0 | 0 | 0 | 0 |

- If the digit to the right has a value of 0 to 4, the digit you are rounding to stays the same. All other digits to the right are replaced with zeros.
- If the digit to the right has a value of 5 to 9, the digit you are rounding to is rounded up by one. All other digits to the right are replaced with zeros.

Number and Base Ten

*Example*

The given chart shows the number of people who were living in five different cities in Ontario in 2006.

| City | Population |
|---|---|
| Mississauga | 1,668,549 |
| Windsor | 1,216,473 |
| Kitchener | 1,204,668 |
| Oshawa | 1,141,590 |
| Thunder Bay | 1,109,140 |

Round the population of Mississauga to the nearest hundred thousand.

*Solution*

### Step 1
Look at the number to the right of the place value you are rounding to.

Look at the number of ten thousands, since 6 is greater than 5 the hundred thousands will round up to 7 hundred thousands.

### Step 2
Replace all the numbers to the right with zeros.

6, 8, 5, 4, 9, would all change to zeros.

1,668,549 rounded to the nearest hundred thousand is 1,700,000.

---

*4.NBT.4 Fluently add and subtract multi–digit whole numbers using the standard algorithm.*

## ADDING THREE- AND FOUR-DIGIT NUMBERS

When numbers with three or four digits are added together, only the digits in the same place value spot can be added.

To add multi-digit numbers together, follow these steps:

1. Line up the numbers based on their place value. If one number has a bigger place value than the other, always place it on top.
2. Add the single digits from right to left (the smallest place value to the biggest place value).

*Example*

What is 528 + 321?

*Solution*

### Step 1
Line up the numbers based on their place value.

```
 528
+321
```

### Step 2
Add the digits in the ones place.

```
 528
+321
   9
```

### Step 3
Add the digits in the tens place.

```
  528
 +321
   49
```

### Step 4
Add the digits in the hundreds place.

```
  528
 +321
  849
```

---

Sometimes, when you add two digits in a place value together, the answer will be bigger than a single digit. When this happens, you will need to regroup. You can only have one digit in each place value. When you regroup, you split the number into its place value parts, and then carry the larger part to the next addition column.

Follow the same steps, and regroup when needed.

*Example*

What is 1,252 + 568?

*Solution*

### Step 1
Line up the numbers based on their place value.

Since 1,252 has one digit in the thousands place value and 568 does not, then 1,252 will go on top.

```
  1,252
 +  568
```

### Step 2
Starting from the right (the ones place), add the single-digit numbers.
2 + 8 = 10

Because 10 is bigger than a single digit answer, it must be regrouped.

Write the 0 below in the ones place, and carry the 1 to the top of the tens place.

```
    1
  1,252
 +  568
      0
```

### Step 3
Add all the digits in the tens place, including the 1 from the regrouped 10.
1 + 5 + 6 = 12

Because 12 is bigger than a single digit answer, it must be regrouped.

Write 2 in the tens place, and carry the 1 to the top of the hundreds place.

```
   11
  1,252
 +  568
     20
```

Number and Base Ten

### Step 4
Add all the digits in the hundreds place, including the 1 from the regrouped 12.
1 + 2 + 5 = 8
Because 8 is a single digit, you do not need to regroup here.
Write the 8 in the hundreds place.

$$\begin{array}{r} \overset{1\,1}{1{,}2}52 \\ +\ 568 \\ \hline 820 \end{array}$$

### Step 5
Only one of the two numbers has a digit in the thousands place value. That means the 1 from the number 1,252 can be carried down to the thousands place value in the answer.

$$\begin{array}{r} \overset{1\,1}{1{,}2}52 \\ +\ 568 \\ \hline 1{,}820 \end{array}$$

---

## SUBTRACTING THREE- AND FOUR-DIGIT NUMBERS

When multi-digit numbers are subtracted, only the digits in the same place value spot can be subtracted. To subtract multi-digit numbers, follow these steps:

1. Line up the numbers based on their place value.
2. Subtract the digits in order from right to left (the smallest place value to the largest).

*Example*
What is 7,892 − 521?

*Solution*

### Step 1
Line up the numbers based on their place value.

7,892
− 521

### Step 2
Subtract the digits in the ones place.

7,892
− 521
      1

### Step 3
Subtract the digits in the tens place.

7,892
− 521
    71

**Step 4**

Subtract the digits in the hundreds place.

7,892
− 521
371

There is only one number in the thousands place value so it can be brought down and written below.

7,892
− 521
7,371

---

Sometimes, when you subtract a digit from another in the same place value, the smaller digit will be on top. When this happens, you need to make the smaller digit bigger by borrowing, or regrouping. You can do this by borrowing a value from the next digit to the left. By adding this value to the digit that needs to be made bigger, you can subtract. If you are borrowing from the tens place, you borrow a value of 10. If you are borrowing from the hundreds place, you borrow a value of 100. Follow the same steps, and regroup when needed.

*Example*

What is 523 − 255?

*Solution*

**Step 1**

Line up the numbers based on their place value.

523
− 255

**Step 2**

Subtract the digits in the ones place.

Since 5 cannot be subtracted from 3, take 1 from the tens place value to the left. Add the 1 ten from the tens place value to the 3 in the ones place value. The result is 13. The number 5 can now be subtracted from 13.

1 13
52 3
− 255
8

**Step 3**

Subtract the digits in the tens place.

The 2 in 523 now has a value of 1 because 1 ten was given to the ones place value. Since 5 cannot be subtracted from 1, take 1 from the hundreds place value to the left. Add the 1 hundred from the hundreds place value to the 1 in the tens place value. The result is 11. The number 5 can now be subtracted from 11.

4 11 13
5 2 3
− 255
68

**Step 4**
Subtract the digits in the hundreds place.
The 5 in 523 now has a value of 4 because 1 hundred was given to the tens place value.

```
  4 11 13
  5 2 3
- 2 5 5
  2 6 8
```

---

*4.NBT.5 Multiply a whole number of up to four digits by a one–digit whole number, and multiply two two–digit numbers, using strategies based on place value and the properties of operations. Illustrate and explain the calculation by using equations, rectangular arrays, and/or area models.*

## MULTIPLYING A TWO-DIGIT NUMBER BY ANOTHER TWO-DIGIT NUMBER

To multiply a two digit whole number by a two-digit number, follow these steps:

1. Multiply the first number by the ones of the second number.
2. Multiply the first number by the tens of the second number.
3. Add the two products.

*Example*
What is the product of 67 × 48?

*Solution*
Think of the multiplier 48 as 4 tens (40) and 8 ones.

**Step 1**
Multiply 67 by the ones of 48.

```
  67
× 8
```

Multiply the 8 by the digit in the ones place.
8 × 7 = 56
Regroup the answer as 5 tens and 6 ones. Write the 6 in the ones place. Carry the 5 tens over to the tens place.

```
  5
  67
× 8
   6
```

Multiply 8 by the digit in the tens place.
8 × 6 = 48
Add this to the 5 tens that you carried over.
48 + 5 = 53

```
  5
  67
× 8
 536
```

**Step 2**

Multiply 67 by the tens of 48.

```
  67
× 40
```

If you multiply 67 × 4 and add a zero on the end, that is the same as multiplying 67 × 40. Put a 0 in the ones place, then multiply 67 × 4.

```
  67
× 40
   0
```

Multiply 4 by the digit in the ones place.

4 × 7 = 28

Regroup the answer as 2 tens and 8 ones. Write the 8 in the tens place. Carry the 2.

```
  2
  67
× 40
  80
```

Multiply 4 by the digit in the tens place.

4 × 6 = 24

Add this to the 2 tens that you carried over.

24 + 2 = 26

```
   2
   67
 × 40
 2,680
```

**Step 3**

Add the products.

536 + 2,680 = 3,216

```
   67
 × 48
 3,216
```

## Dropping and Then Adding Zero

When one of the factors in a multiplication problem is a multiple that ends in a zero or zeros, you can drop the zero or zeros, multiply the remaining fact, and then add the dropped zero or zeros to the end of the product.

## Multiples of 10

When one factor ends in a multiple of 10, drop the zero, multiply the basic fact, and then add the zero to the end of the product.

*Example*

Apply the strategy of dropping and then adding zero to solve the problem 6 × 80.

*Solution*

**Step 1**

Drop the zero from 80.

80 → 8

**Step 2**

Multiply the remaining fact.

6 × 8 = 48

**Step 3**
Add the dropped zero to the end of the product.
48 → 480
Therefore, 6 × 80 = 480.

---

## MULTIPLES OF 100

When one of the factors is a multiple of 100, drop the two zeros, multiply the remaining fact, and then add the two zeros to the end of the product.

*Example*
   Apply the strategy of dropping and then adding zero to solve the problem 900 × 9.

*Solution*
   **Step 1**
   Drop the two zeros from 900.
   900 → 9

   **Step 2**
   Multiply the remaining fact.
   9 × 9 = 81

   **Step 3**
   Add the two dropped zeros to the end of the product.
   81 → 8,100
   Therefore, 900 × 9 = 8,100.

---

## MULTIPLES OF 1,000

When one of the factors is a multiple of 1,000, drop the three zeros, multiply the remaining fact, and then add the three dropped zeros to the end of the product.

*Example*
   Apply the strategy of dropping and then adding zero to solve 4 × 2,000.

*Solution*
   **Step 1**
   Drop the three zeros from 2,000.
   2,000 → 2

   **Step 2**
   Multiply the remaining fact.
   4 × 2 = 8

   **Step 3**
   Add the three dropped zeros to the end of the product.
   8 → 8,000
   Therefore, 4 × 2,000 = 8,000.

# Using Mental Math Strategies to Multiply Whole Numbers by 10, 100, and 1,000

One mental math strategy you can use is to look for patterns when multiplying whole numbers by multiples of 10. Look at the pattern that forms when you multiply the same number by 1, 10, 100, and 1,000.

4 × 1 = 4
4 × 10 = 40
4 × 100 = 400
4 × 1 0 = 4 0

| Multiplier | Explanation | Example |
|---|---|---|
| × 10 | There is one zero in 10. Add one zero to the end of the other number. | 36 × 10 = 360 |
| × 100 | There are two zeros in 100. Add two zeros to the end of the other number. | 93 × 10 = 9 30 |
| × 1 0 | There are three zeros in 1000. Add three zeros to the end of the other number. | 7 × 10 = 70 |

One mental strategy for quickly and easily multiplying numbers by 10, 100, or 1,000 is to count the number of zeros. Then, add the same number of zeros to the end of the other number.

*Example*

In a concert hall there are 73 rows with 100 seats.

In total, how many seats are there in the concert hall?

*Solution*

73 × 100 = ☐

**Step 1**
Count the number of zeros in 100.
There are 2 zeros.

**Step 2**
Add 2 zeros to 73.
73 × 100 = 7,300.
There are 7,300 seats in total.

---

# Representing Multiplication Using an Area Model

Multiplication equations can be represented by an area model. An area model follows the same idea as the area formula $A = \text{length} \times \text{width}$. When using an area model to represent multiplication, one number is used to represent the width of the rectangle, and the other number is used to represent the length of the rectangle. Multiply the length by the width to find the total area of the rectangle.

*Example*
To represent the equation 5 × 252 using an area model, draw a rectangle with a width of 5 and a length of 252.

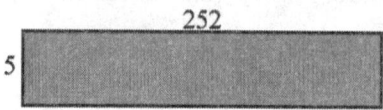

It is difficult to multiply 5 by a big number like 252. To make it easier, you can split 252 into smaller parts that are easier to multiply. The easiest way is to split it up into hundreds, tens, and ones.
252 = 200 + 50 + 2

Now, you can split your rectangle into smaller parts that are easier to multiply.

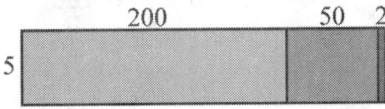

To find the area of the whole rectangle, you can find the area of each smaller part and then add them together. That means that 5 × 252 is the same as 5 × 200 plus 5 × 50 plus 5 × 2.

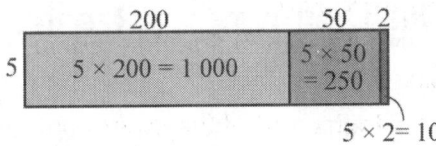

Add these all together to find the total.
A = 1,000 + 250 + 10
A = 1,260

The answer was found using the area model to represent the equation.
5 × 252 = 1,260

---

## MULTIPLYING A ONE-DIGIT NUMBER BY A TWO-DIGIT NUMBER WITH REGROUPING

To multiply a two-digit number by a one-digit number, follow these steps:

1. Line up the numbers based on their place value.
2. Multiply the one-digit number by the ones. Regroup if necessary.
3. Multiply the one-digit number by the tens. Regroup if necessary.

Only single-digit numbers can be written in each place value. When you multiply two numbers and the product is greater than nine, you must regroup the product. For example, if you are multiplying 3 × 4, the product will be 12. Regroup the number down into single digits so it can be recorded correctly. The product 12 can be broken down into 1 ten and 2 ones. The 2 ones would be written in the ones place value, and the 1 ten would be carried over and written above the tens place value.

*Example*
   Solve the multiplication equation 22 × 8 = □.

*Solution*
   **Step 1**
   Line up the numbers based on their place value.
   ```
     22
   ×  8
   ```
   **Step 2**
   Multiply the one-digit number by the ones.
   8 × 2 = 16
   Regroup the 16 into 1 ten and 6 ones. Carry the 1 ten over to the tens place.
   ```
     1
     22
   ×  8
      6
   ```

**Step 3**

Multiply the one-digit number by the tens.
8 × 2 = 16
Add the 1 ten that was carried over.
You have 17 tens. This is regrouped as 7 tens and 1 hundred.

```
  1
 22
× 8
───
176
```

## MULTIPLYING TWO DIGITS BY ONE DIGIT WITHOUT REGROUPING

To multiply a two-digit number by a one-digit number, use the following steps:

1. Line up the numbers based on place value.
2. Multiply the one-digit number by the ones.
3. Multiply the one-digit number by the tens.

*Example*

Solve the multiplication equation 40 × 2 = ☐.

*Solution*

**Step 1**

Line up the numbers based on place value.

```
 40
× 2
```

**Step 2**

Multiply the one-digit number by the ones place value.
2 × 0 = 0
Write the 0 below the ones place value.

```
 40
× 2
───
  0
```

**Step 3**

Multiply the one-digit number by the tens place value.
4 × 2 = 8
Write the 8 below the tens place value.

```
 40
× 2
───
 80
```

## MULTIPLYING A FOUR-DIGIT NUMBER BY A ONE-DIGIT NUMBER

Use the following steps to multiply a four-digit number by a one-digit number:

1. Line up the numbers according to place value.
2. Multiply the one-digit number by the ones place value. Regroup if necessary.
3. Multiply the one-digit number by the tens place value. Regroup if necessary.
4. Multiply the one-digit number by the hundreds place value. Regroup if necessary.
5. Multiply the one-digit number by the thousands place value. Regroup if necessary.

*Example*

Multiply 3 × 1,223.

*Solution*

**Step 1**
Multiply the one-digit number by the ones.
3 × 3 = 9
Place the product under the ones place value.
```
  1,223
×     3
_____
      9
```

**Step 2**
Multiply the one-digit number by the tens.
3 × 2 = 6
Place the product under the tens place value.
```
  1,223
×     3
_____
     69
```

**Step 3**
Multiply the one-digit number by the hundreds.
3 × 2 = 6
Place the product under the hundreds place value.
```
  1,223
×     3
_____
    669
```

**Step 4**
Multiply the one-digit number by the thousands.
3 × 1 = 3
Place the product under the thousands place value.
```
  1,223
×     3
_____
  3,669
```

## REPRESENTING THE DISTRIBUTIVE PROPERTY BY USING AN AREA MODEL

The distributive property says that when you multiply a large number, you can break the expression down into smaller multiplication facts. For example, 2 × 41 is the same as (2 × 40) + (2 × 1).

To represent the distributive property by using an area model, follow these steps:

1. Draw a rectangle to represent the multiplication expression.
2. Break the rectangle into sections that are easier to multiply.
3. Calculate the area of the first section.
4. Calculate the area of the second section.
5. Add the products.

*Example*

Represent the multiplication expression 2 × 65 by using the distributive property.

*Solution*

**Step 1**
Draw a rectangle to represent the multiplication expression.

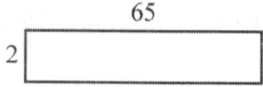

**Step 2**
Break the rectangle into sections that are easy to multiply.
It is usually easiest to break up the rectangle by place value.
65 = 60 + 5

| | 60 | 5 |
|---|---|---|
| 2 | | |

**Step 3**
Calculate the area of the first section.
$A = l \times w$
$A = 2 \times 60$
$A = 120$

| | 60 | 5 |
|---|---|---|
| 2 | 2 × 60 = 120 | |

**Step 4**
Calculate the area of the second section.
$A = l \times w$
$A = 2 \times 5$
$A = 10$

| | 60 | 5 |
|---|---|---|
| 2 | 120 | 2 × 5 = 10 |

**Step 5**
Add the products.
120 + 10 = 130

| | 60 | 5 |
|---|---|---|
| 2 | 120 | 10 |

This means that 2 × 65 = 130.

| | 65 |
|---|---|
| 2 | 130 |

# MULTIPLYING A THREE-DIGIT NUMBER BY A ONE-DIGIT NUMBER

To multiply a three-digit number by a one-digit number, follow these steps:

1. Line up the numbers based on place value.
2. Multiply the one-digit number by the ones. Place the product below in the ones place value. Regroup if necessary.
3. Multiply the one-digit number by the tens. Place the product below in the tens place value. Regroup if necessary.
4. Multiply the one-digit number by the hundreds. Place the product below in the hundreds place value.

*Example*
Solve the multiplication equation 122 × 8 = □.

*Solution*

**Step 1**
Line up the numbers based on their place value.

```
  122
×   8
```

**Step 2**
Multiply the one-digit number by the ones.
8 × 2 = 16
Regroup 16 into 1 ten and 6 ones. The one ten is carried over to the tens place value.

```
   1
  122
×   8
    6
```

**Step 3**
Multiply the one-digit number by the tens.
8 × 2 = 16 plus the 1 that was carried over. There are 17 tens.
This is regrouped as 7 tens and 1 hundred. The 1 is carried over to the hundreds place value.

```
  1 1
  122
×   8
   76
```

**Step 4**
Multiply the one-digit number by the hundreds.
8 × 1 = 8 plus the 1 that was carried over. There are 9 hundreds.

```
  1 1
  122
×   8
  976
```

*4.NBT.6 Find whole-number quotients and remainders with up to four-digit dividends and one-digit divisors, using strategies based on place value, the properties of operations, and/or the relationship between multiplication and division. Illustrate and explain the calculation by using equations, rectangular arrays, and/or area models.*

## DIVIDING 3-DIGIT BY 1-DIGIT WHOLE NUMBERS

**Division** separates a group of objects into several equal, smaller groups. The starting group is called the **dividend**. The number that represents the groups that are separated out is called the **divisor**. The number that represents the objects in each smaller group is called the **quotient**.

$$\text{Divisor} \rightarrow 4\overline{)8} \leftarrow \text{Dividend} \quad \text{(Quotient = 2)}$$

$$\underset{\text{Dividend}}{8} \div \underset{\text{Divisor}}{4} = \underset{\text{Quotient}}{2}$$

You can divide using **place value**.

First, look at the divisor to see if it is greater than (>) or less than (<) the first digit of the dividend.

- If the divisor is less than the first digit of the dividend, the first digit of the quotient (answer) will be placed above the digit in the hundreds place.
- If the divisor is greater than the first digit of the dividend, the first digit of the quotient (answer) will be placed above the digit in the tens place.

*Example*

In the dividend 235, the 2 is in the hundreds place, the 3 is in the tens place, and the 5 is in the ones place.

Divide 235 by 5.

$$5\overline{)235}$$

*Solution*

Follow these steps to see the division process.

**Step 1**
There are 23 tens in the dividend 235.
How many groups of 5 can you make out of 23 tens?
$20 \div 5 = 4$, $4 \times 5 = 20$
You can make 4 groups of 5 tens.
Put the 4 above the 3 of 23.
Put the 20 below the 23.

$$\begin{array}{r} 4\phantom{00} \\ 5\overline{)235} \\ 20\phantom{0} \end{array}$$

### Step 2
Subtract 20 from 23.
(23 − 20 = 3)
Bring down the 5 ones from 235.
Put the 5 to the right of the 3 tens.
You now have 35 ones.

$$\begin{array}{r} 4\phantom{00} \\ 5\overline{)235} \\ \underline{20}\phantom{0} \\ 35 \end{array}$$

### Step 3
How many groups of 5 can you make out of 35 ones?
35 ÷ 5 = 7, 7 × 5 = 35
You can make 7 groups of 5 ones.
Put the 7 above the 5 of 235 (to the right of the 4).
Put the 35 below the 35.

$$\begin{array}{r} 47 \\ 5\overline{)235} \\ \underline{20}\phantom{0} \\ 35 \\ \underline{35} \end{array}$$

### Step 4
Subtract 35 from 35.
You do not have a remainder.
235 ÷ 5 = 47

$$\begin{array}{r} 47 \\ 5\overline{)235} \\ \underline{20}\phantom{0} \\ 35 \\ \underline{35} \\ 0 \end{array}$$

---

*Example*

Hannah has 132 stickers. She pastes 8 stickers on each page.

How many pages will she need in order to paste all the stickers?

*Solution*

To solve this problem, Hannah needs to divide 132 by 8. One way to divide is to use place value.

$$\begin{array}{r} 16 \\ 8\overline{)132} \\ \underline{8}\phantom{00} \leftarrow 8 \times 1 = 8 \\ 52 \leftarrow 13 - 8 = 5; \text{Bring down the 2 ones.} \\ \underline{48} \leftarrow 8 \times 6 = 48 \\ 4 \leftarrow 52 - 48 = 4; \text{There are 4 stickers left over.} \end{array}$$

Hannah needs 17 pages. Can you see why Hannah needs 17 pages, not 16 pages? She needs the extra page to paste the 4 stickers that are left over after she pastes 8 on each of the 16 pages.

# Representing Division Using an Area Model

Division equations can be represented by an area model. An area model follows the same idea as the area formula, which is $A = \text{length} \times \text{width}$.

When using an area model to represent division, the dividend is used to represent the area (the total), and the divisor represents the width. Divide the area of the rectangle by the width to find the length.

$$\frac{\text{area}}{\text{width}} = \text{length}$$

*Example*

To represent the equation $255 \div 5$ using an area model, draw a rectangle with a width of 5 and an area of 255.

$$5 \;|\; 255 \;|$$

It is difficult to divide a large number like 255 by 5. To make it easier, you can split 255 into smaller parts that are easier to divide. The easiest way is to split it up into hundreds, tens, and ones.
$255 = 200 + 50 + 5$

Now, you can split your rectangle into smaller parts that are easier to divide.

$$5 \;|\; 200 \;|\; 50 \;|\; 5 \;|$$

To find the length of the whole rectangle, you can find the length of each smaller part and then add them together. That means that $255 \div 5$ is the same as $200 \div 5$ plus $50 \div 5$ plus $5 \div 5$.

|   | 40 | 10 | 1 |
|---|----|----|---|
| 5 | 200 | 50 | 5 |
|   | $200 \div 5$ = 40 | $50 \div 5$ = 10 | $5 \div 5$ = 1 |

You can write the quotients above the rectangles to show the length of each part.

|   | 40 | 10 | 1 |
|---|----|----|---|
| 5 | 200 | 50 | 5 |

Add these all together to find the total length.
$l = 40 + 10 + 1$
$l = 51$

The answer was found using the area model to represent the equation $255 \div 5 = 51$.

# Dividing Multi-Digit Numbers by One-Digit Numbers

When you divide a whole number, you are breaking the whole number into smaller parts. The starting group is called the **dividend**. The number of small parts the dividend is being broken into is called the **divisor**. The number of objects in each smaller group is called the **quotient**.

$$\text{Divisor} \longrightarrow 4\overline{)8} \longleftarrow \text{Dividend} \quad (\text{Quotient} = 2)$$

$$8 \div 4 = 2$$
(Dividend ÷ Divisor = Quotient)

To divide a multi-digit number by a one-digit number, follow these steps:

1. Write the division sentence as long division.
2. Find out how many times the divisor goes into the first digit of the dividend. Write the answer on top. (Sometimes, the divisor will be too large to fit into the first digit. If this is the case, find out how many times the divisor goes into the first two digits of the dividend).
3. Multiply the number on top by the divisor. Write the answer below. Subtract.
4. Bring down the next number from the dividend. Write it next to the answer from step 4. This is the new dividend.
5. Repeat steps 2, 3, and 4 until the new dividend is 0. The final answer will be left on top.

*Example*
   Divide 8,274 by 3.

*Solution*

   **Step 1**
   Write the division sentence as long division.

   $3\overline{)8\,274}$

   **Step 2**
   Find out how many times the divisor goes into the first digit of the dividend. Write the answer on top.

   $3\overline{)8\,274}$ with 2 on top

   The number 3 goes into 8 two times. Write the number 2 above the 8.

   **Step 3**
   Multiply the number on top by the divisor. Write your answer below. Subtract.

   $3\overline{)8\,274}$
   $\phantom{3)}-6$
   $\phantom{3)\,}\,2$

   Since 3 × 2 = 6, write 6 below the 8. Subtract to find a difference of 2.

### Step 4
Bring down the next number from the dividend. Write it next to the answer from step 3. This is the new dividend.

```
    2
3)8 274
  -6 ↓
    2 2
```

Bring down the 2.

### Step 5
Repeat steps 2, 3, and 4 until the new dividend is 0. The final answer will be left on top.

The number 3 goes into 22 seven times. $3 \times 7 = 21$

Write the 7 on top, and subtract 21 from 22. Bring down the next digit from the dividend.

```
    2 7
3)8 274
  -6 ↓
    2 2
   -2 1 ↓
      1 7
```

The number 3 goes into 17 five times. $3 \times 5 = 15$

Write the 5 on top, and subtract 15 from 17. Bring down the next digit from the dividend.

```
    2 75
3)8 274
  -6 ↓
    2 2
   -2 1 ↓
      1 7
     -1 5 ↓
        2 4
```

The number 3 goes into 24 eight times. $3 \times 8 = 24$

Write the 8 on top, and subtract 24 from 24. Since the new dividend is 0, and there are no more digits to bring down from the dividend, the final answer is the number left on top.

```
    2 758
3)8 274
  -6 ↓
    2 2
   -2 1 ↓
      1 7
     -1 5 ↓
        2 4
       -2 4
          0
```

The number 8,274 divided by 3 is 2,758.

## DIVIDING TWO-DIGIT NUMBERS BY ONE-DIGIT NUMBERS

When you have a division problem, you can sometimes solve it easily in your head. For example, you may know the answer to a question such as 36 ÷ 4 just by looking at it. If you have a problem with a bigger number, such as 92 ÷ 4, you need a different way to find the answer.

These are some strategies for solving division problems with big numbers:

- Long division
- Short division
- Repeated subtraction

To use any of the division strategies, you need to know what a dividend, a divisor, and a quotient are.

$$\text{Divisor} \longrightarrow 4\overline{)8} \longleftarrow \text{Dividend} \quad \text{(Quotient = 2)}$$

$$8 \div 4 = 2$$

where 8 is the Dividend, 4 is the Divisor, and 2 is the Quotient.

## LONG DIVISION

To use long division, follow these steps:

1. Write the division sentence as long division.
2. Find out how many times the divisor goes into the first digit of the dividend. Write the answer on top.
3. Multiply the number on top by the divisor. Write the answer below, and then subtract.
4. Bring down the next number from the dividend.
5. Repeat steps 2 to 4 until you get a difference of zero. The quotient is the number above the dividend.

*Example*

Use long division to solve the expression 92 ÷ 4.

*Solution*

**Step 1**
Write the division sentence as long division.

$$4\overline{)92}$$

**Step 2**
Find out how many times the divisor goes into the first digit of the dividend. Write the answer on top. The number 4 goes into 9 twice. Write the number 2 above the 9.

$$4\overline{)92}^{\,2}$$

**Step 3**
Multiply the number on top by the divisor. Write the answer below, and subtract.
Write 8 below the 9 because 4 × 2 = 8. Subtract to find a difference of 1.

$$\begin{array}{r} 2\phantom{0} \\ 4\overline{)92} \\ -8\phantom{0} \\ \hline 1\phantom{0} \end{array}$$

### Step 4
Bring down the next number from the dividend. Write it next to the difference from step 3. This is the new dividend.
Bring down the 2.

$$\begin{array}{r} 2\phantom{0} \\ 4\overline{)92} \\ -8\downarrow \\ \hline 12 \end{array}$$

### Step 5
Find out how many times the divisor goes into the new dividend. Write this answer on top.
The number 4 goes into 12 three times. Write the number 3 above the 2.

$$\begin{array}{r} 23 \\ 4\overline{)92} \\ -8\phantom{0} \\ \hline 12 \end{array}$$

### Step 6
Multiply the new number on top by the divisor. Write the answer below, and subtract.
Write 12 at the bottom because 4 × 3 = 12. Subtract to find a difference of 0.

$$\begin{array}{r} 23 \\ 4\overline{)92} \\ -8\phantom{0} \\ \hline 12 \\ -12 \\ \hline 0 \end{array}$$

When there is a difference of zero, there are no more steps. The answer is written on top.
The correct answer is 23.

$$\begin{array}{r} 23 \\ 4\overline{)92} \\ -8\phantom{0} \\ \hline 12 \\ -12 \\ \hline 0 \end{array}$$

---

## SHORT DIVISION

Short division is similar to long division, but you skip some of the steps in short division. Short division is a good strategy to use if you are very good at remembering division facts and calculating division with remainders.

To use short division, follow these steps:

1. Write the division sentence as short division.
2. Divide the first digit of the dividend by the divisor. Write the whole number on top, and write the remainder between the first and second digits of the dividend. The remainder and the second digit of the divisor make a new number.
3. Divide the new number by the divisor, and write the answer on top.

*Example*

Use short division to solve the expression 92 ÷ 4.

*Solution*

**Step 1**

Write the division sentence as short division.

4)‾92

**Step 2**

Divide the first digit of the dividend by the divisor.

9 ÷ 4 = 2 R1

Write the whole number on top, and write the remainder between the first and second digits of the dividend. Write the 2 above the 9. Write the 1 between the 9 and the 2 in the dividend.

$\phantom{4)}2\phantom{0}$
4)‾9¹2

The remainder and the second digit of the divisor make a new number.

**Step 3**

Divide the new number by the divisor, and write the answer on top.

12 ÷ 4 = 3

Write the 3 above the 2.

$\phantom{4)}2\,3$
4)‾9①②

The answer is 23.

---

## REPEATED SUBTRACTION

Repeated subtraction is a good strategy to use if you have trouble remembering the steps for long division and short division.

To use repeated subtraction, follow these steps:

1. Write the dividend at the top. Subtract any number that is easy to divide by the divisor.
2. Keep subtracting until you get a difference of zero.
3. Divide each of the numbers you subtracted by the divisor.
4. Find the sum of your answers from step 3.

*Example*

Use repeated subtraction to solve the expression 92 ÷ 4.

*Solution*

**Step 1**

Write the dividend at the top. Subtract any number that is easy to divide by the divisor.

The divisor is 4, so try subtracting 40.

```
  92
- 40
  52
```

### Step 2
Subtract any number that is easy to divide by the divisor.
Try subtracting 40 again.

```
  92
- 40
  52
- 40
  12
```

### Step 3
Subtract any number that is easy to divide by the divisor.
The number 12 is easy to divide by 4.  Subtract 12.

```
  92
- 40
  52
- 40
  12
- 12
   0
```

### Step 4
Divide each of the numbers that you subtracted by the divisor.
To go from 92 to 0, you subtracted 40, 40, and 12.  The divisor is 4.

```
  92
- 40   40 ÷ 4 = 10
  52
- 40   40 ÷ 4 = 10
  12
- 12   12 ÷ 4 = 3
   0
```

### Step 5
Add the underlined numbers together to find the solution.
10 + 10 + 3 = 23
The correct answer is 23.

# EXERCISE #1—NUMBER AND OPERATIONS IN BASE TEN

29. Which of the following expanded notations shows the number 100,024?
    A. 100,000 + 20,000 + 4,000
    B. 100,000 + 2,000 + 4
    C. 100,000 + 20 + 4
    D. 100 + 20 + 4

30. In which of the following sets of numbers is the digit 4 in the same place value position for every number in the set?
    A. 96,407, 43,543, 26,421
    B. 86,194, 576,436, 26,421
    C. 23,407, 875,436, 126,421
    D. 572,194, 254,250, 975,436

*Use the following information to answer the next question.*

> After reading a book on the solar system, Ethan learned that the moon is about three hundred eighty-four thousand four hundred ten kilometers from Earth.

31. What is the distance to the moon written in number form?
    A. 348,010
    B. 348,410
    C. 380,410
    D. 384,410

*Use the following information to answer the next question.*

> A student is given the numbers 985,633, 984,633, 986,633, and 987,633 and asked to compare them.

32. Which of these numbers is the **greatest**?
    A. 984,633
    B. 985,633
    C. 986,633
    D. 987,633

33. Expressed in words, the number 970,012 is
    A. ninety-seven hundred twelve
    B. ninety-seven thousand twelve
    C. nine hundred seven thousand twelve
    D. nine hundred seventy thousand twelve

34. What is 4,621,933 rounded to the nearest ten thousand?
    A. 462,000
    B. 4,620,000
    C. 4,621,900
    D. 4,622,000

35. Rounded to the nearest hundred, the number 5,455,233 is _____.

36. What is 1,743,362 rounded to the nearest thousand?
    A. 1,740,000
    B. 1,743,000
    C. 1,743,360
    D. 1,743,400

37. What is 5,887,412 rounded to the nearest hundred thousand? _____

38. What is the sum of 452 + 698? _____

39. The expression 4,514 − 629 equals _____.

40. The product of 39 × 52 is
    A. 273
    B. 793
    C. 1,418
    D. 2,028

41. What is 50 × 9? _____

42. What is the product of 100 × 5? _____

43. What is the product of 17 × 8?
    A. 142
    B. 136
    C. 122
    D. 112

44. What is the solution to the multiplication equation 11 × 7 = □?
    A. 75
    B. 77
    C. 82
    D. 88

45. What is 2 multiplied by 2,863? _____

*Use the following information to answer the next question.*

| Mackenzie is learning how to use area models to represent the distributive property in her math class. |
|---|
| |       | 80  | 8  |
| | 3     | 240 | 24 | |

46. What problem would Mackenzie be solving by using the given area model?
    A. 3 × 88
    B. 80 × 8
    C. 3 × 240
    D. 240 × 24

Exercise #1      76      Castle Rock Research

47. What is 319 × 8? _____

48. Which of the following area models represents the multiplication equation 2 × 629?

A.  
| 600 | 20 | 9 |
|---|---|---|
| 1,200 | 40 | 18 |
(2)

B.  
| 600 | 2 | 9 |
|---|---|---|
| 1,200 | 4 | 18 |
(2)

C.  
| 60 | 29 |
|---|---|
| 120 | 4 | 18 |
(2)

D.  
| 60 | 20 | 90 |
|---|---|---|
| 120 | 40 | 180 |
(2)

*Use the following information to answer the next question.*

> Monica bought a box of apples. The box contained 365 apples. She divided the apples equally among her five brothers.

49. How many apples did each brother receive?
   A. 37
   B. 73
   C. 136
   D. 145

*Use the following information to answer the next question.*

> Peggy has 555 bottle caps in her collection. She wants to put them into groups of 5 to sell at the county fair. She writes an equation to help her divide the bottle caps.

50. Which of the following area models represents Peggy's equation?

A.  
| 100 | 10 | 1 |
|---|---|---|
| 500 | 50 | 5 |
(5)

B.  
| 10 | 10 | 1 |
|---|---|---|
| 50 | 50 | 5 |
(5)

C.  
| 1 | 1 | 1 |
|---|---|---|
| 5 | 5 | 5 |
(5)

D.  
| 10 | 10 | 10 |
|---|---|---|
| 50 | 50 | 50 |
(5)

*Use the following information to answer the next question.*

> Candice bought 8 stereos on sale for a total of $2,680. She paid the same price for each stereo.

51. How much did each of Candice's stereos cost? $_____

52. What is 72 ÷ 2? _____

# EXERCISE #1—NUMBER AND OPERATIONS IN BASE TEN
## ANSWERS AND SOLUTIONS

| | | | |
|---|---|---|---|
| 29. C | 35. 5455200 | 41. 450 | 47. 2552 |
| 30. C | 36. B | 42. 500 | 48. A |
| 31. D | 37. 5900000 | 43. B | 49. B |
| 32. D | 38. 1150 | 44. B | 50. A |
| 33. D | 39. 3885 | 45. 5726 | 51. 335 |
| 34. B | 40. D | 46. A | 52. 36 |

**29. C**

**Step 1**
Put the number into a place value chart.

| Thousands | | | Ones | | |
|---|---|---|---|---|---|
| H | T | O | H | T | O |
| 1 | 0 | 0 | 0 | 2 | 4 |

**Step 2**
Write the number in expanded notation.

- The 1 in the hundred thousands position equals 100,000.
- There are 0 ten thousands, 0 thousands, and 0 hundreds. The zeros do not need to be shown in the expanded notation.
- The 2 in the tens position equals 20.
- The 4 in the ones position equals 4.
100,000 + 20 + 4

**30. C**

**Step 1**
Make a place value chart to compare the digits in each number.

| Thousands | | | Ones | | |
|---|---|---|---|---|---|
| H | T | O | H | T | O |
| | 9 | 6 | 4 | 0 | 7 |
| | 4 | 3 | 5 | 4 | 3 |
| | 2 | 6 | 4 | 2 | 1 |

The digit 4 is not in the same place value position in the numbers 96,407, 43,543, and 26,421.

| Thousands | | | Ones | | |
|---|---|---|---|---|---|
| H | T | O | H | T | O |
| | 8 | 6 | 1 | 9 | 4 |
| 5 | 7 | 6 | 4 | 3 | 6 |
| | 2 | 6 | 4 | 2 | 1 |

The digit 4 is not in the same place value position in the numbers 86,194, 576,436, and 26,421.

| Thousands | | | Ones | | |
|---|---|---|---|---|---|
| H | T | O | H | T | O |
| | 2 | 3 | 4 | 0 | 7 |
| 8 | 7 | 5 | 4 | 3 | 6 |
| 1 | 2 | 6 | 4 | 2 | 1 |

The digit 4 is in the same place value position in the numbers 23,407, 875,436, and 126,421.

| Thousands | | | Ones | | |
|---|---|---|---|---|---|
| H | T | O | H | T | O |
| 5 | 7 | 2 | 1 | 9 | 4 |
| 2 | 5 | 4 | 2 | 5 | 0 |
| 9 | 7 | 5 | 4 | 3 | 6 |

The digit 4 is not in the same place value position in the numbers 572,194, 254,250, and 975,436.

**Step 2**
Identify the value of the digit 4.
In the numbers 23,407, 875,436, and 126,421, the digit 4 is in the hundreds place and has a value of 400 in each number.

### 31. D

**Step 1**
Break the number words into their periods.
Three hundred eighty-four thousand is in the thousands period.
Four hundred ten is in the ones period.

| Thousands | | | Ones | | |
|---|---|---|---|---|---|
| H | T | O | H | T | O |
| 3 | 8 | 4 | 4 | 1 | 0 |

**Step 2**
Write the number as a numeral.
In numerals, the distance to the moon is 384,410.

### 32. D

**Step 1**
Create a place value chart.

| Thousands | | | Ones | | |
|---|---|---|---|---|---|
| H | T | O | H | T | O |
| 9 | 8 | 5 | 6 | 3 | 3 |
| 9 | 8 | 4 | 6 | 3 | 3 |
| 9 | 8 | 6 | 6 | 3 | 3 |
| 9 | 8 | 7 | 6 | 3 | 3 |

**Step 2**
Start at the left, and compare the numbers in the hundred thousands place.
All numbers have a 9 in the hundred thousands place.

**Step 3**
Compare the ten thousands place.
All numbers have an 8 in the ten thousands place.

**Step 4**
Compare the numbers in the thousands place.
7 > 5, 7 > 4, and 7 > 6
Because 7 is greater than all the other numbers in the thousands place, 987,633 is the greatest number.

### 33. D

**Step 1**
Place the number in a place value chart.

| Thousands | | | Ones | | |
|---|---|---|---|---|---|
| H | T | O | H | T | O |
| 9 | 7 | 0 | 0 | 1 | 2 |

**Step 2**
To write a number in words, start from the left and work toward the right.
The number in the thousands period is 970. Since 970 represents thousands, the word *thousand* is added after the number. It is written as nine hundred seventy thousand.
The number in the ones period is 12. It is written as twelve.

**Step 3**
Put the two written forms together.
Write the thousands period first, followed by the ones period.
Expressed in words, the number 970,012 is nine hundred seventy thousand twelve.

### 34. B

**Step 1**
Place the number in a place value chart.

| Millions | Thousands | | | Ones | | |
|---|---|---|---|---|---|---|
| O | H | T | O | H | T | O |
| 4 | 6 | 2 | 1 | 9 | 3 | 3 |

**Step 2**
Look at the number to the right of the place value that is being rounded to.
Look at the number of thousands. Since 1 is less than 5, the 2 ten thousands will stay the same.

**Step 3**
Replace all other digits to the right with zeros.
Replace the 1 thousands, 9 hundreds, 3 tens, and 3 ones with zeros.
Rounded to the nearest ten thousand, 4,621,933 becomes 4,620,000.

**35.** 5455200

**Step 1**
Place the number in a place value chart.

| Millions | Thousands | | | Ones | | |
|---|---|---|---|---|---|---|
| O | H | T | O | H | T | O |
| 5 | 4 | 5 | 5 | 2 | 3 | 3 |

**Step 2**
Look at the number to the right of the place value that is being rounded to.
Look at the number of tens. Since 3 is less than 5, the 2 hundreds will stay the same.

**Step 3**
Replace all other digits to the right of the hundreds with zeros.
Replace the 3 tens and 3 ones with zeros.
Rounded to the nearest hundred, 5,455,233 becomes 5,455,200.

**36.** B

**Step 1**
Place the number in a place value chart.

| Millions | Thousands | | | Ones | | |
|---|---|---|---|---|---|---|
| O | H | T | O | H | T | O |
| 1 | 7 | 4 | 3 | 3 | 6 | 2 |

**Step 2**
Look at the number to the right of the place value that is being rounded to.
Look at the number of hundreds. Since 3 is less than 5, the thousands will stay the same.

**Step 3**
Replace all numbers to the right with zeros.
Replace the 3 hundreds, 6 tens, and 2 ones with zeros.
Rounded to the nearest thousand, 1,743,362 becomes 1,743,000.

**37.** 5900000

**Step 1**
Place the number in a place value chart.

| Millions | Thousands | | | Ones | | |
|---|---|---|---|---|---|---|
| O | H | T | O | H | T | O |
| 5 | 8 | 8 | 7 | 4 | 1 | 2 |

**Step 2**
Look at the number to the right of the place value you are rounding to.
Look at the number of ten thousands, since that is to the right of the hundred thousands. Since 8 is greater than 5, the hundred thousands will round up to 9 hundred thousands.

**Step 3**
Replace all numbers to the right of the hundred thousands with zeros.
The 8 ten thousands, 7 thousands, 4 hundreds, 1 tens, and 2 ones will be replaced with zeros.
Rounded to the nearest hundred thousand, 5,887,412 becomes 5,900,000.

**38.** 1150

**Step 1**
Line up the numbers based on place value.
$$\begin{array}{r}452\\+698\end{array}$$

**Step 2**
Add the ones.
8 + 2 = 10
You have 10 ones. You can only have single-digit numbers in each place value, so you will need to regroup 10 as 1 ten and 0 ones. Bring the 1 ten over to the tens place.
$$\begin{array}{r}\phantom{0}1\phantom{00}\\452\\+698\\\hline 0\end{array}$$

**Step 3**
Add the tens.
9 + 5 + 1 = 15
You have 15 tens. You can only have single-digit numbers in each place value, so you will need to regroup 15 tens as 1 hundred and 5 tens.
$$\begin{array}{r}11\phantom{0}\\452\\+698\\\hline 50\end{array}$$

### Step 4
Add the hundreds.

4 + 6 + 1 = 11

You have 11 hundreds. You can only have single-digit numbers in each place value, so you will need to regroup 11 hundreds as 1 thousand and 1 hundred.

```
  11
  452
 +698
 1,150
```

### 39. 3885

#### Step 1
Line up the numbers based on their place values.

```
  4 5 1 4
-   6 2 9
```

#### Step 2
Subtract the ones.

It is impossible to subtract 9 from 4. Borrow 1 from the tens place. Remember that 1 ten equals 10 ones, which gives a total of 14 ones and 0 tens.

14 − 9 = 5

```
        0 14
  4 5 1 4
-   6 2 9
          5
```

#### Step 3
Subtract the tens.

The 1 in the tens place value is now a zero because you borrowed to complete step 2. It is impossible to subtract 2 from 0. Borrow 1 from the hundreds place. Remember that 1 hundred equals 10 tens.

There are now 10 in the tens place and 4 in the hundreds place.

10 − 2 = 8

```
     4 10 14
  4 5 1 4
-   6 2 9
        8 5
```

### Step 4
Subtract the hundreds.

There are now 4 hundreds because you borrowed 1 in step 3. It is impossible to subtract 6 from 4. Borrow 1 from the thousands place. Remember that 1 thousand equals 10 hundreds.

That gives a total of 14 hundreds and 3 thousands.

14 − 6 = 8

```
  3 14 10 14
  4 5 1 4
-   6 2 9
      8 8 5
```

### Step 5
Subtract the thousands.

In step 4, you borrowed 1 thousand. There are 3 thousands left.

3 − 0 = 3

```
  3 14 10 14
  4 5 1 4
-   6 2 9
  3 8 8 5
```

The expression 4,514 − 629 equals 3,885.

### 40. D

#### Step 1
Multiply 39 by 2.

```
   1
   39
 x  2
   78
```

#### Step 2
Multiply 39 by 50.

```
    4
   39
 x 50
 1,950
```

#### Step 3
Add the two products.

78 + 1,950 = 2,028

### 41. 450

#### Step 1
Drop the zero.

50 → 5

#### Step 2
Do the remaining multiplication.

5 × 9 = 45

**Step 3**

Add the zero that was dropped back onto the product.

45 → 450

50 × 9 = 450

**42.** 500

There are two zeros after the 1. To find the product, simply place two zeros after the 5.

100 × 5 = 500

**43.** B

**Step 1**

Line up the numbers based on their place value.

17
× 8

**Step 2**

Multiply the one-digit number by the number in the ones place value.

8 × 7 = 56

Regroup 56 into 5 tens and 6 ones. Carry the 5 tens over to the tens place value.

⁵
17
× 8
---
6

**Step 3**

Multiply the one-digit number by the number in the tens place value.

8 × 1 = 8

Add the 5 tens that were carried over.

8 + 5 = 13

You have 13 tens. This is regrouped as 1 hundred and 3 tens.

⁵
17
× 8
---
136

The product of 17 × 8 is 136.

**44.** B

**Step 1**

Line up the numbers based on their place values.

11
× 7

**Step 2**

Multiply the one-digit number by the ones place value.

1 × 7 = 7

Write the 7 below the ones place value.

11
× 7
---
7

**Step 3**

Multiply the one-digit number by the tens place value.

1 × 7 = 7

Write the 7 below the tens place value.

11
× 7
---
77

**45.** 5726

**Step 1**

Multiply the one-digit number by the ones.

2 × 3 = 6

Place the 6 below the line of the ones place value.

2863
×    2
-----
6

**Step 2**

Multiply the one-digit number by the tens.

2 × 6 = 12

Place the 2 below the line of the tens place, and carry the 1 to the top of the hundreds place.

¹
2863
×    2
-----
26

**Step 3**

Multiply the one-digit number by the hundreds. Do not forget to add the 1 that was carried over from the tens.

2 × 8 = 16

16 + 1 = 17

Place the 7 below the line of the hundreds place, and carry the 1 to the top of the thousands place.

¹¹
2863
×    2
-----
726

### Step 4
Multiply the one-digit number by the thousands. Do not forget to add the 1 that was carried over from the hundreds.
2 × 2 = 4
4 + 1 = 5
Place the 5 below the line of the thousands place.

```
  11
 2863
×   2
─────
 5,726
```

### 46. A
In the area model, the large number has been broken into easier multiplication facts.

The top two numbers on the area model are 80 and 8. When you add those numbers together, you get 88.

The number on the left side of the area model is 3.

An area model is used to calculate *A = l × w*.

The problem Mackenzie would be solving by using the given area model is 3 × 88.

### 47. 2552

**Step 1**
Line up the numbers based on their place value.
```
 319
×  8
```

**Step 2**
Multiply the 8 by 9.
8 × 9 = 72
Regroup 72 into 7 tens and 2 ones. The 7 tens are carried over to the tens place.
```
  7
 319
×  8
────
   2
```

### Step 3
Multiply the 8 by 1, and then add the 7 tens you carried over.
Since 8 × 1 = 8, adding the 7 tens that were carried over equals 15 tens.
This is regrouped as 1 hundred and 5 tens. The 1 hundred is carried over to the hundreds place.
```
  17
 319
×  8
────
  52
```

### Step 4
Multiply the 8 by 3, and then add the 1 hundred you carried over.
Since 8 × 3 = 24, adding the 1 hundred that was carried over makes 25 hundreds.
```
  17
 319
×  8
─────
 2,552
```

### 48. A
**Step 1**
Write the larger number in expanded notation. When using an area model to represent multiplication, the multiplicand is used to represent the length, and the multiplier represents the width. Break up the multiplicand into its place values.
629 = 600 + 20 + 9

**Step 2**
Draw the area model using the place values.

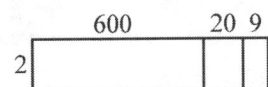

Calculate the products of each place value.
2 × 600 = 1,200
2 × 20 = 40
2 × 9 = 18

**Step 3**
Complete the area model.
Write the products in the area model to show the total area.
This area model represents 2 × 629.

|   | 600   | 20 | 9  |
|---|-------|----|----|
| 2 | 1,200 | 40 | 18 |

### 49. B

**Step 1**
Determine the expression to use to find the number of apples each brother received.
The total number of apples is 365, and the number of brothers is 5.
To determine the expression, divide the total number of apples by the number of brothers.
5)365

**Step 2**
Divide 365 by 5.
The number 5 can go into 36 seven times. Write a 7 above the 36.
Since $5 \times 7 = 35$, subtract 35 from 36, and bring down the 5.

```
    7
5)365
 -35
   15
```

The number 5 can go into 15 three times. Write a 3 above the 5.
Since $5 \times 3 = 15$, subtract 15 from 15. There is 0 left over.

```
   73
5)365
 -35
   15
  -15
    0
```

Each brother received 73 apples.

### 50. A

**Step 1**
Write the larger number in expanded notation. Split the larger number into hundreds, tens, and ones.
$555 = 500 + 50 + 5$

**Step 2**
Draw the area model.
Write the smaller number along the width of the rectangle. Write the hundreds, tens, ones of the larger number inside the rectangle.
This is the area model that represents Peggy's equation.

|   | 100 | 10 | 1 |
|---|---|---|---|
| 5 | 500 | 50 | 5 |

If you need help, this is how the quotients are found:
$500 \div 5 = 100$
$50 \div 5 = 10$
$5 \div 5 = 1$

**Step 3**
To find the quotient of $555 \div 5$, add the individual quotients from the expanded area.
$100 + 10 + 1 = 111$
$555 \div 5 = 111$

### 51. 335

**Step 1**
Write the division sentence as long division.
8)2,680

**Step 2**
Find out how many times the divisor goes into the dividend. Write your answer on top.
Since 8 does not go into the first digit (2), you must look at the first two digits (26). The number 8 goes into 24 three times, so write the number 3 above the 6.

```
    3
8)2,680
```

**Step 3**
Multiply the number on top by the divisor. Write your answer below, and subtract. Since $8 \times 3 = 24$, write 24 below 26. Subtract to find a difference of 2.

```
    3
8)2,680
  -24
    2
```

## Step 4
Bring down the next number from the dividend. Bring down the 8. Write it next to your answer from step 3. This is your new dividend.

$$\begin{array}{r} 3 \\ 2\overline{)2{,}680} \\ -24 \\ \hline 28 \end{array}$$

## Step 5
Repeat steps 2, 3, and 4 until you reach 0. The final answer will be left on top.

$$\begin{array}{r} 335 \\ 8\overline{)2{,}680} \\ -24 \\ \hline 28 \\ -24 \\ \hline 40 \\ -40 \\ \hline 0 \end{array}$$

Each of the stereos cost Candice $335.

## 52. 36

### Method 1
Use long division.

| Write the division sentence as long division. | $2\overline{)72}$ |
|---|---|
| Two goes into seven 3 times. Write the number 3 above the 7. | $\begin{array}{r}3\\2\overline{)72}\end{array}$ |
| Since 2 × 3 = 6, write 6 below the 7. Subtract to find a difference of 1. | $\begin{array}{r}3\\2\overline{)72}\\-6\\\hline 1\end{array}$ |
| Bring down the 2. | $\begin{array}{r}3\\2\overline{)72}\\-6\downarrow\\\hline 12\end{array}$ |
| Two goes into 12 six times. Write the number 6 above the 2. | $\begin{array}{r}36\\2\overline{)72}\\-6\\\hline 12\end{array}$ |
| Since 2 × 6 = 12, write 12 at the bottom. Subtract to find a difference of 0. The correct answer is 36. | $\begin{array}{r}36\\2\overline{)72}\\-6\\\hline 12\\-12\\\hline 0\end{array}$ |

### Method 2
Use short division.

| Write the division sentence as short division. | $2\overline{)72}$ |
|---|---|
| Two goes into seven 3 times with a remainder of 1. Write the 3 above the 7. Write the 1 next to the 2. | $\begin{array}{r}3\\2\overline{)7^12}\end{array}$ |
| Two goes into 12 six times, and there is no remainder. Write the 6 above the 2. The correct answer is 36. | $\begin{array}{r}3\ 6\\2\overline{)7^12}\end{array}$ |

**Method 3**

Use repeated subtraction.
When you use repeated subtraction, you can use any numbers that make sense to you.
This is only one possible way to find the answer. The important thing is to keep subtracting until you reach zero.

| | |
|---|---|
| Start with the number 72 at the top. Subtract any number that is easy to divide by 2. Try subtracting 40. | 72<br>− 40<br>32 |
| Subtract another number that is easy to divide by 2. Try subtracting 20. | 72<br>− 40<br>32<br>− 20<br>12 |
| The number 12 is already easy to divide by 2. Subtract 12. | 72<br>− 40<br>32<br>− 20<br>12<br>− 12<br>0 |
| To get from 72 to zero, you subtracted 40, then 20, and then 12. Write the solutions to 40 ÷ 2, 20 ÷ 2, and to 12 ÷ 2. | 72<br>−40 → 40 ÷ 2 = **20**<br>32<br>−20 → 20 ÷ 2 = **10**<br>12<br>−12 → 12 ÷ 2 = **6**<br>0 |
| Add the underlined numbers together to find the solution. The correct answer is 36. | 20 + 10 + 6 = 36 |

# EXERCISE #2—NUMBER AND OPERATIONS IN BASE TEN

53. Written in expanded notation, the number 236,079 is
    A. 200,000 + 30,000 + 6,000 + 700 + 90
    B. 20,000 + 30,000 + 6,000 + 700 + 90
    C. 200,000 + 30,000 + 6,000 + 70 + 9
    D. 20,000 + 3,000 + 600 + 70 + 9

54. What digit is in the tens place value in the number 245,697?
    A. 5
    B. 6
    C. 7
    D. 9

55. For an election campaign, five hundred eighty-seven thousand five hundred pamphlets were printed. The number of pamphlets printed, written in number form, is
    A. 515,875
    B. 500,587
    C. 587,500
    D. 875,500

*Use the following information to answer the next question.*

Ross learned that in one particular week, the bottle depot near his house received the following numbers of beverage containers:

- 154,370 pop cans
- 154,073 glass bottles
- 150,347 plastic bottles
- 134,075 milk cartons

56. The bottle depot received the **greatest** amount of which beverage container?
    A. 134,075
    B. 150,347
    C. 154,073
    D. 154,370

57. Expressed in words, the number 42,678 is written as
    A. forty-two six hundred seventy-eight
    B. forty-two thousand six hundred seventy-eight
    C. four hundred twenty-six thousand seventy-eight
    D. four hundred and two thousand six hundred seventy-eight

58. What is the number 3,233,143 rounded to the nearest ten thousand?
    A. 3,200,000
    B. 3,230,000
    C. 3,231,000
    D. 3,233,100

59. What is the value of the number 1,892,143 rounded to the nearest hundred?
    A. 1,892,145
    B. 1,892,140
    C. 1,892,100
    D. 1,892,000

60. What is 1,688,888 rounded to the nearest thousand?
    A. 1,688,889
    B. 1,688,890
    C. 1,688,900
    D. 1,689,000

61. What is 4,751,582 rounded to the nearest hundred thousand? _____

62. The sum of 8,125 + 1,214 is _____.

63. What is the difference of 9,654 − 2,133? _____

64. What is the product of 76 × 84?
    A. 6,384
    B. 6,080
    C. 984
    D. 912

65. What is 40 × 7? _____

66. What is 18 × 100?
    A. 80
    B. 180
    C. 1,800
    D. 180,000

67. What is 596 × 7? _____

*Use the following information to answer the next question.*

Sam is learning how to use area models to represent the distributive property in his math class.

68. Which of the following area models represents 4 × 92?

    A.  | 20 | 20 |
        |----|----|
        | 80 | 80 |
        (4 on left)

    B.  | 50 | 40 |
        |----|----|
        | 50 | 40 |
        (1 on left)

    C.  | 50 | 25 |
        |----|----|
        | 200| 100|
        (4 on left)

    D.  | 90 | 2 |
        |----|---|
        | 360| 8 |
        (4 on left)

69. What is 6 × 1,243?
    A. 7,458
    B. 7,218
    C. 6,248
    D. 6,218

*Use the following information to answer the next question.*

Brittany is asked to solve the multiplication equation 4 × 191 = ☐.

70. Which of the following area models represents Brittany's multiplication equation?

A.
|   | 100 | 9 | 1 |
|---|---|---|---|
| 4 | 400 | 36 | 4 |

B.
|   | 10 | 90 | 1 |
|---|---|---|---|
| 4 | 40 | 360 | 4 |

C.
|   | 1 | 9 | 1 |
|---|---|---|---|
| 4 | 4 | 36 | 4 |

D.
|   | 100 | 90 | 1 |
|---|---|---|---|
| 4 | 400 | 360 | 4 |

71. Solve the multiplication equation 22 × 8 = ☐.

72. Solve the multiplication equation 40 × 2 = ☐.

*Use the following information to answer the next question.*

Mrs. Baxter had a bag of 120 candies. She gave all the candies to the students in her class. Each student received 8 candies.

73. How many students are in Mrs. Baxter's class?
    A. 10
    B. 15
    C. 20
    D. 25

74. Which of the following area models represents 288 ÷ 4?

    A.
    |   | 5 | 2 | 2 |
    |---|---|---|---|
    | 4 | 20 | 8 | 8 |

    B.
    |   | 50 | 2 | 2 |
    |---|----|---|---|
    | 4 | 200 | 8 | 8 |

    C.
    |   | 5 | 20 | 2 |
    |---|---|----|---|
    | 4 | 20 | 80 | 8 |

    D.
    |   | 50 | 20 | 2 |
    |---|----|----|---|
    | 4 | 200 | 80 | 8 |

75. When 3,462 is divided by 4, the quotient is
    A. 265, with a remainder of 4
    B. 365, with a remainder of 4
    C. 465, with a remainder of 2
    D. 865, with a remainder of 2

76. What is 84 ÷ 6? _____

Exercise #2

# EXERCISE #2—NUMBER AND OPERATIONS IN BASE TEN ANSWERS AND SOLUTIONS

| 53. C | 59. C | 65. 280 | 71. See solution |
| 54. D | 60. D | 66. C | 72. See solution |
| 55. C | 61. 4800000 | 67. 4172 | 73. B |
| 56. D | 62. 9339 | 68. D | 74. D |
| 57. B | 63. 7521 | 69. A | 75. D |
| 58. B | 64. A | 70. D | 76. 14 |

## 53. C

**Step 1**
Place the number into a place value chart.

| Thousands | | | Ones | | |
|---|---|---|---|---|---|
| H | T | O | H | T | O |
| 2 | 3 | 6 | 0 | 7 | 9 |

**Step 2**
Find the value of each digit in the place value chart.

- The 2 in the hundred thousands place is equal to 200,000.
- The 3 in the ten thousands place is equal to 30,000.
- The 6 in the thousands place is equal to 6,000.
- The 0 does not need to be included.
- The 7 in the tens place is equal to 70.
- The 9 in the ones place is equal to 9.

**Step 3**
Write the expanded notation.
200,000 + 30,000 + 6,000 + 70 + 9

## 54. D

**Step 1**
Place the number into a place value chart.

| Thousands | | | Ones | | |
|---|---|---|---|---|---|
| H | T | O | H | T | O |
| 2 | 4 | 5 | 6 | 9 | 7 |

**Step 2**
Identify the place value of each digit in the number 245,697.

- The digit 7 is in the ones position.
- The digit 9 is in the tens position.
- The digit 6 is in the hundreds position.
- The digit 5 is in the thousands position.
- The digit 4 is in the ten thousands position.
- The digit 2 is in the hundred thousands position.

The digit 9 is in the tens position in the number 245,697.

## 55. C

To write the numeral for the number five hundred eighty-seven thousand five hundred, you can use a place value chart.

Since there are 587 thousands, write 587 in the thousands period.

Since there are 500 ones, write 500 in the ones period.

| Thousands | | | Ones | | |
|---|---|---|---|---|---|
| Hundreds | Tens | Ones | Hundreds | Tens | Ones |
| 5 | 8 | 7 | 5 | 0 | 0 |

The numeral in the place value chart is 587,500.

### 56. D

**Step 1**
Use a table of values.
Write each digit of each number in the correct place value position.

| Thousands | | | Ones | | |
|---|---|---|---|---|---|
| H | T | O | H | T | O |
| 1 | 5 | 4 | 3 | 7 | 0 |
| 1 | 5 | 4 | 0 | 7 | 3 |
| 1 | 5 | 0 | 3 | 4 | 7 |
| 1 | 3 | 4 | 0 | 7 | 5 |

**Step 2**
Compare the digits in the greatest place value position.
The greatest place value position is the hundred thousands.
All four numbers have a 1 in the hundred thousands position.

**Step 3**
Compare the digits in the ten thousands position.
Since 5 > 3, eliminate 134,075 and continue comparing 154,370, 154,073, and 150,347.

**Step 4**
Compare the digits in the thousands position.
Since 4 > 0, eliminate 150,347 and continue comparing only 154,370 and 154,073.

**Step 5**
Compare the digits in the hundreds position.
Since 3 > 0, the number 154,370 has the greatest value.

### 57. B

**Step 1**
Place the number in a place value chart.

| Thousands | | | Ones | | |
|---|---|---|---|---|---|
| H | T | O | H | T | O |
| 0 | 4 | 2 | 6 | 7 | 8 |

**Step 2**
To write a number in words, start from the left and work to the right.

The number in the thousands period is 42. Since 42 represents thousands, the word *thousand* is added after the number. It is written as forty-two thousand.

The number in the ones period is 678. It is written as six hundred seventy-eight.

**Step 3**
Put the two written forms together.
Write the thousands period first, followed by the ones period.

Expressed in words, the number 42,678 is written as forty-two thousand six hundred seventy-eight.

### 58. B

**Step 1**
Place the number in a place value chart.

| Millions | Thousands | | | Ones | | |
|---|---|---|---|---|---|---|
| O | H | T | O | H | T | O |
| 3 | 2 | 3 | 3 | 1 | 4 | 3 |

**Step 2**
Look at the number to the right of the place value that the number is being rounding to.

In this case, the number is being rounded to the nearest ten thousand, so the place value to the right is the one thousands.

Look at the number of one thousands. Since 3 is less than 5, the 3 ten thousands will stay the same.

**Step 3**
Replace all other digits to the right of the ten thousands with zeros.

The 3 thousands, 1 hundreds, 4 tens, and 3 ones will be replaced with zeros.

Rounded to the nearest ten thousand, 3,233,143 becomes 3,230,000.

### 59. C

**Step 1**
Put the number in a place value chart.

| Millions | Thousands | | | Ones | | |
|---|---|---|---|---|---|---|
| O | H | T | O | H | T | O |
| 1 | 8 | 9 | 2 | 1 | 4 | 3 |

**Step 2**
Look at the numbers to the right of the place value you are rounding to.
Since the number is being rounded to the hundreds, the tens place will be looked at.
The number in the tens place is 4, which is less than 5, so the 1 hundred will stay the same.

**Step 3**
Replace all digits to the right with zeros.
The 4 tens and 3 ones will then be replaced with zeros.
Rounded to the nearest hundred, 1,892,143 becomes 1,892,100.

60. **D**

**Step 1**
Place the number in a place value chart.

| Millions | Thousands | | | Ones | | |
|---|---|---|---|---|---|---|
| O | H | T | O | H | T | O |
| 1 | 6 | 8 | 8 | 8 | 8 | 8 |

**Step 2**
Look at the number to the right of the place value that is being rounded to.
Look at the number of hundreds. Since 8 is greater than 5, the number of thousands will round up to 9.

**Step 3**
Replace all numbers to the right of the thousands place with zeros.
The 8 hundreds, 8 tens, and 8 ones will be replaced with zeros.
Rounded to the nearest thousand, 1,688,888 becomes 1,689,000.

61. **4800000**

**Step 1**
Enter the number into a place value chart.

| Millions | Thousands | | | Ones | | |
|---|---|---|---|---|---|---|
| O | H | T | O | H | T | O |
| 4 | 7 | 5 | 1 | 5 | 8 | 2 |

**Step 2**
Look at the number to the right of the hundred thousands place value.
This is the number in the ten thousands place.
The number in the ten thousands place is equal to 5, so the number in the hundred thousands place will round up to 8.

**Step 3**
Replace all numbers to the right of the hundred thousands place value with zeros.
Rounded to the nearest hundred thousand, 4,751,582 becomes 4,800,000.

62. **9339**

**Step 1**
Line up the numbers using place value.
  8,125
+1,214

**Step 2**
Add the digits in the ones place.
  8,125
+1,214
      9

**Step 3**
Add the digits in the tens place.
  8,125
+1,214
    39

**Step 4**
Add the digits in the hundreds place.
  8,125
+1,214
  339

**Step 5**
Add the digits in the thousands place.
  8,125
+1,214
9,339

63. **7521**

**Step 1**
Line up the numbers based on their place value.
  9,654
− 2,133

**Step 2**
Subtract the ones.
  9,654
− 2,133
      1

**Step 3**
Subtract the tens.
  9,654
− 2,133
    21

**Step 4**
Subtract the hundreds.
```
  9,654
- 2,133
    521
```

**Step 5**
Subtract the thousands.
```
  9,654
- 2,133
  7,521
```

64. **A**

  **Step 1**
  Multiply 4 by 76.
  ```
   ²76
  ×   4
    304
  ```

  **Step 2**
  Multiply 80 by 76.
  ```
   ⁴76
  ×  80
  6,080
  ```

  **Step 3**
  Add the two products.
  6,080 + 304 = 6,384

65. **280**

  **Step 1**
  Drop the zero.
  40 → 4

  **Step 2**
  Do the remaining multiplication.
  4 × 7 = 28

  **Step 3**
  Add back onto the product the zero that was dropped.
  28 → 280
  This means that 40 × 7 = 280.

66. **C**

  When you are multiplying by multiples of 10, the multiple and the answer always contain the same number of zeros.

  Determine how many zeros are in the multiple. Add this amount of zeros to the product.

  Since there are two zeros in 100, add two zeros to 18.
  18 × 100 = 1,800

67. **4172**

  **Step 1**
  Line up the numbers based on their place value.
  ```
  596
  × 7
  ```

  **Step 2**
  Multiply the 7 by 6.
  7 × 6 = 42
  Regroup 42 into 4 tens and 2 ones. The 4 tens are carried over to the tens place.
  ```
    ⁴
  596
  × 7
    2
  ```

  **Step 3**
  Multiply the 7 by 9, and then add the 4 tens you carried over.
  Since 7 × 9 = 63, adding the 4 tens that were carried over equals 67 tens.
  This is regrouped as 6 hundreds and 7 tens. The 6 hundreds are carried over to the hundreds place.
  ```
   ⁶⁴
  596
  ×  7
   72
  ```

  **Step 4**
  Multiply the 7 by 5, and then add the 6 hundreds you carried over.
  Since 7 × 5 = 35, adding the 6 hundreds that were carried over makes 41 hundreds.
  ```
   ⁶⁴
  596
  ×   7
  4,172
  ```

68. **D**

  **Step 1**
  Break the larger number into easier multiplication facts.
  The expression 4 × 92 can be broken down into 4 × 90 and 4 × 2 because 90 + 2 = 92.

**Step 2**
Draw two rectangles side by side representing the area of the new multiplication facts.

```
       90    2
   4 |_____|__|
```

This area model represents 4 × 92.

```
       90    2
   4 | 360 | 8 |
```

**69. A**

**Step 1**
Multiply the one-digit number by the ones.
6 × 3 = 18
Write the 8 below the line of the ones place, and carry the 1 to the top of the tens place.

```
    ¹
   1243
 ×    6
   ─────
      8
```

**Step 2**
Multiply the one-digit number by the tens. Remember to add the 1 that was carried over from the ones.
6 × 4 = 24
24 + 1 = 25
Write the 5 below the line of the tens place, and carry the 2 to the top of the hundreds place.

```
   ²¹
   1243
 ×    6
   ─────
     58
```

**Step 3**
Multiply the one-digit number by the hundreds. Remember to add the 2 that was carried over from the tens.
6 × 2 = 12
12 + 2 = 14
Write the 4 below the line of the hundreds place, and carry the 1 to the top of the thousands place.

```
  ¹²¹
   1243
 ×    6
   ─────
    458
```

**Step 4**
Multiply the one-digit number by the thousands. Remember to add the 1 that was carried over from the hundreds.
6 × 1 = 6
6 + 1 = 7
Write the 7 below the line of the thousands place.

```
  ¹²¹
   1243
 ×    6
   ─────
   7,458
```

**70. D**

**Step 1**
Write the larger number in expanded notation.
Split the larger number into hundreds, tens, and ones.
191 = 100 + 90 + 1

**Step 2**
Draw an area model.
Split and label the rectangle.
Write the smaller number along the width of the rectangle. Write the ones, tens, and hundreds of the larger number along the top of the rectangle.
This area model represents 4 × 191.

```
       100    90   1
   4 | 400 | 360 | 4 |
```

Write out the multiplication equations.
4 × 100 = 400
4 × 90 = 360
4 × 1 = 4

All the products are written in the rectangle under the length to show the total area.

**Step 3**
Find the product.
To find the product of 4 × 191, add up each of the individual products from the expanded length.
400 + 360 + 4 = 764
4 × 191 = 764

**71.**

**Step 1**
Line up the numbers based on their place value.

```
    22
  ×  8
```

**Step 2**
Multiply the one-digit number by the ones.
8 × 2 = 16
Regroup the 16 into 1 ten and 6 ones. Carry the 1 ten over to the tens place.
```
  1
  22
×  8
   6
```

**Step 3**
Multiply the one-digit number by the tens.
8 × 2 = 16
Add the 1 ten that was carried over.
You have 17 tens. This is regrouped as 7 tens and 1 hundred.
```
  1
  22
×  8
 176
```

**72.**
**Step 1**
Line up the numbers based on place value.
```
 40
× 2
```

**Step 2**
Multiply the one-digit number by the ones place value.
2 × 0 = 0
Write the 0 below the ones place value.
```
 40
× 2
  0
```

**Step 3**
Multiply the one-digit number by the tens place value.
4 × 2 = 8
Write the 8 below the tens place value.
```
 40
× 2
 80
```

**73. B**
**Step 1**
Write out the expression to determine the number of students.
The total number of candies is 120.
The number of candies received by each student is 8.
The number of students in the class is equal to the value of the expression 120 ÷ 8.

**Step 2**
Determine the number of students by dividing 120 by 8.
```
     15
 8)120
   − 8
    40
   −40
     0
```
When 120 is divided by 8, 15 is the quotient and 0 is the remainder.
The value of the expression is 15.
Therefore, there are 15 students in Mrs. Baxter's class.

**74. D**
**Step 1**
Write the larger number in expanded notation.
Split the larger number into hundreds, tens, and ones.
288 = 200 + 80 + 8

**Step 2**
Draw an area model.
Write the smaller number along the width of the rectangle. Write the ones, tens, and hundreds of the larger number inside the rectangle.
This area model represents 288 ÷ 4.

|   | 50 | 20 | 2 |
|---|----|----|---|
| 4 | 200 | 80 | 8 |

If you need help, this is how the quotients are found:
200 ÷ 4 = 50
 80 ÷ 4 = 20
  8 ÷ 4 = 2
All the individual quotients are written on top of the area being divided.

## Step 3
To find the quotient of 288 ÷ 4, add the individual quotients from the expanded area.
50 + 20 + 2 = 72
288 ÷ 4 = 72

## 75. D
### Step 1
Set up the division equation.
Write the divisor (4) in front of the division bracket and the dividend (3,462) below the division bracket.
divisor)dividend
4)3,462

### Step 2
Determine if the first digit in the dividend can be divided by the divisor. If not, use the first two digits of the dividend.
The first digit in the dividend (3) is smaller than 4 (the divisor).
You will need to use the first two digits of the dividend (34).

### Step 3
Determine how many times the divisor can go into the first two numbers of the dividend.
The number 4 can go into 34 eight times.
Multiply the 4 by the 8, and write the product (32) below the dividend.
```
    8
4)3,462
   32
```

### Step 4
Subtract the two numbers.
34 − 32 = 2
Bring down the number 6. Thus, 26 will be the new dividend.
```
    8
4)3,462
  −32
   26
```

### Step 5
Repeat the previous steps until you cannot divide any longer.
The answer will be above the dividend.
```
   865
4)3,462
  −32
   26
  −24
    22
   −20
     2
```
The quotient is 865, with a remainder of 2.

## 76. 14
### Method 1
Use long division.

| Write the division sentence as long division. | 6)84 |
| Six goes into 8 once. Write the number 1 above the 8. | 1<br>6)84 |
| Write 6 below the 8 because 6 × 1 = 6. Subtract to find a difference of 2. | 1<br>6)84<br>−6<br>2 |
| Bring down the 4. | 1<br>6)84<br>−6↓<br>24 |
| Six goes into 24 four times. Write the number 4 next to the 1. | 14<br>6)84<br>−6<br>24 |
| Write 24 at the bottom because 6 × 4 = 24. Subtract to find a difference of 0.<br>The correct answer is 14. | 14<br>6)84<br>−6<br>24<br>−24<br>0 |

## Method 2
Use short division.

| Write the division sentence as short division. | $6 \overline{)84}$ |
|---|---|
| Six goes into 8 once with a remainder of 2. Write the 1 above the 8. Write the 2 next to the 4. | $6 \overline{)8^24}$ with 1 above |
| Six goes into 24 four times, and there is no remainder. Write the 4 next to the 1. The correct answer is 14. | $6 \overline{)8^24}$ with 14 above |

## Method 3
Use repeated subtraction.
When using repeated subtraction, you can use any numbers that make sense to you. This is only one possible way to find the answer.
The important thing is to keep subtracting until you reach 0.

| Start with the number 84 at the top. Subtract any number that is easy to divide by 6. Try subtracting 60. | 84<br>− 60<br>24 |
|---|---|
| The number 24 is already easy to divide by 6. Subtract 24. | 84<br>− 60<br>24<br>− 24<br>0 |
| To get from 84 to zero, you subtracted 60 and then 24. Write the solutions to 60 ÷ 6 and to 24 ÷ 6. | 84<br>− 60  60 ÷ 6 = 10<br>24<br>− 24  24 ÷ 6 = 4<br>0 |
| Add the underlined numbers together to find the solution. The correct answer is 14. | 10 + 4 = 14 |

# Number and Fractions

# NUMBER AND OPERATIONS—FRACTIONS

## Table of Correlations

| Standard | | Concepts | Exercise #1 | Exercise #2 |
|---|---|---|---|---|
| 4.NF | Number and Operations—Fractions | | | |
| 4.NF.1 | Explain why a fraction a/b is equivalent to a fraction (n × a)/(n × b) by using visual fraction models, with attention to how the number and size of the parts differ even though the two fractions themselves are the same size. Use this principle to recognize and generate equivalent fractions. | Equivalent Fractions Represent the Same Quantity | 77 | 104 |
| | | Identifying Equivalent Fractions for a Given Fraction | 78 | 105 |
| | | Identifying Equivalent Fractions Using Fraction Strips | 79 | 106 |
| 4.NF.2 | Compare two fractions with different numerators and different denominators. | Using Equivalent Fractions to Compare Fractions with Unlike Denominators | 80 | 107 |
| | | Comparing Fractions with Unlike Denominators Using a Number Line | 81 | 108 |
| | | Writing Fractions with a Common Denominator | 95 | 122 |
| 4.NF.3A | Understand a fraction a/b with a > 1 as a sum of fractions 1/b. Understand addition and subtraction of fractions as joining and separating parts referring to the same whole. | Representing the Subtraction of Fractions with Like Denominators | 84 | 109 |
| | | Representing the Addition of Fractions with Like Denominators | 83 | 110 |
| | | Adding Fractions with Like Denominators | 85 | 111 |
| | | Subtracting Fractions with Like Denominators | 82 | 112 |
| 4.NF.3B | Understand a fraction a/b with a > 1 as a sum of fractions 1/b. Decompose a fraction into a sum of fractions with the same denominator in more than one way, recording each decomposition by an equation. Justify decompositions. | Adding Fractions with Like Denominators | 85 | 111 |
| | | Understanding Fractions as Unit Fractions | 86 | 113 |
| | | Understanding Mixed Numbers | 87 | 114 |
| 4.NF.3C | Understand a fraction a/b with a > 1 as a sum of fractions 1/b. Add and subtract mixed numbers with like denominators. | Adding Mixed Numbers with the Same Denominators | 88 | 115 |
| | | Subtracting Mixed Numbers with Like Denominators | 89 | 116 |
| 4.NF.3D | Understand a fraction a/b with a > 1 as a sum of fractions 1/b. Solve word problems involving addition and subtraction of fractions referring to the same whole and having like denominators. | Solving Problems Involving the Subtraction of Fractions with Like Denominators | 90 | 117 |
| | | Solving Problems Involving the Addition of Fractions with Like Denominators | 91 | 118 |
| 4.NF.4B | Apply and extend previous understandings of multiplication to multiply a fraction by a whole number. Understand a multiple of a/b as a multiple of 1/b, and use this understanding to multiply a fraction by a whole number. | Multiplying a Fraction by a Whole Number Using Repeated Addition | 93 | 119 |
| | | Multiplying Whole Numbers by Fractions | 92 | 120 |
| 4.NF.4C | Apply and extend previous understandings of multiplication to multiply a fraction by a whole number. Solve word problems involving multiplication of a fraction by a whole number. | Solving Problems Involving Multiplying Whole Numbers by Fractions | 94 | 121 |

| 4.NF.5 | Apply and extend previous understandings of multiplication to multiply a fraction by a whole number. Express a fraction with denominator 10 as an equivalent fraction with denominator 100, and use this technique to add two fractions with respective denominators 10 and 100. | Writing Fractions with a Common Denominator | 95 | 122 |
|---|---|---|---|---|
| | | Adding Fractions with Denominators That Are Multiples of Each Other | 96 | 123 |
| 4.NF.6 | Apply and extend previous understandings of multiplication to multiply a fraction by a whole number. Use decimal notation for fractions with denominators 10 or 100. | Writing Fractions with Denominators of 100 as Decimals | 97 | 124 |
| | | Relating Decimals to Fractions | 98 | 125 |
| | | Writing Fractions with a Denominator of 10 as Decimals | 99 | 126 |
| | | Expressing Decimals to the Hundredths as Equivalent Fractions | 100 | 127 |
| | | Showing Decimals on a Number Line | 101 | 128 |
| 4.NF.7 | Apply and extend previous understandings of multiplication to multiply a fraction by a whole number. Compare two decimals to hundredths by reasoning about their size. Recognize that comparisons are valid only when the two decimals refer to the same whole. Record the results of comparisons with the symbols >, =, or <, and justify the conclusions. | Order decimals to the 100ths | 102 | 129 |
| | | Order Decimals to the Tenths | 103 | 130 |

**4.NF.1** *Explain why a fraction a/b is equivalent to a fraction (n × a)/(n × b) by using visual fraction models, with attention to how the number and size of the parts differ even though the two fractions themselves are the same size. Use this principle to recognize and generate equivalent fractions.*

## Equivalent Fractions Represent the Same Quantity

**Equivalent fractions** are fractions that represent the **same part** of a whole or the same part of a set. For example, the fractions $\frac{1}{3}$ and $\frac{4}{12}$ are **equivalent fractions**. **Fraction strips** can be used to show that the fractions represent the same amount.

To find out which fractions are equivalent to $\frac{6}{8}$ using the fraction strips, go to the strip that shows **eighths**. Count 6 of the squares. Look for another strip that ends at the same place as the 6 squares. The strip that ends at the **same place** is the fourths strip. The three squares in the fourths strip line up with the 6 squares in the eighths strip. The fraction $\frac{6}{8}$ is equivalent to $\frac{3}{4}$.

$$\frac{6}{8} = \frac{3}{4}$$

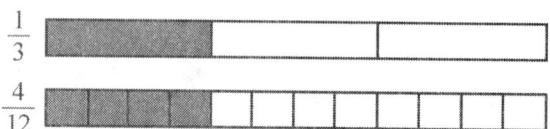

*Example*

The shaded parts of this unlabelled fraction strip chart shows **three equivalent fractions**.

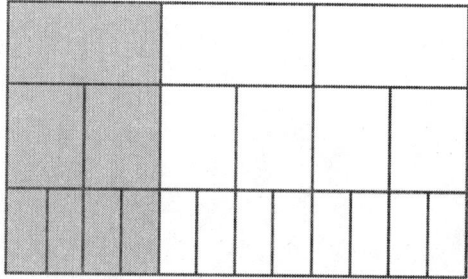

What three equivalent fractions are represented by the shaded parts of the fraction chart?

Label the chart to show the three equivalent fractions.

*Solution*

**Step 1**

Identify the equivalent fractions.

Count the number of parts in each fraction line. The number of parts is the numerator of the fractions; the total number of parts is the denominator of the fractions.

$$\frac{1}{3} = \frac{2}{6} = \frac{4}{12}$$

**Step 2**

Label the three fraction strips to show the three equivalent fractions.

| $\frac{1}{3}$ | | $\frac{1}{3}$ | | $\frac{1}{3}$ | | $\frac{1}{3}$ |
|---|---|---|---|---|---|---|
| $\frac{1}{6}$ | $\frac{1}{6}$ | $\frac{1}{6}$ | $\frac{1}{6}$ | $\frac{1}{6}$ | $\frac{1}{6}$ | $\frac{2}{6}$ |

$\frac{1}{12}$ $\frac{1}{12}$ $\frac{1}{12}$ $\frac{1}{12}$ $\frac{1}{12}$ $\frac{1}{12}$ $\frac{1}{12}$ $\frac{1}{12}$ $\frac{1}{12}$ $\frac{1}{12}$ $\frac{1}{12}$ $\frac{1}{12}$ $\frac{4}{12}$

---

Equivalent fractions can also be represented with fraction wheels.

*Example*

Write a fraction to represent the shaded part of the fraction wheel shown. Write a new fraction that is equivalent to the first fraction.

Draw a fraction wheel to show the equivalent fraction.

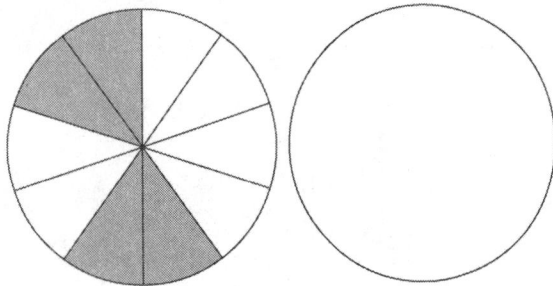

*Solution*

The fraction that represents the shaded part of the fraction wheel is $\frac{4}{10}$.

A fraction that is equivalent to $\frac{4}{10}$ is $\frac{2}{5}$.

The fraction $\frac{2}{5}$ is shown on this fraction wheel.

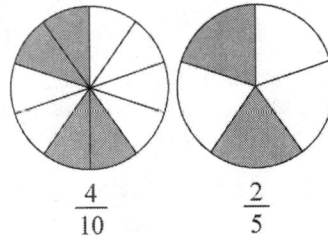

$\frac{4}{10}$  $\frac{2}{5}$

# IDENTIFYING EQUIVALENT FRACTIONS FOR A GIVEN FRACTION

When you are trying to identify an equivalent fraction for a given fraction, it helps to think about how equivalent fractions are created.

Remember that when you create an equivalent fraction, you multiply the denominator and the numerator by the same number.

To identify an equivalent fraction for a given fraction, follow these steps:

1. Determine what the original denominator was multiplied by to get the new fraction.
2. Multiply the original numerator by that same number.
3. If the denominator and the numerator of the equivalent fraction were multiplied by the same number, it is an equivalent fraction.

*Example*

A series of fractions is given.

$$\frac{6}{10}, \frac{4}{15}, \frac{4}{10}, \frac{6}{20}$$

Which of the given fractions is equivalent to $\frac{2}{5}$?

*Solution*

**Step 1**

Determine what the denominator, 5, was multiplied by to get each of the other denominators:

- To get the denominator 10: $5 \times 2 = 10$
- To get the denominator 15: $5 \times 3 = 15$
- To get the denominator 20: $5 \times 4 = 20$

**Step 2**

Determine what the numerator would be if it was multiplied by the same number as the denominator. The numerator is 2. If the denominator is 10, the numerator would be $2 \times 2 = 4$. If the denominator is 15, the numerator would be $2 \times 3 = 6$. If the denominator is 20, the numerator would be $2 \times 4 = 8$.

**Step 3**

Create the equivalent fractions to determine which of the given fractions is equivalent to $\frac{2}{5}$.

$$\frac{4}{10}, \frac{6}{15}, \frac{8}{20}$$

Of the fractions listed in the series, the only fraction that is equivalent to $\frac{2}{5}$ is $\frac{4}{10}$.

Not for Reproduction

## IDENTIFYING EQUIVALENT FRACTIONS USING FRACTION STRIPS

**Equivalent fractions** are fractions that represent the same amount.

*Example*

The fractions $\frac{1}{4}$ and $\frac{2}{8}$ are different, but you can see that these fractions are equal to the same amount when you compare diagrams of them.

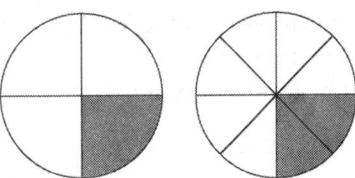

---

You can use fraction strips to help identify equivalent fractions.

*Example*

On this fraction strip, the first row is split into quarters, and the second row is split into eighths. When you shade $\frac{3}{4}$, you can see that it is the same as shading $\frac{6}{8}$.

| $\frac{1}{4}$ | | $\frac{1}{4}$ | | $\frac{1}{4}$ | | $\frac{1}{4}$ | |
|---|---|---|---|---|---|---|---|
| $\frac{1}{8}$ | $\frac{1}{8}$ | $\frac{1}{8}$ | $\frac{1}{8}$ | $\frac{1}{8}$ | $\frac{1}{8}$ | $\frac{1}{8}$ | $\frac{1}{8}$ |

This means that $\frac{3}{4} = \frac{6}{8}$.

---

*Example*

Use fraction strips to find three fractions that are equal to $\frac{2}{3}$.

*Solution*

**Step 1**

Shade $\frac{2}{3}$ on the fraction strip.

**Step 2**

Draw a line from the right edge of $\frac{2}{3}$.

**Step 3**

Find three fractions that have their right edges on the same line.

Three fractions that are equivalent to $\frac{2}{3}$ are $\frac{4}{6}$, $\frac{6}{9}$, and $\frac{8}{12}$.

---

*4.NF.2    Compare two fractions with different numerators and different denominators.*

## USING EQUIVALENT FRACTIONS TO COMPARE FRACTIONS WITH UNLIKE DENOMINATORS

At times, you may be asked to compare fractions that have different denominators. For example, if you are told that Adam ate $\frac{2}{3}$ of a pizza and Samantha ate $\frac{3}{4}$, you would have to find a way to tell who ate the bigger amount.

To answer a question like that, the fractions have to be part of the same whole. In other words, both fractions need the same denominator. To do this, you must create equivalent fractions. A fraction that looks different but has the same value is called an **equivalent fraction**.

Look at the two diagrams shown.

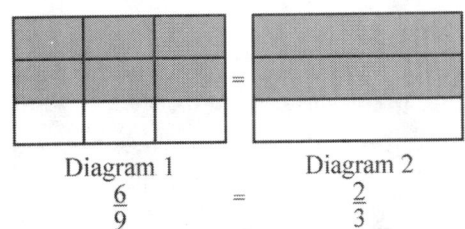

Diagram 1 $\frac{6}{9}$ = Diagram 2 $\frac{2}{3}$

In the second diagram, 2 of the 3 rectangles are shaded. In diagram 1, 6 of the 9 rectangles are shaded. Each drawing shows the same amount shaded. Therefore, the fraction $\frac{2}{3}$ is equivalent to the fraction $\frac{6}{9}$.

To compare fractions using equivalent fractions, follow these steps:

1. Rewrite the fractions with a common denominator.
2. Compare the numerators.

*Example*

$\frac{2}{4} \square \frac{3}{8}$

Insert a >, <, or = sign to make the given statement true.

*Solution*

**Step 1**
Rewrite the fractions with a common denominator.
Find the lowest common denominator (LCD). Use divisibility rules to determine if the smaller denominator (4) is a factor of the larger denominator (8).
8 is divisible by 4.
Because 4 is a factor of 8, multiply the numerator and denominator by 2 to create an equivalent fraction with a denominator of 8.

$\frac{2 \times 2}{4 \times 2} = \frac{4}{8}$

**Step 2**
Compare the numerators.

$\frac{4}{8}, \frac{3}{8}$

3 is smaller than 4.

Link the equivalent fraction to its original fraction. The fraction $\frac{4}{8}$ is equivalent to $\frac{2}{4}$.

$\frac{2}{4} > \frac{3}{8}$

*Example*

$\dfrac{2}{3} \square \dfrac{3}{4}$

Insert a >, <, or = sign to make the given statement true.

*Solution*

**Step 1**
Rewrite the fractions with a common denominator.
Write the multiples of each denominator until a common one appears.

- Multiples of 3: 3, 6, 9, **12**, and 15
- Multiples of 4: 4, 8, **12**, 16, and 20

The lowest common denominator (LCD) for 3 and 4 is 12.
Use the LCD to create new equivalent fractions.
Multiply the numerator and the denominator by the same factor.

$\dfrac{2 \times 4}{3 \times 4} = \dfrac{8}{12}, \dfrac{3 \times 3}{4 \times 3} = \dfrac{9}{12}$

**Step 2**
Compare the numerators.

$\dfrac{8}{12}, \dfrac{9}{12}$

9 is larger than 8.
Link the equivalent fraction to its original fraction.

The fraction $\dfrac{8}{12}$ is equivalent to $\dfrac{2}{3}$. The fraction $\dfrac{9}{12}$ is equivalent to $\dfrac{3}{4}$.

$\dfrac{2}{3} < \dfrac{3}{4}$

---

## COMPARING FRACTIONS WITH UNLIKE DENOMINATORS USING A NUMBER LINE

It is possible to show a fraction on a number line. To compare fractions using number lines, follow these steps:

1. Draw a number line for each of the fractions you compare.
2. Label the fractions on the number lines.
3. Compare the fractions.

*Example*

Use number lines to compare the fractions $\frac{2}{3}$ and $\frac{3}{4}$.

*Solution*

**Step 1**
Draw a number line for each of the fractions.
The number lines should be the same length. Both number lines should start at 0 and go to 1.

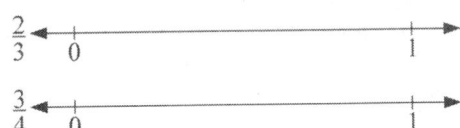

Split the number lines into sections based on the denominator of each fraction. The number line for $\frac{2}{3}$ should have 3 equal sections. The number line for $\frac{3}{4}$ should have 4 equal sections.

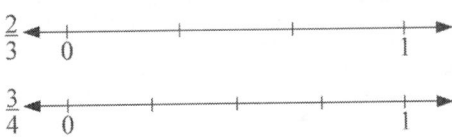

**Step 2**
Label the fractions on the number lines.
Look at the numerator of each fraction. Count that number of ticks from the left. For $\frac{2}{3}$, count 2 ticks. For $\frac{3}{4}$, count 3 ticks.

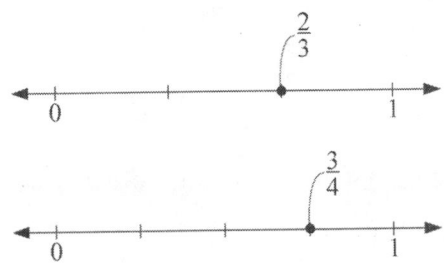

**Step 3**
Compare the fractions.
The fraction that is closest to 0 has the least value, the fraction that is closest to 1 has the greatest value.
The fraction $\frac{2}{3}$ is closer to 0 than the fraction $\frac{3}{4}$.

$\frac{2}{3} < \frac{3}{4}$

*4.NF.3A Understand a fraction a/b with a > 1 as a sum of fractions 1/b. Understand addition and subtraction of fractions as joining and separating parts referring to the same whole.*

## REPRESENTING THE SUBTRACTION OF FRACTIONS WITH LIKE DENOMINATORS

Fractions show how many parts are being compared to the whole. The denominator represents the whole, and the numerator represents the number of parts. For example, a pizza is cut into 8 slices. John eats 2 pieces, and his sister eats 3 pieces. The fraction that represents the number of pieces John ate is $\frac{2}{8}$.

The fraction that represents the number of pieces that John's sister ate is $\frac{3}{8}$.

You can represent the subtraction of fractions using diagrams. To subtract fractions with the same denominators, use the following steps:

1. Draw a grid based on the factors of the denominator.
2. Color in the parts equivalent to the first numerator.
3. Cross out the shaded parts equivalent to the second numerator.
4. Add the total number of remaining shaded parts.

*Example*

Draw a diagram to solve the expression $\frac{4}{9} - \frac{1}{9}$.

*Solution*

**Step 1**
Draw a grid based on the factors of the denominator.
3 × 3 = 9

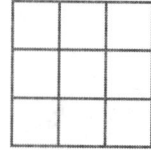

**Step 2**
Color in the parts equivalent to the first numerator.
The first numerator is 4.

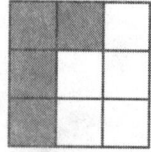

**Step 3**
Cross out the shaded parts equivalent to the second numerator.
The second numerator is 1.

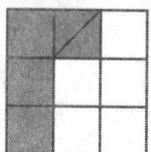

**Step 4**
Add the total number of remaining shaded parts.
4 shaded squares minus 1 crossed out squares equals 3 shaded squares.
$$\frac{4}{9} - \frac{1}{9} = \frac{3}{9}$$
Notice that 1 column is left shaded. The fraction $\frac{3}{9}$ can be reduced to $\frac{1}{3}$.
$$\frac{4}{9} - \frac{1}{9} = \frac{1}{3}$$

## REPRESENTING THE ADDITION OF FRACTIONS WITH LIKE DENOMINATORS

Fractions compare the number of parts to the whole. The denominator is the number on the bottom of the fraction; it represents the whole. The numerator is the number on the top of the fraction; it represents the number of parts.

Pictures can be used to add fractions with like denominators. Just like when you use real-life objects, the whole picture will represent the denominator, and the parts of the pictures will represent the numerator.

*Example*
Draw a diagram to solve the expression $\frac{4}{9} + \frac{2}{9}$.

*Solution*
**Step 1**
Draw a grid based on the factors of the denominator.
3 × 3 = 9

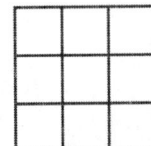

**Step 2**
Color in the parts equivalent to each numerator.
The numerators are 4 and 2. Use a different color for each numerator.

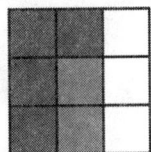

**Step 3**
Add the total number of shaded parts.
4 red squares plus 2 blue squares equals 6 shaded squares.
$$\frac{4}{9} + \frac{2}{9} = \frac{6}{9}$$
Notice that 2 out of the 3 columns are shaded. The fraction $\frac{6}{9}$ can be reduced to $\frac{2}{3}$.
$$\frac{4}{9} + \frac{2}{9} = \frac{2}{3}$$

## ADDING FRACTIONS WITH LIKE DENOMINATORS

Fractions show how many parts are being compared to the whole. The denominator (the number on the bottom) represents the whole. The numerator (the number on the top) represents the number of parts.

*Example*

A pizza is cut into eight slices. John ate two slices, and Trina ate three slices. You can use fractions to show how much of the pizza each of them ate.

Portion of the pizza John ate = $\frac{2}{8}$    Portion of the pizza Trina ate = $\frac{3}{8}$

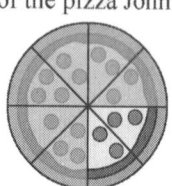 

You can also use a fraction to show how much of the pizza John and Trina ate altogether.

Altogether = $\frac{5}{8}$

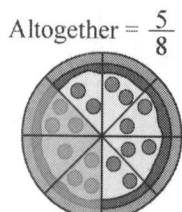

The number sentence that shows how many slices they ate altogether is $\frac{2}{8} + \frac{3}{8} = \frac{5}{8}$.

---

To add fractions with the same denominator, follow these rules:

- Keep the denominator the same.
- Add the numerators together.

*Example*

What is $\frac{1}{5} + \frac{3}{5}$?

*Solution*

Both fractions have a denominator of 5, so the answer will also have a denominator of 5.
$\frac{1}{5} + \frac{3}{5} = \frac{?}{5}$

To find the answer, add the numerators.
$\frac{1}{5} + \frac{3}{5} = \frac{4}{5}$

Not for Reproduction

## SUBTRACTING FRACTIONS WITH LIKE DENOMINATORS

Fractions show how many parts are being compared to the whole. The denominator represents the whole, and the numerator represents the number of parts.

*Example*

A pizza was cut into 10 slices. Some of the slices have already been eaten. Seven slices of pizza are left. Martin eats one of the remaining slices. You can use fractions to show how much pizza there was to start with and how much of the pizza Martin ate.

$\frac{7}{10}$ of a pizza    Martin ate $\frac{1}{10}$

 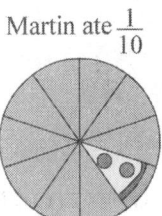

You can also use a fraction to show how much pizza is left.

$\frac{6}{10}$ are left

The number sentence that shows how much pizza is left is $\frac{7}{10} - \frac{1}{10} = \frac{6}{10}$.

---

To subtract fractions with the same denominator, follow these rules:

1. Keep the denominator the same.
2. Subtract the numerators.

*Example*

What is $\frac{5}{6} - \frac{4}{6}$?

*Solution*

**Step 1**
The denominator of both fractions is 6. Therefore, the answer will also have a denominator of 6.
$\frac{5}{6} - \frac{4}{6} = \frac{?}{6}$

**Step 2**
To find the answer, subtract the numerators.
$\frac{5}{6} - \frac{4}{6} = \frac{1}{6}$

*4.NF.3B Understand a fraction a/b with a > 1 as a sum of fractions 1/b. Decompose a fraction into a sum of fractions with the same denominator in more than one way, recording each decomposition by an equation. Justify decompositions.*

## UNDERSTANDING FRACTIONS AS UNIT FRACTIONS

Any fraction can be represented by the sum of unit fractions. A unit fraction always has 1 as its numerator, but it can have various numbers as its denominator. For example, both $\frac{1}{2}$ and $\frac{1}{8}$ are unit fractions.

To represent a given fraction as the sum of unit fractions, use the following steps:

1. Determine the number of unit fractions by using the value of the numerator.
2. Keep the denominator the same, and write the number of fractions.

For example, to show the fraction $\frac{3}{4}$ as the sum of unit fractions, write $\frac{1}{4} + \frac{1}{4} + \frac{1}{4}$.

*Example*

Represent the fraction $\frac{4}{8}$ as the sum of unit fractions.

*Solution*

### Step 1
Determine the number of unit fractions.

By looking at the numerator of the fraction $\frac{4}{8}$, you know that there are 4 unit fractions.

### Step 2
Use the denominator of the given fraction to write 4 unit fractions.

$\frac{4}{8} = \frac{1}{8} + \frac{1}{8} + \frac{1}{8} + \frac{1}{8}$

The sum of unit fractions $\frac{1}{8} + \frac{1}{8} + \frac{1}{8} + \frac{1}{8}$ represent the fraction $\frac{4}{8}$.

---

## UNDERSTANDING MIXED NUMBERS

A **mixed number** is a way to write a fraction bigger than 1. The number $2\frac{1}{3}$ is an example of a mixed number.

Mixed numbers have two parts: the whole number and the fraction.

In $2\frac{1}{3}$, the whole number is 2, and the fraction is $\frac{1}{3}$. A picture of $2\frac{1}{3}$ looks like this:

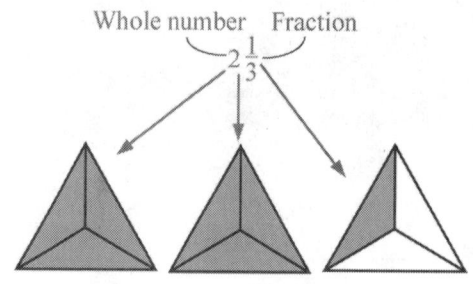

*Example*

Draw the mixed number $3\frac{1}{2}$.

*Solution*

**Step 1**
Draw the shapes.

The denominator in $3\frac{1}{2}$ is 2, so each shape should have 2 pieces.

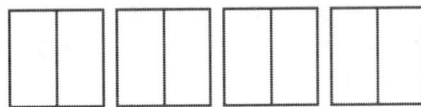

**Step 2**
Color in the wholes.

The mixed number $3\frac{1}{2}$ has 3 wholes, so shade in 3 whole squares.

**Step 3**
Color in the fractional part.

The fraction in the mixed number $3\frac{1}{2}$ is $\frac{1}{2}$, so shade in 1 out of 2 pieces of another square.

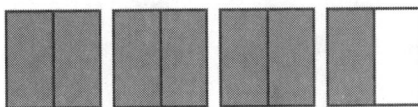

---

*Example*

One page of a photo album can have 4 pictures.

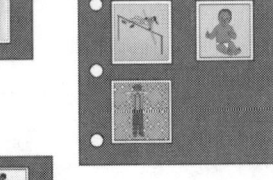

How many pages of pictures are there?

*Solution*

There are some whole pages of pictures, and there are also some part pages. The number of pages of pictures will be a mixed number.

**Step 1**
Count the number of wholes.
There are 2 pages that are full.

**Step 2**
Decide what the fraction will be.

The last page has only 3 out of 4 pictures. That means the fraction is $\frac{3}{4}$.

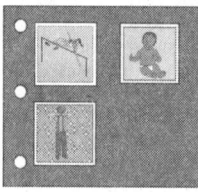

**Step 3**
Put the whole and the part together. Write the whole first and then the fraction.

There are $2\frac{3}{4}$ pages of pictures.

---

*4.NF.3C Understand a fraction a/b with a > 1 as a sum of fractions 1/b. Add and subtract mixed numbers with like denominators.*

## ADDING MIXED NUMBERS WITH THE SAME DENOMINATORS

A mixed number is made up of a whole number and a proper fraction. For example, $2\frac{6}{10}$ is a mixed number.

The shaded parts of the circles shown here represent the mixed number $2\frac{6}{10}$. There are 2 whole circles that are shaded and 6 out of 10 parts shaded in the third circle.

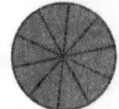  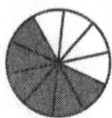

Imagine you were asked to solve $2\frac{5}{6} + 1\frac{2}{6}$. You could use pictures, number lines, or number sense to find the answer.

## USING PICTURES

To add $2\frac{5}{6} + 1\frac{2}{6}$ by using pictures, you need to draw a representation of each fraction.

The mixed number $2\frac{5}{6}$ can be represented by 2 whole circles and a third circle with 5 out of 6 parts shaded.

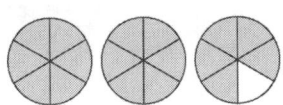

The mixed number $1\frac{2}{6}$ can be represented by 1 whole circle and a second circle with 2 out of 6 parts shaded.

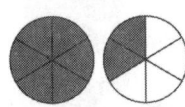

To add means to put together. Put the pictures for each fraction together, and count the number of whole circles and the number of parts shaded.

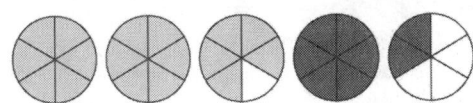

There are 3 whole circles and 7 parts shaded in total. This gives the mixed number $3\frac{7}{6}$.

It takes 6 parts to make 1 whole circle. This means that $3\frac{7}{6}$ is the same as $4\frac{1}{6}$.

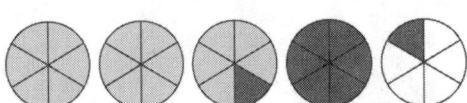

By using pictures, you can find that $2\frac{5}{6} + 1\frac{2}{6} = 4\frac{1}{6}$.

## USING A NUMBER LINE

To add $2\frac{5}{6} + 1\frac{2}{6}$ by using a number line, start by finding $2\frac{5}{6}$ on the number line.

To add $1\frac{2}{6}$, you will need to move 1 whole jump and $\frac{2}{6}$ of a jump.

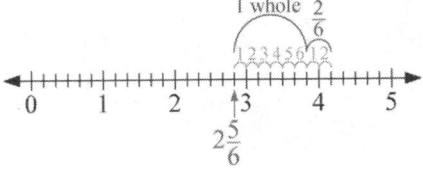

On the number line, you can see that 1 whole happens every 6 ticks.
The answer is the number you land on after your final jump.

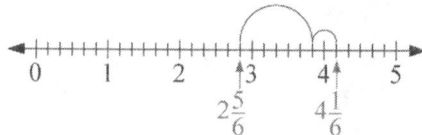

By using the number line, you can find that $2\frac{5}{6} + 1\frac{2}{6} = 4\frac{1}{6}$.

## USING NUMBER SENSE

To add $2\frac{5}{6} + 1\frac{2}{6}$ by using number sense, start by adding the whole numbers.

$2 + 1 = 3$

Next, add the fractions. Since the denominators are the same, you can just add the numerators.

$\frac{5}{6} + \frac{2}{6}$

$= \frac{5+2}{6}$

$= \frac{7}{6}$

Put the whole number and the fraction together to find the answer.

$2\frac{5}{6} + 1\frac{2}{6} = 3\frac{7}{6}$

The numerator in the fraction is larger than the denominator. You cannot give an answer like this. It needs to be simplified.

The fraction $\frac{7}{6}$ means there are 7 sixths. This picture shows $\frac{7}{6}$.

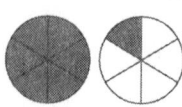

From the picture, you can see that $\frac{7}{6}$ is the same as $1\frac{1}{6}$.

This means that $3\frac{7}{6} = 3 + 1\frac{1}{6} = 4\frac{1}{6}$.

Therefore, $2\frac{5}{6} + 1\frac{2}{6} = 4\frac{1}{6}$.

## SUBTRACTING MIXED NUMBERS WITH LIKE DENOMINATORS

A mixed number is a way of writing fractions larger than 1. For example, $2\frac{6}{10}$ is a mixed number.

The shaded parts of the following circles represent the mixed number $2\frac{6}{10}$. There are 2 whole circles that are shaded and 6 out of 10 parts shaded in the third circle.

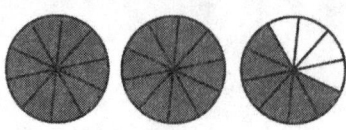

Not for Reproduction

Imagine you were asked to solve $3\frac{1}{4} - 1\frac{3}{4}$. You could use pictures, a number line, or number sense to find the answer.

## USING PICTURES

To subtract $3\frac{1}{4} - 1\frac{3}{4}$ using pictures, start by drawing a representation of $3\frac{1}{4}$.

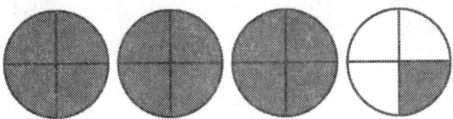

Then, take away 1 whole circle and $\frac{3}{4}$ of a circle.

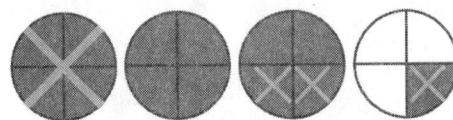

The remaining shaded sections show the solution. There is 1 whole and 2 out of 4 parts shaded. $3\frac{1}{4} - 1\frac{3}{4} = 1\frac{2}{4}$

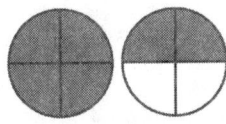

## USING A NUMBER LINE

To subtract $3\frac{1}{4} - 1\frac{3}{4}$ using a number line, start by finding $3\frac{1}{4}$ on the number line.

To subtract, you will need to move 1 whole jump and $\frac{3}{4}$ of a jump to the left. On the number line, you can see that 1 whole happens every 4 ticks.

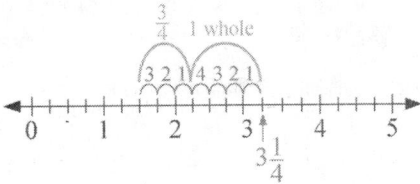

The number you land on after your final jump is the answer. $3\frac{1}{4} - 1\frac{3}{4} = 1\frac{2}{4}$

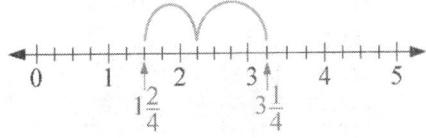

## USING NUMBER SENSE

To subtract mixed numbers, you can always subtract the whole numbers and then subtract the fractions. The problem with $3\frac{1}{4} - 1\frac{3}{4}$ is that you cannot subtract $\frac{1}{4} - \frac{3}{4}$. Try rewriting $3\frac{1}{4}$ in a different way.

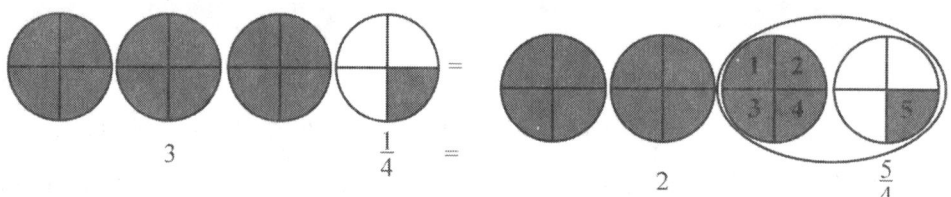

The mixed number $3\frac{1}{4}$ is the same as $2\frac{5}{4}$. Now, you can find the solution. The new subtraction sentence is $2\frac{5}{4} - 1\frac{3}{4}$.

Start by subtracting the whole numbers.
$2 - 1 = 1$

Then, subtract the fractions. Since the denominators are the same, you can just subtract the numerators.

$\frac{5}{4} - \frac{3}{4}$
$= \frac{5-3}{4}$
$= \frac{2}{4}$

Put the whole number and the fraction together to find the answer.
$2\frac{5}{4} - 1\frac{3}{4} = 1\frac{2}{4}$

*4.NF.3D Understand a fraction a/b with a > 1 as a sum of fractions 1/b. Solve word problems involving addition and subtraction of fractions referring to the same whole and having like denominators.*

## SOLVING PROBLEMS INVOLVING THE SUBTRACTION OF FRACTIONS WITH LIKE DENOMINATORS

Fractions are made up of two numbers. The top number is called the **numerator**, and the bottom number is called the **denominator**. The numerator represents the number of items or pieces of the whole that are present. The denominator represents the total number of items or pieces in the whole.

To solve problems involving the subtraction of fractions that have like (the same) denominators, follow these steps:

1. Identify the fractions in the problem.
2. Subtract the numerators.
3. Put the difference over the like denominator.

*Example*

Emily had a pizza party for her birthday. She shared a 10-piece pizza with some friends. Emily ate 5 pieces of pizza, and her friend Andrew ate 2 pieces.

In fraction form, how much more of the pizza did Emily eat than Andrew?

*Solution*

**Step 1**

Identify the fractions in the problem.
The denominator of the fraction is 10 because 10 pieces make up the whole pizza.

Emily ate 5 out of 10 pieces, so the fraction of pizza she ate is $\frac{5}{10}$. Andrew ate 2 out of 10 pieces, so the fraction of pizza he ate is $\frac{2}{10}$.

**Step 2**

Subtract the numerators.
$5 - 2 = 3$

**Step 3**

Put the difference over the like denominator.

The difference is 3, and the like denominator is 10. The fraction is $\frac{3}{10}$.

Emily ate $\frac{3}{10}$ more of the pizza than Andrew.

## SOLVING PROBLEMS INVOLVING THE ADDITION OF FRACTIONS WITH LIKE DENOMINATORS

Fractions are made up of two numbers. The top number is called the *numerator*, and the bottom number is called the *denominator*. The numerator represents the number of items or pieces that you have. The denominator represents the number of items or pieces that complete the whole. When fractions have like denominators, they can be added together.

To solve problems involving the addition of fractions that have like denominators, follow these steps:

1. Identify the fractions in the problem.
2. Add the numerators.
3. Put the total over the like denominator.

*Example*

Mena and her sister were baking a batch of 12 cupcakes to have as snacks during the week. At the end of the week, Mena had eaten 4 of the cupcakes, and her sister had eaten 3 of the cupcakes.

What fraction of the cupcakes did the girls eat in total?

*Solution*

**Step 1**

Identify the fractions in the problem.
The denominator in the problem is 12 because there are 12 cupcakes.

Mena ate 4 out of the 12 cupcakes, so the fraction of cupcakes she ate is $\frac{4}{12}$.

Mena's sister ate 3 out of the 12 cupcakes, so the fraction of cupcakes she ate is $\frac{3}{12}$.

**Step 2**
Add the numerators.
4 + 3 = 7

**Step 3**
Put the total over the like denominator.

The total is 7, and the denominator is 12, so the fraction is $\frac{7}{12}$.

The girls ate $\frac{7}{12}$ of the cupcakes.

---

*4.NF.4B Apply and extend previous understandings of multiplication to multiply a fraction by a whole number. Understand a multiple of a/b as a multiple of 1/b, and use this understanding to multiply a fraction by a whole number.*

## MULTIPLYING A FRACTION BY A WHOLE NUMBER USING REPEATED ADDITION

When multiplying a fraction by a whole number using repeated addition, the whole number will tell you how many fractions to add together. For example, to multiply $\frac{1}{4} \times 3$ by using repeated addition, add $\frac{1}{4}$ three times.

$$\frac{1}{4} + \frac{1}{4} + \frac{1}{4}$$

When you add fractions with like denominators, remember to keep the denominators the same and add together all the numerators.

$$\frac{1}{4} + \frac{1}{4} + \frac{1}{4} = \frac{3}{4}$$

*Example*

Determine the product of $\frac{1}{3} \times 5 = \square$ using repeated addition.

*Solution*

**Step 1**
Rewrite the multiplication equation as addition.

The whole number tells you how many fractions to add together. You should add $\frac{1}{3}$ five times.

$$\frac{1}{3} + \frac{1}{3} + \frac{1}{3} + \frac{1}{3} + \frac{1}{3} = \square$$

**Step 2**
Solve the addition equation.

The denominator remains the same (3). Add all the numerators together, and place the sum over the denominator.

$$1 + 1 + 1 + 1 + 1 = 5$$
$$\frac{1}{3} + \frac{1}{3} + \frac{1}{3} + \frac{1}{3} + \frac{1}{3} = \frac{5}{3}$$

## MULTIPLYING WHOLE NUMBERS BY FRACTIONS

Fractions can be shown with simple pictures. You can divide a shape into equal parts to represent the denominator, and you can represent the numerator by shading in a number of sections.

The given diagram represents the fraction $\frac{4}{6}$.

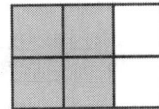

Multiplying fractions can be represented using an area model. An area model is a rectangle where the length is one factor, the width is the other factor, and the product is the area.

To multiply fractions by whole numbers using an area model, follow these steps:

1. Draw enough rectangles to represent the whole number, and color each of the rectangles entirely.
2. Multiply each of the rectangles by the fraction by dividing each of the wholes into the number of parts represented by the denominator.
3. Determine the product.

*Example*

Use an area model to solve $4 \times \frac{2}{3}$.

*Solution*

**Step 1**
Draw rectangles to represent the whole number.
Because the whole number is 4, there needs to be 4 whole rectangles.
Draw 4 whole rectangles, and shade them entirely.

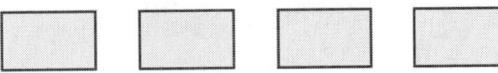

**Step 2**
Multiply each of the rectangles by $\frac{2}{3}$.

Divide each rectangle into 3 horizontal strips, which is equal to the value of the denominator. Shade 2 horizontal strips darker, which is equal to the value of the numerator.

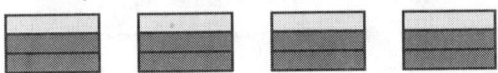

**Step 3**
Determine the product.
The darker shaded sections represent the product.

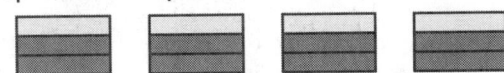

In total, 2 sections are overlapping out of 3 sections in each rectangle.
$2 + 2 + 2 + 2 = 8$
Place the number 8 over the denominator (3).

$4 \times \frac{2}{3} = \frac{8}{3}$

*4.NF.4C Apply and extend previous understandings of multiplication to multiply a fraction by a whole number. Solve word problems involving multiplication of a fraction by a whole number.*

## SOLVING PROBLEMS INVOLVING MULTIPLYING WHOLE NUMBERS BY FRACTIONS

Whenever you have a word problem, read the question carefully before deciding which operation to use. When a problem has a fraction and a whole number, there are two common situations that will tell you that you need to multiply.

In the first situation, you are given the fraction and asked to multiply it by a whole number. This kind of problem is similar to other multiplication problems you might have seen with whole numbers. For example, Alex leaves $\frac{1}{3}$ of his pop every lunch for 5 days. To find out how what fraction of pop is left at the end of the week, you would multiply $\frac{1}{3}$ by 5.

*Example*

Julia's mother always cuts sandwiches into pieces to put in Julia's school lunches. Each piece is $\frac{1}{4}$ of a sandwich. Every day, Julie gets 3 pieces.

What fraction of a sandwich does Julia get in her lunch?

*Solution*

Julia gets 3 pieces that are each $\frac{1}{4}$ of a sandwich. To find out how much she gets in total, you need to multiply $\frac{1}{4}$ by 3.

$$\frac{1}{4} \times 3 = \frac{1}{4} \times \frac{3}{1}$$
$$= \frac{1 \times 3}{4 \times 1}$$
$$= \frac{3}{4}$$

Julia gets $\frac{3}{4}$ of a sandwich in her lunch every day.

In the second situation, you are given the whole number and asked to multiply it by a fraction. In this kind of problem, the keyword *of* will show you that you need to multiply. For example, Kate has 5 packs of candies, and each pack of candies is $\frac{1}{3}$ full. To find how many packs of candy Kate has, you would multiply 5 by $\frac{1}{3}$.

*Example*

Anita has a piece of ribbon that is 6 yd long. She uses $\frac{2}{5}$ of it to wrap a present.

How much ribbon did Anita use?

*Solution*

Find $\frac{2}{5}$ of 6 yd. To find out how much ribbon Anita used, multiply 6 by $\frac{2}{5}$.

$$6 \times \frac{2}{5} = \frac{6}{1} \times \frac{2}{5}$$
$$= \frac{6 \times 2}{1 \times 5}$$
$$= \frac{12}{5}$$

Anita used $\frac{12}{5}$ yd of ribbon.

---

**4.NF.5** Apply and extend previous understandings of multiplication to multiply a fraction by a whole number. Express a fraction with denominator 10 as an equivalent fraction with denominator 100, and use this technique to add two fractions with respective denominators 10 and 100.

## WRITING FRACTIONS WITH A COMMON DENOMINATOR

It is hard to add, subtract, or compare fractions with different denominators. One way to handle the problem is to rewrite the fractions so they have the same denominator. This strategy is called finding a **common denominator**.

To write fractions with common denominators, follow these steps:

1. Choose a common denominator.
2. Rewrite the first fraction.
3. Rewrite the second fraction.

It is often easiest to choose the lowest common denominator (LCD) when you rewrite the fractions.

*Example*

Write the fractions $\frac{1}{3}$ and $\frac{2}{5}$ with a common denominator.

*Solution*

**Step 1**

Choose a common denominator.

The denominator of $\frac{1}{3}$ is 3. The denominator of $\frac{2}{5}$ is 5. Find a number that is a multiple of both 3 and 5 by looking at the multiples of each number:

- Some multiples of 3 are 3, 6, 9, 12, and 15.
- Some multiples of 5 are 5, 10, 15, and 20.

The number 15 is the lowest multiple of both 3 and 5. Use this as the common denominator.

**Step 2**

Rewrite the first fraction with a denominator of 15.

$$\frac{1}{3} = \frac{?}{15}$$

To go from a denominator of 3 to a denominator of 15, you need to multiply by 5. Multiply the numerator and denominator by 5.

$$\frac{1}{3} = \frac{1 \times 5}{3 \times 5} = \frac{5}{15}$$

**Step 3**

Rewrite the second fraction with a denominator of 15.

$$\frac{2}{5} = \frac{?}{15}$$

To go from a denominator of 5 to a denominator of 15, you need to multiply by 3. Multiply the numerator and denominator by 3.

$$\frac{2}{5} = \frac{2 \times 3}{5 \times 3} = \frac{6}{15}$$

Written with a common denominator, the fractions $\frac{1}{3}$ and $\frac{2}{5}$ are equal to $\frac{5}{15}$ and $\frac{6}{15}$.

Not for Reproduction

## ADDING FRACTIONS WITH DENOMINATORS THAT ARE MULTIPLES OF EACH OTHER

When two fractions have the same denominator, you can add the fractions by adding the numerators. For example, $\frac{1}{6} + \frac{4}{6} = \frac{5}{6}$. However, when you have fractions with different denominators, adding the numerators does not work. You need to think of a way to give the fractions the same denominator.

*Example*

The fractions $\frac{1}{2}$ and $\frac{1}{4}$ have different denominators. It is easy to split a half fraction into quarters. If you take a fraction circle that shows $\frac{1}{2}$ and split it in half again, it will show an equal fraction in quarters.

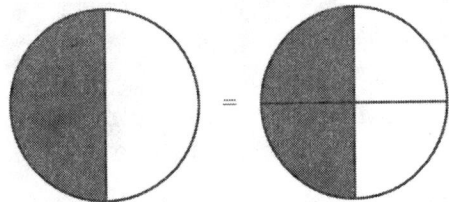

From the diagram, you can see that $\frac{1}{2} = \frac{2}{4}$.

You can now add the fractions easily.

$\frac{1}{2} + \frac{1}{4}$

$= \frac{2}{4} + \frac{1}{4}$

$= \frac{3}{4}$

---

Another way to give the fractions the same denominator is to use equivalent fractions.

*Example*

Add $\frac{1}{3}$ and $\frac{1}{9}$.

*Solution*

**Step 1**
Create equivalent fractions.
The denominators are multiples of each other, so look at the fraction with the smaller denominator.
The fraction with the smaller denominator is $\frac{1}{3}$.

Multiply the numerator and denominator by the same number to create equivalent fractions.
Multiply the denominator (3) by 3. The denominator now becomes 9. Multiply the numerator by 3 as well. The numerator now becomes 3.

$\frac{1 \times 3}{3 \times 3} = \frac{3}{9}$

**Step 2**
Add the fractions.

$$\frac{1}{3} + \frac{1}{9} = \frac{3}{9} + \frac{1}{9}$$
$$= \frac{3+1}{9}$$
$$= \frac{4}{9}$$

The sum of the given fractions is $\frac{4}{9}$.

---

*4.NF.6   Apply and extend previous understandings of multiplication to multiply a fraction by a whole number.  Use decimal notation for fractions with denominators 10 or 100.*

# WRITING FRACTIONS WITH DENOMINATORS OF 100 AS DECIMALS

Fractions and decimals can be used to represent the same amount of equal parts.  To write a fraction with a denominator of 100 as an equivalent decimal, the last digit in the numerator must be in the hundredths place.  For example, if the numerator is 56, the last digit (6) would have to be in the hundredths place.  If the numerator is only a single digit, it still needs to go into the hundredths place.  This means that you would have to use zeros to fill in the tenths place.

Remember that when you are writing a decimal, you should put a zero in the ones place followed by a period.  The hundredths place is the second place value to the right of the period.

*Example*

Relate the fraction $\frac{8}{100}$ to a decimal.

*Solution*

**Step 1**
Determine the place value of the decimal.
Look at the denominator.
The fraction has a denominator of 100.  This means that the decimal will have its last digit in the hundredths place.

**Step 2**
Determine the digits in the decimal.
The digits in the numerator will be the digits of the decimal.  The number 8 is the only digit in the numerator.
In step 1, you determined that the last digit must be in the hundredths place, so 8 will then be in the hundredths place.

**Step 3**
Write the decimal.
The decimal that relates to the fraction $\frac{8}{100}$ is 0.08.

*Example*

Relate the fraction $\frac{32}{100}$ to a decimal.

*Solution*

**Step 1**
Determine the place value of the decimal.
Look at the denominator.
The fraction has a denominator of 100. This means that the last digit of the decimal will go in the hundredths place.

**Step 2**
Determine the digits in the decimal.
The digits in the numerator will be the digits of the decimal. The number 32 is the numerator. Since the last digit of the decimal must be in the hundredths place, the number 3 will be in the tenths place, and 2 will be in the hundredths place.

**Step 3**
Write the decimal.
The decimal that relates to the fraction $\frac{32}{100}$ is 0.32.

---

## RELATING DECIMALS TO FRACTIONS

You can use decimals and fractions to represent the same amount. For example, $0.3 = \frac{3}{10}$.

To convert a decimal to a fraction, follow these steps:

1. Use the place value of the last digit in the decimal number as the denominator of the fraction. If the last digit in the decimal is in the tenths position, the denominator of the fraction will be 10.
2. Remove the decimal point. The digits to the right of the decimal become the numerator.
3. Reduce the fraction to lowest terms.

*Example*
To convert the decimal 0.7 to a fraction, look at the place value of the last digit in the decimal number.

The last digit is a 7, and it is in the tenths place. Therefore, 10 becomes the denominator.

To determine the numerator of the fraction, remove the decimal point. The number to the right becomes the numerator.

$0.7 = \left(\frac{7}{10}\right)$

---

## WRITING FRACTIONS WITH A DENOMINATOR OF 10 AS DECIMALS

Fractions and decimals can be used to represent the same amount of equal parts. To write a fraction with a denominator of 10 as an equivalent decimal, write the numerator of the given fraction in the tenths place value.

When you are writing a decimal, you should put a zero in the ones place value followed by a period. The tenths place value is the first place value to the right of the period.

*Example*

The given square is divided into 10 equal parts with 4 parts shaded. The fraction $\frac{4}{10}$ can be used to represent the shaded parts.

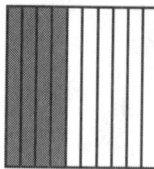

What is the decimal that represents the shaded parts of the square?

*Solution*

Write the numerator of the fraction and place it in the tenths place value.

$\frac{4}{10} = 0.4$

*Example*

Write the fraction $\frac{7}{10}$ as a decimal.

*Solution*

Write the numerator of the fraction in the tenths place value.

$\frac{7}{10} = 0.7$

## EXPRESSING DECIMALS TO THE HUNDREDTHS AS EQUIVALENT FRACTIONS

Decimals and fractions are two different ways of showing the same number. For example, six hundredths could be written as the fraction $\frac{6}{100}$ or as the decimal 0.06.

To convert a decimal to a fraction, follow these steps:

1. Figure out the denominator. The place value of the last digit of the decimal is the same as the denominator of the fraction.
2. Figure out the numerator. The digits in the decimal will be the numerator of the fraction.

*Example*

Write 0.09 as a fraction.

*Solution*

**Step 1**
Figure out the denominator.
The place value of the last digit of the decimal is the same as the denominator of the fraction.
The last digit of 0.09 is 9, and it is in the hundredths place. The denominator of the fraction is 100.

$\frac{?}{100}$

Number and Fractions

**Step 2**
Figure out the numerator.
The digits in the decimal will be the numerator of the fraction.
The digits in 0.09 are 0, 0, and 9. You do not have to write the zeros that come at the beginning of the decimal. That means that 9 is the only digit you have to write in the numerator.
The fraction is $\frac{9}{100}$.

---

*Example*
Write 0.73 as a fraction.

*Solution*

**Step 1**
Figure out the denominator.
The place value of the last digit of the decimal is the same as the denominator of the fraction.
The last digit of 0.73 is 3, and it is in the hundredths place. The denominator of the fraction is 100.
$$\frac{?}{100}$$

**Step 2**
Figure out the numerator.
The digits in the decimal will be the numerator of the fraction.
The digits in 0.73 are 0, 7, and 3. You do not have to write the zeros that come at the beginning of the decimal. That means that 73 is the numerator.
The fraction is $\frac{73}{100}$.

---

## SHOWING DECIMALS ON A NUMBER LINE

Any number can be shown as a point on a number line. Decimal numbers can be placed on points between two whole numbers.

You can divide the section of a number line between two whole numbers into tenths to show a decimal number with one place.

*Example*
The decimal number 3.2 is greater than 3 and less than 4. It falls between 3 and 4 on a number line, and it is closer to 3 than 4.

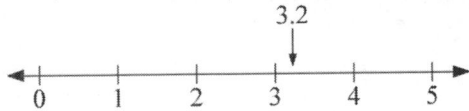

To show the exact location of 3.2, you can take the part of the number line between the 3 and the 4 and break it up into 10 tenths. The number 3.2 will be 2 tenths greater than 3.

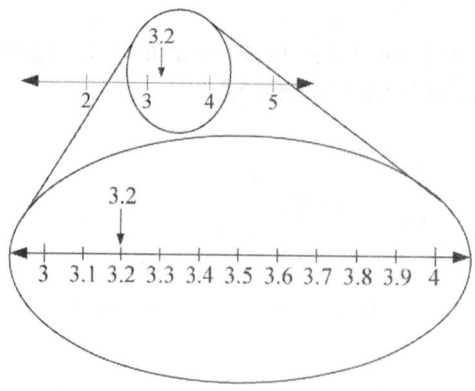

You can divide the section of a number line between 2 tenths into hundredths to show a decimal number with two places.

*Example*

The decimal number 3.29 is greater than 3.2 and less than 3.3. It falls between 3.2 and 3.3 on a number line, and it is closer to 3.3 than 3.2.

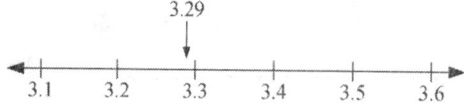

To show the exact location of 3.29, you can take the part of the number line between 3.2 and 3.3 and break it up into 10 hundredths. The number 3.29 will be 9 hundredths greater than 3.2.

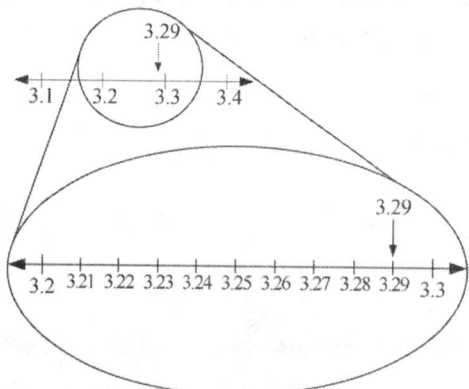

You can divide the section of a number line between 2 hundredths into thousandths to show a decimal number with three places.

*Example*

The decimal number 3.294 is greater than 3.29 and less than 3.3. It falls between 3.29 and 3.3 on a number line, and it is about halfway between 3.29 and 3.3.

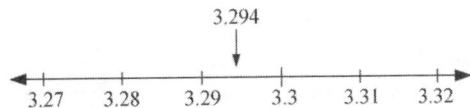

To show the exact location of 3.294, you can take the part of the number line between 3.29 and 3.3 and break it up into 10 thousandths. The number 3.294 will be 4 thousandths greater than 3.29.

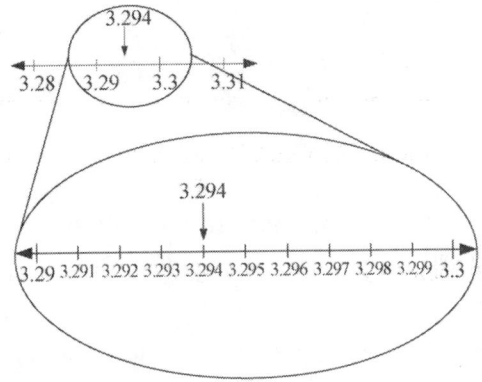

---

You can continue to divide a number line into smaller and smaller sections to show decimals with any number of places. For example, 3.2947 is between 3.294 and 3.295. You can divide the section of the number line between 3.2947 and 3.2948 into hundred thousandths to show the location of 3.29471.

To show any decimal on a number line, follow these steps:

1. Draw a number line.
2. Find the decimal on the number line.

*Example*

Draw a number line to show 8.37.

*Solution*

**Step 1**
Draw a number line.
The number 8.37 is bigger than 8.3 and smaller than 8.4. Divide a section of a number line between 8.3 and 8.4 into hundredths.

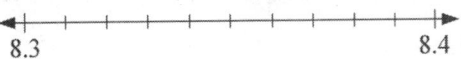

**Step 2**
Find the decimal on the number line.
The number 8.37 is seven hundredths greater than 8.3. It should go on the seventh tick.

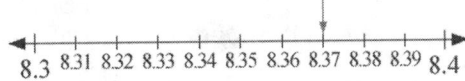

*4.NF.7* *Apply and extend previous understandings of multiplication to multiply a fraction by a whole number. Compare two decimals to hundredths by reasoning about their size. Recognize that comparisons are valid only when the two decimals refer to the same whole. Record the results of comparisons with the symbols >, =, or <, and justify the conclusions.*

## ORDER DECIMALS TO THE 100THS

Numbers can be ordered from least value to greatest value or from greatest value to least value. For example, order the following decimal numbers from greatest value to least value: 0.53, 1.47, 0.41.

**Place value** can be used to first compare decimal numbers and then order them.

*Example*

|  | 0.53 | 1.47 | 0.41 |
|---|---|---|---|
| Start at the left. Compare the digits in the ones place. Since 1 is greater than 0, the number with the greatest value is 1.47. | 0.53 | 1.47 | 0.41 |
| Since 0.53 and 0.41 both have a 0 in the ones place, move to the right and compare the digits in the tenths place. Since 5 is greater than 4, 0.53 is greater than 0.41. You do not need to continue comparing the hundredths. | 0.53 |  | 0.41 |

From greatest value to least value, the order of the decimal numbers is 1.47, 0.53, 0.41.

---

*Example*

Place the following decimal numbers in order from **least** to **greatest**.

237.46, 237.53, 237.48, 237.35, and 237.43

*Solution*

From least to greatest, the numbers are 237.35, 237.43, 237.46, 237.48, and 237.53.

Since each number has the same digit in the hundreds, tens, and ones places, look at the digits in the tenths place. Order the numbers from least value to greatest value: 3, 4, 5.

Least number: 237.35

Middle numbers: 237.4…

Greatest number: 237.53

Now order the middle numbers that have the digit 4 in the tenths place. Order the digits in the hundredths place from least value to greatest value: 3, 6, 8

237.43, 237.46, and 237.48

---

## ORDER DECIMALS TO THE TENTHS

There are two different ways to order decimal numbers.

1. **Descending Order**: from greatest value to least value.
2. **Ascending Order**: from least value to greatest value.

## Example

A place value chart can be used to help organize the decimal numbers, making them easier to order. For example to order the decimal numbers 1.4, 0.5, and 0.4 in **descending order** a place value chart can be used.

Place each decimal into the place value chart.

| Ones | | | . | Parts of a Whole | | |
|---|---|---|---|---|---|---|
| H | T | O | . | Tth | Hth | Thth |
| | | 0 | . | 5 | | |
| | | 1 | . | 4 | | |
| | | 0 | . | 4 | | |

Start at the left. Compare the digits in the ones place. Since 1 is greater than 0, the number with the greatest value is 1.47

Since 0.5 and 0.4 both have a 0 in the ones place, move to the right and compare the digits in the tenths place. Since 5 is greater than 4 you can determine that 0.5 > 0.4

The descending order of decimals is:
1.4 > 0.5 > 0.4

---

You can also use a number line to show the order of numbers.

## Example

If you need to place the decimal numbers 0.8, 1.3, and 0.3 in order from least value to greatest value, you can use a number line like the one shown. Remember that the number closest to the left side has the least value, and the number closest to the right side has the greatest value.

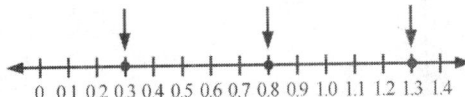

The decimals in least to greatest order as shown on the number line is: 0.3, 0.8, 1.3.

# EXERCISE #1—NUMBER AND OPERATIONS—FRACTIONS

77. Which of the following sets of blocks represents a fraction that is equivalent to the fraction $\frac{4}{5}$?

   A.
   B.
   C.
   D.

78. Which of the following fractions is equivalent to $\frac{2}{7}$?

   A. $\frac{4}{21}$
   B. $\frac{6}{21}$
   C. $\frac{6}{14}$
   D. $\frac{8}{14}$

*Use the following information to answer the next question.*

Cohen is using fraction strips to find equivalent fractions.

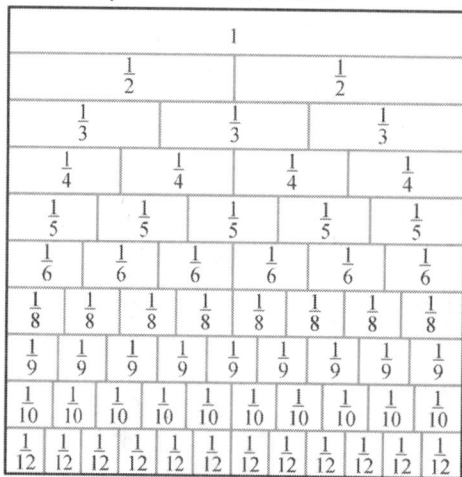

79. Which of the following pairs of fractions are equivalent?

   A. $\frac{2}{5}$ and $\frac{4}{10}$
   B. $\frac{2}{5}$ and $\frac{3}{8}$
   C. $\frac{5}{6}$ and $\frac{2}{3}$
   D. $\frac{5}{6}$ and $\frac{11}{12}$

*Use the following information to answer the next question.*

Jason wants to compare $\frac{5}{6}$ and $\frac{7}{9}$. He decides to start by finding a common denominator.

80. Which of the following pairs of fractions correctly compares $\frac{5}{6}$ and $\frac{7}{9}$ by using the lowest common denominator?

    A. $\frac{8}{9} > \frac{7}{9}$
    B. $\frac{15}{18} > \frac{14}{18}$
    C. $\frac{22}{27} > \frac{21}{27}$
    D. $\frac{30}{36} > \frac{28}{36}$

*Use the following information to answer the next question.*

Three different fractions are shown on three number lines.

Number line 1
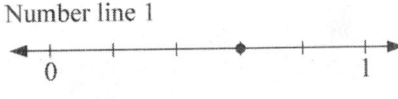

Number line 2

Number line 3
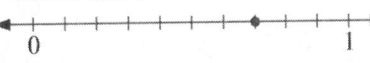

81. Which of the following statements about these fractions is **true**?

    A. The fraction $\frac{7}{10}$ is greater than $\frac{3}{5}$.
    B. The fraction $\frac{1}{5}$ is greater than $\frac{7}{10}$.
    C. The fraction $\frac{7}{10}$ is less than $\frac{1}{5}$.
    D. The fraction $\frac{3}{5}$ is less than $\frac{1}{5}$.

82. When the fractions $\frac{4}{7}$ and $\frac{3}{7}$ are subtracted, the difference is

    A. $\frac{7}{14}$
    B. $\frac{1}{14}$
    C. $\frac{1}{7}$
    D. $\frac{1}{0}$

*Use the following information to answer the next question.*

Lisa and Jenny shared a vegetable and pepperoni pizza. Lisa ate 2 pieces, and Jenny had 1 piece.

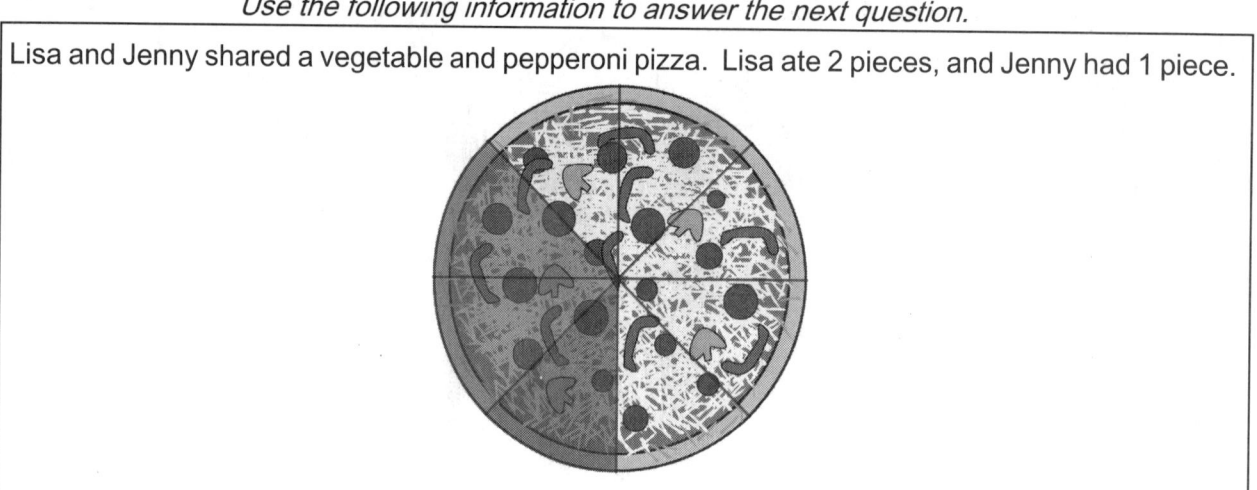

83. What fraction of the pizza did Lisa and Jenny eat?

*Use the following information to answer the next question.*

A fraction problem is given.

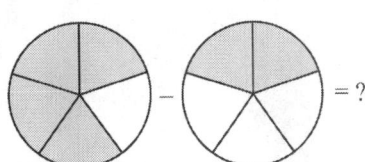 = ?

84. Which of the following diagrams represents the solution to this fraction problem?

A.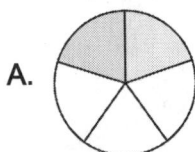

B. 

C.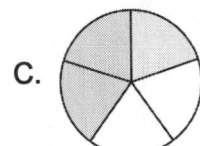

D. 

85. What is the sum of $\frac{2}{4} + \frac{1}{4}$?

  A. $\frac{3}{4}$

  B. $\frac{3}{8}$

  C. $\frac{2}{8}$

  D. $\frac{2}{16}$

86. What fraction can be broken up into $\frac{1}{10} + \frac{1}{10} + \frac{1}{10}$?

  A. $\frac{3}{10}$

  B. $\frac{1}{3}$

  C. $\frac{3}{1}$

  D. $\frac{10}{3}$

87. Which of the following pictures shows $2\frac{1}{3}$ packages of tennis balls?

A.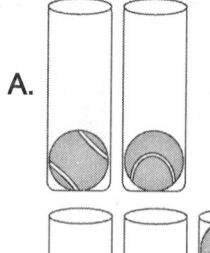

B.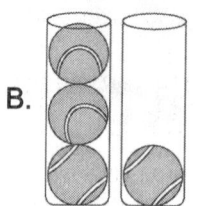

C.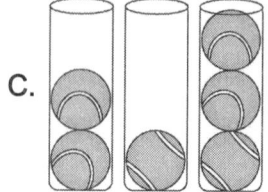

D.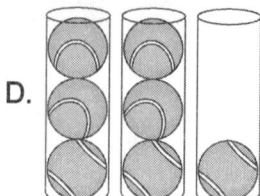

88. What is $3\frac{3}{5} + \frac{4}{5}$?

    A. $3\frac{2}{5}$

    B. $4\frac{2}{5}$

    C. $4\frac{7}{5}$

    D. $6\frac{4}{5}$

89. What is $5 - 1\frac{1}{2}$?

    A. $1\frac{1}{2}$

    B. $2\frac{1}{2}$

    C. $3\frac{1}{2}$

    D. $4\frac{1}{2}$

*Use the following information to answer the next question.*

> Matthew and Luke bought a large pie. They cut the pie into 8 pieces. Matthew ate 3 pieces, and Luke ate 4. Together they ate 7 pieces.

90. How much pie is left?

    A. $\frac{7}{8}$

    B. $\frac{5}{8}$

    C. $\frac{3}{8}$

    D. $\frac{1}{8}$

*Use the following information to answer the next question.*

> Keisha's favorite colors are orange and purple. She counts her T-shirts and finds that $\frac{3}{8}$ of them are orange, $\frac{2}{8}$ of them are purple, and $\frac{3}{8}$ of them are another color.

91. What fraction of Keisha's T-shirts are one of her favorite colors?

    A. $\frac{1}{8}$  
    B. $\frac{5}{8}$  
    C. $\frac{6}{8}$  
    D. $\frac{8}{8}$

*Use the following information to answer the next question.*

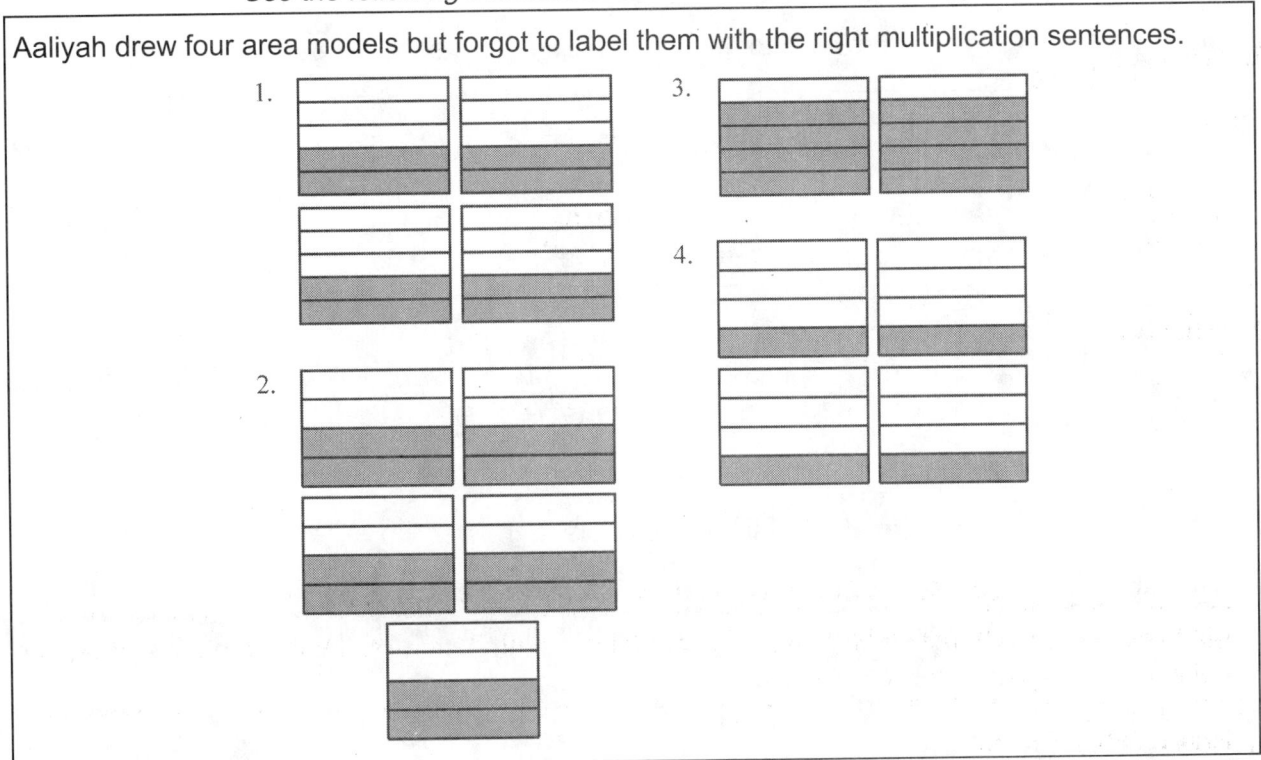

Aaliyah drew four area models but forgot to label them with the right multiplication sentences.

92. Which of the given area models shows the solution to $\frac{2}{5} \times 4$?

    A. 1  
    B. 2  
    C. 3  
    D. 4

93. Which of the following expressions is equal to $\frac{1}{6} + \frac{1}{6} + \frac{1}{6}$?

    A. $\frac{1}{6} + 3$  
    B. $\frac{1}{6} \times 3$  
    C. $\frac{3}{6} + 3$  
    D. $\frac{3}{6} \times 3$

*Use the following information to answer the next question.*

Isaiah buys a 4 oz bag of jellybeans. When he gets home, he eats $\frac{5}{6}$ of the bag.

94. How many ounces of jellybeans did Isaiah eat?
    A. $\frac{20}{24}$ oz
    B. $\frac{5}{24}$ oz
    C. $\frac{20}{6}$ oz
    D. $\frac{9}{6}$ oz

*Use the following information to answer the next question.*

Alice wants to write $\frac{3}{5}$ and $\frac{7}{10}$ with common denominators. She knows that 10 can be a common denominator, so she does not have to rewrite $\frac{7}{10}$. She only needs to rewrite $\frac{3}{5}$.

95. When Alice writes $\frac{3}{5}$ with a denominator of 10, the numerator will be _____.

96. What is the solution to the expression $\frac{1}{2} + \frac{4}{10}$?
    A. $\frac{5}{10}$
    B. $\frac{6}{10}$
    C. $\frac{7}{10}$
    D. $\frac{9}{10}$

97. Which of the following decimal numbers is equivalent to the fraction $\frac{60}{100}$?
    A. 0.06
    B. 0.60
    C. 6.00
    D. 60.0

98. Which of the following fractions is equal to 0.5?
    A. $\frac{1}{5}$
    B. $\frac{5}{1}$
    C. $\frac{5}{10}$
    D. $\frac{10}{5}$

*Use the following information to answer the next question.*

During a math lesson, a teacher showed the given set of suns to his students.

99. Which of the following decimal numbers represents the number of shaded suns in the given set?
    A. 0.05
    B. 0.5
    C. 0.55
    D. 5.0

100. What is 0.02 written as a fraction?

A. $\dfrac{2}{100}$

B. $\dfrac{2}{10}$

C. $\dfrac{10}{2}$

D. $\dfrac{100}{2}$

*Use the following information to answer the next question.*

A number line is given.

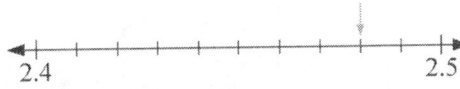

101. What number is the arrow pointing to? _____

102. Which of the following sets of numbers is in order from **greatest** to **least** value?

A. 0.24, 0.65, 0.41, 0.960.86

B. 0.24, 0.41, 0.65, 0.960.86

C. 0.96, 0.86, 0.65, 0.410.24

D. 0.96, 0.86, 0.41, 0.650.24

103. Which of the following sets of decimal numbers is listed from **least** to **greatest**?

A. 0.2, 1.6, 1.9, 2.3, 2.8

B. 0.2, 2.3, 1.6, 2.8, 1.9

C. 1.6, 1.9, 2.3, 2.8, 0.2

D. 2.8, 2.3, 1.9, 1.6, 0.2

# EXERCISE #1—NUMBER AND OPERATIONS—FRACTIONS
## ANSWERS AND SOLUTIONS

| 77. D | 84. C | 91. B | 98. C |
| 78. B | 85. A | 92. A | 99. B |
| 79. A | 86. A | 93. B | 100. A |
| 80. B | 87. D | 94. C | 101. 2.48 |
| 81. A | 88. B | 95. 6 | 102. C |
| 82. C | 89. C | 96. D | 103. A |
| 83. See solution | 90. D | 97. B | |

**77. D**

Step 1

Find an equivalent fraction to the fraction $\frac{4}{5}$.

Multiply both the numerator and the denominator by the same number.

$$\frac{4 \times 2}{5 \times 2} = \frac{8}{10}$$

The fraction $\frac{8}{10}$ is equivalent to the fraction $\frac{4}{5}$.

Step 2

Identify which of the given sets of blocks represents the fraction $\frac{8}{10}$.

Remember that the number of shaded blocks is the numerator and the total number of blocks is the denominator of the fraction.

The set of blocks in choice D has 10 blocks in total, and 8 of these are shaded. Therefore, set D represents the fraction $\frac{8}{10}$, which is equivalent to the fraction $\frac{4}{5}$.

**78. B**

To find an equivalent fraction, multiply the denominator and the numerator by the same number.

Step 1

Multiply the denominator and the numerator of the fraction $\frac{2}{7}$ by 2.

$$\frac{2 \times 2}{7 \times 2} = \frac{4}{14}$$

Since there are no given fractions that match $\frac{4}{14}$, continue to multiply.

Step 2

Multiply the denominator and the numerator of the fraction $\frac{2}{7}$ by 3.

$$\frac{2 \times 3}{7 \times 3} = \frac{6}{21}$$

Since the fraction $\frac{6}{21}$ is given as a possible answer, there is no need to go any further.

**79. A**

Line up the fraction strips. Fractions with right edges that line up are equivalent.

The fractions $\frac{2}{3}$, $\frac{5}{6}$, and $\frac{11}{12}$ are all different lengths. None of these fractions are equivalent.

| $\frac{1}{5}$ | | $\frac{1}{5}$ | |
|---|---|---|---|
| $\frac{1}{8}$ | $\frac{1}{8}$ | $\frac{1}{8}$ | |
| $\frac{1}{10}$ | $\frac{1}{10}$ | $\frac{1}{10}$ | $\frac{1}{10}$ |

The fractions $\frac{2}{5}$ and $\frac{4}{10}$ are equivalent because the right edges line up.

### 80. B

**Step 1**

Find the lowest common denominator for $\frac{5}{6}$ and $\frac{7}{9}$.

- Factors of 6 are 6, 12, and 18.
- Factors of 9 are 9, 18, and 27.

The lowest common denominator is 18.

**Step 2**

Write both fractions with a denominator of 18.

$\frac{5}{6} = \frac{5 \times 3}{6 \times 3} = \frac{15}{18}$

$\frac{7}{9} = \frac{7 \times 2}{9 \times 2} = \frac{14}{18}$

The fractions $\frac{5}{6}$ and $\frac{7}{9}$ become $\frac{15}{18}$ and $\frac{14}{18}$ when they are written with the lowest common denominator.

Since $\frac{15}{18} > \frac{14}{18}$, then $\frac{5}{6} > \frac{7}{9}$.

### 81. A

Determine what fractions the number lines are showing. They are all showing fractions because they all show numbers between 0 and 1.

Find out how many parts the number line is broken into. This number will be the denominator. The tick where the dot is placed on the number line will be the numerator.

**Step 1**
Find out what fraction the first number line shows.

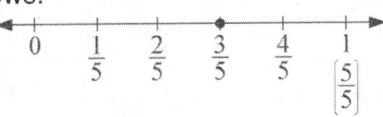

The number line is broken into 5 parts. The dot on the number line is 3 ticks over from the left.

The number line shows $\frac{3}{5}$.

**Step 2**
Find out what fraction the second number line shows.

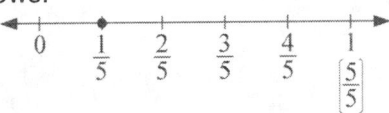

The number line is broken into 5 parts. The dot on the number line is 1 tick over from the left.

The number line shows $\frac{1}{5}$.

**Step 3**
Find out what fraction the third number line shows.

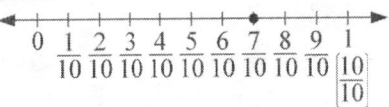

The number line is broken up into 10 parts. The dot on the number line is 7 ticks over from the left. The number line shows $\frac{7}{10}$.

**Step 4**
Compare the fractions by lining up the number lines.
It is important to make sure the number lines are the same size when you are comparing fractions with unlike denominators.

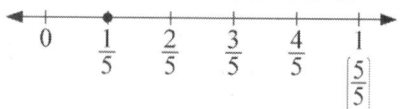

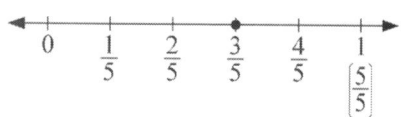

After comparing the three number lines, it is clear that $\frac{7}{10}$ is greater than $\frac{1}{5}$ and $\frac{3}{5}$ because it is closest to 1 on the number line.

The only true statement is that $\frac{7}{10}$ is greater than $\frac{3}{5}$.

**82. C**

**Step 1**
Subtract the numerators of the fractions while keeping the common denominator the same.
$$\frac{4}{7} - \frac{3}{7} = \frac{4-3}{7}$$
$$= \frac{1}{7}$$

**Step 2**
Reduce the resulting fraction to lowest terms if possible.
The fraction is already in lowest terms since both the numerator and the denominator cannot be divided by a common factor other than 1.
Therefore, $\frac{4}{7} - \frac{3}{7} = \frac{1}{7}$.

**83.**

**Step 1**
Find the denominator.
The denominator is the total number of pieces of pizza.
$$\frac{\phantom{0}}{8}$$
In total, there were 8 pieces of pizza.

**Step 2**
Find the numerator.
The numerator is the total number of pieces eaten. To find the numerator, add together the number of pieces of the pizza that each girl ate.
Lisa ate 2 of the 8 pieces, and Jenny ate 1 of the 8 pieces.
$$\frac{2}{8} + \frac{1}{8} = \frac{3}{8}$$
There were 3 pieces of pizza eaten in total.

**Step 3**
Write the fraction.
In words, 3 out of the 8 pieces of pizza were eaten.
Using fractional notation, $\frac{3}{8}$ of the pizza was eaten.

**84. C**

**Step 1**
Determine the equation.
Both fractions have 5 parts that make a whole. The denominator of both fractions is 5.
The first fraction has 4 shaded areas, so the fraction is $\frac{4}{5}$. The second fraction has 2 shaded areas, so the fraction is $\frac{2}{5}$.
$$\frac{4}{5} - \frac{2}{5} = ?$$

**Step 2**
Determine the solution, and reduce when possible.
Because the fractions have the same denominator, the numerators can be subtracted.
$$\frac{4}{5} - \frac{2}{5} = \frac{2}{5}$$

**Step 3**
Model the solution.
The denominator 5 means there are 5 parts in total that make the fraction whole.
The numerator 2 means 2 of the 5 parts are shaded.

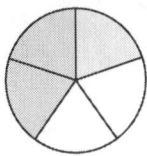

**85. A**
**Step 1**
Add the numerators of the fractions while keeping the denominators the same.
$\frac{2}{4} + \frac{1}{4} = \frac{2+1}{4} = \frac{3}{4}$

**Step 2**
Reduce the resulting fraction to lowest terms. The fraction is already in lowest terms. There is no need to reduce the fraction.
The sum of $\frac{2}{4} + \frac{1}{4} = \frac{3}{4}$.

**86. A**

The fraction $\frac{1}{10}$ means one part of a shape that is split up into 10 sections. If you have 3 sections of $\frac{1}{10}$, that means you have three parts of a shape that is split into 10 sections.

That fraction is written as $\frac{3}{10}$.

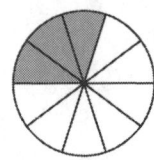

**87. D**
A whole package of tennis balls has 3 balls. The mixed number $2\frac{1}{3}$ has 2 wholes and $\frac{1}{3}$ of another whole.

Find a picture that has 2 full packages. There should also be 1 out of 3 balls in another package.

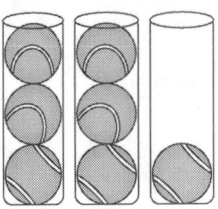

**88. B**
**Method 1**
Use pictures.
Draw a picture of each fraction.

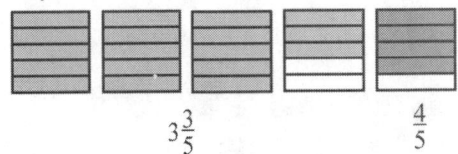

$3\frac{3}{5}$ $\qquad$ $\frac{4}{5}$

Put the two fractions together. $3\frac{3}{5} + \frac{4}{5} = 4\frac{2}{5}$

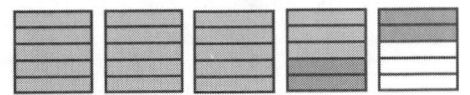

**Method 2**
Use a number line.
Label $3\frac{3}{5}$ on a number line divided into fifths.

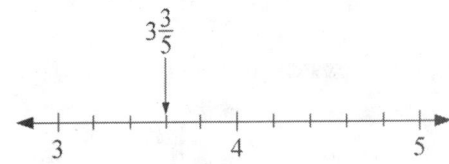

Count up 4 fifths. $3\frac{3}{5} + \frac{4}{5} = 4\frac{2}{5}$

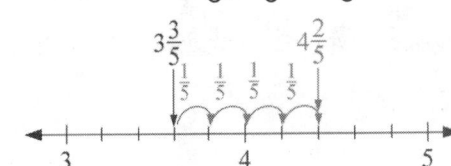

**Method 3**
Use number sense.

Add the wholes. There are zero wholes in $\frac{4}{5}$.

$3 + 0 = 3$
Add the fractions.
$\frac{3}{5} + \frac{4}{5} = \frac{7}{5}$

The answer is $3\frac{7}{5}$. The fraction part of a mixed number always has to be a proper fraction, with a numerator smaller than the denominator.

Try writing $3\frac{7}{5}$ a different way. $3\frac{3}{5} + \frac{4}{5} = 4\frac{2}{5}$

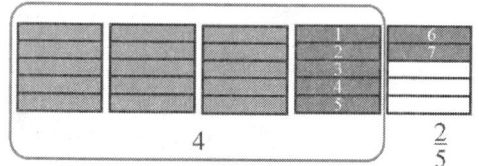

**89. C**

**Method 1**
Use pictures.

**Step 1**
Draw a picture with 5 wholes split into halves.

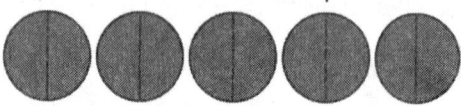

**Step 2**
Cross out 1 whole and 1 half.

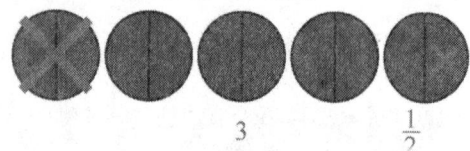

There are 3 wholes and 1 half left over.
$5 - 1\frac{1}{2} = 3\frac{1}{2}$

**Method 2**
Use a number line.

**Step 1**
Label 5 on a number line divided into halves.

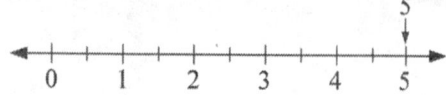

**Step 2**
Count back 1 whole and 1 half.

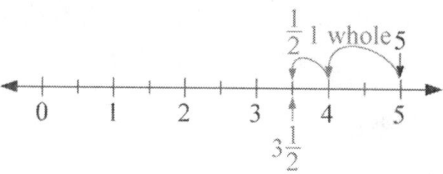

$5 - 1\frac{1}{2} = 3\frac{1}{2}$

**Method 3**
Use number sense.

**Step 1**
Subtract the whole numbers, and subtract the fractions. The problem with $5 - 1\frac{1}{2}$ is that 5 does not have a fractional part. Try rewriting it a different way.

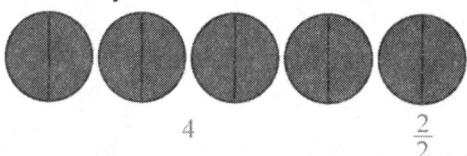

The number 5 is the same as $4\frac{2}{2}$. Now, you can find the solution. The new subtraction sentence is $4\frac{2}{2} - 1\frac{1}{2}$.

**Step 2**
Subtract the wholes.
$4 - 1 = 3$

**Step 3**
Subtract the fractions.
$\frac{2}{2} - \frac{1}{2} = \frac{1}{2}$

**Step 4**
Put the wholes and the fractions back together.
$5 - 1\frac{1}{2} = 3\frac{1}{2}$

## 90. D

**Step 1**
Identify the fractions from the problem.
The pie was cut into 8 pieces. The fraction for the whole is $\frac{8}{8}$.

Together Matthew and Luke ate 7 pieces.
The fraction for the pieces eaten is $\frac{7}{8}$.

**Step 2**
Subtract the two fractions.
Subtract the two numerators while keeping the same denominator.

$$\frac{8}{8} - \frac{7}{8} = \frac{8-7}{8}$$
$$= \frac{1}{8}$$

There is $\frac{1}{8}$ of the pie left.

## 91. B

Keisha's favorite colors are orange and purple. To find out what fraction of her T-shirts are one of her favorite colors, add the fraction that are orange to the fraction that are purple.

$$\frac{3}{8} + \frac{2}{8} = \frac{5}{8}$$

A total of $\frac{5}{8}$ of Keisha's T-shirts are one of her favorite colors.

## 92. A

The correct area model shows the multiplication of a whole number by a fraction.

**Step 1**
Draw rectangles to represent the whole number.
The whole number is 4, so draw four whole rectangles.

**Step 2**
Multiply each of the rectangles by $\frac{2}{5}$.

The denominator is 5, so divide each rectangle into five horizontal strips. The numerator is 2, so shade two of the strips.

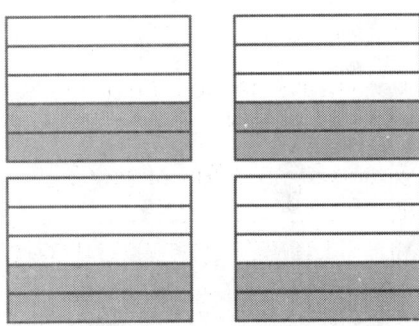

You can use the area model to find the product of $\frac{2}{5} \times 4$. The shaded sections represent the product.

In total, two sections out of five sections in each rectangle are shaded.
$2 + 2 + 2 + 2 = 8$
Place the number 8 over the denominator (5).

$$\frac{2}{5} \times 4 = \frac{8}{5}$$

This product is shown in area model 1.

## 93. B

The fraction $\frac{1}{6}$ is added together 3 times.
This is the same as saying that there are 3 groups of $\frac{1}{6}$. You should multiply by 3.

Write the multiplication sentence.
$\frac{1}{6} \times 3$

If you want to solve the multiplication problem, you can add the fractions.

$$\frac{1}{6} \times 3 = \frac{1}{6} + \frac{1}{6} + \frac{1}{6}$$
$$= \frac{1+1+1}{6}$$
$$= \frac{3}{6}$$

## 94. C

The question is asking for $\frac{5}{6}$ of 4 oz. To find out how much Isaiah ate, you need to multiply 4 by $\frac{5}{6}$.

$$4 \times \frac{5}{6} = \frac{4}{1} \times \frac{5}{6}$$
$$= \frac{4 \times 5}{1 \times 6}$$
$$= \frac{20}{6}$$

$\frac{20}{6}$ can also be written as $3\frac{2}{6}$.

Isaiah ate $\frac{20}{6}$ oz of jellybeans.

## 95. 6

Rewrite $\frac{3}{5}$ with a denominator of 10.

$$\frac{3}{5} = \frac{?}{10}$$

To go from a denominator of 5 to a denominator of 10, you need to multiply by 2. Multiply the numerator and denominator by 2.

$$\frac{3}{5} = \frac{3 \times 2}{5 \times 2} = \frac{6}{10}$$

The numerator of Alice's new fraction will be 6.

## 96. D

**Step 1**
Create equivalent fractions.

Look at $\frac{1}{2}$ because the denominator is smaller.

$$\frac{1}{2} = \frac{2}{4} = \frac{3}{6} = \frac{4}{8} = \frac{5}{10}$$

**Step 2**
Add the fractions.

$$\frac{1}{2} + \frac{4}{10}$$
$$= \frac{5}{10} + \frac{4}{10}$$
$$= \frac{5+4}{10}$$
$$= \frac{9}{10}$$

## 97. B

Both the fraction $\frac{60}{100}$ and the decimal number 0.60 represent 60 out of 100 squares on a hundreds grid.

The decimal 0.60 is equivalent to the fraction $\frac{60}{100}$.

## 98. C

**Step 1**
Find the denominator.
The place value of the last digit in the decimal is the denominator of the fraction.
The 5 in 0.5 is in the tenths position, so the denominator is 10.

$$\frac{?}{10}$$

**Step 2**
Find the numerator.
Remove the decimal point. The digits to the right of the decimal point become the numerator.
When the decimal point is removed from 0.5, the 5 is left. The number 5 is the numerator.

$$\frac{5}{10}$$

## 99. B

There are 5 shaded suns and 10 suns in total. Therefore, the fraction that represents the number of shaded suns is $\frac{5}{10}$.

The decimal that represents the fraction $\frac{5}{10}$ is 0.5. The number 0 tells you that the whole set of suns is not shaded (there is no whole number). The number 5 tells you that 5 of the 10 suns are shaded.

## 100. A

**Step 1**
Figure out the denominator.

The place value of the last digit of the decimal is the same as the denominator of the fraction.

The last digit of 0.02 is 2, and it is in the hundredths place. The denominator of the fraction is 100.

$$\frac{?}{100}$$

**Step 2**
Figure out the numerator.

The digits in the decimal will be the numerator of the fraction.

The digits in 0.02 are 0, 0, and 2. It is not necessary to write the zeros that come in the beginning of the decimal. This means that 2 is the only digit in the numerator.

The fraction is $\frac{2}{100}$.

## 101. 2.48

The number line shows the numbers between 2.4 and 2.5. The line is divided into hundredths, and the arrow is pointing to the number that is 8 hundredths greater than 2.4.

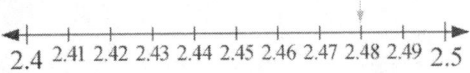

The number is 2.48.

## 102. C

**Step 1**
To determine which set of numbers is in order from greatest to least value, first place each decimal into a place value chart. Only digits in the same place value can be compared.

| Ones | . | Parts of a Whole | |
|------|---|------|-----|
|  O   | . | Tth  | Hth |
|  0   | . |  2   |  4  |
|  0   | . |  6   |  5  |
|  0   | . |  4   |  1  |
|  0   | . |  9   |  6  |
|  0   | . |  8   |  6  |

**Step 2**
Compare the numbers from left to right, that is, from the largest place value to the smallest place value.

All the decimals have the same number in the ones place value (0). Compare the numbers in the tenths place value.
9 > 8 > 6 > 4 > 2

The five given decimals can now be arranged in order from greatest to least value.
0.96 > 0.86 > 0.65 > 0.41 > 0.24

## 103. A

**Step 1**
Place all the decimals in a place value chart to organize the numbers.

| Ones | . | Tenths |
|------|---|--------|
|  1   | . |   6    |
|  1   | . |   9    |
|  2   | . |   3    |
|  2   | . |   8    |
|  0   | . |   2    |

**Step 2**
Order the decimals from least to greatest.
Since the numbers need to be ordered from least to greatest, look for the smallest number in the ones column. The number 0 is the smallest number, and there is only one 0, so 0.2 will be the first number in the order.

Next, look for the next smallest digit in the ones column. The number 1 is the next smallest digit after 0. Since there are two decimals with a 1 in the ones column, look at the tenths position. The number 1.6 will come after 0.2, and 1.9 will come after 1.6 because 6 < 9.

Finally, look at the numbers starting with 2. The number 2.3 will come after 1.9, and the number 2.8 will come after 2.3 because 3 < 8.

Therefore, the correct order is 0.2, 1.6, 1.9, 2.3, 2.8.

# EXERCISE #2—NUMBER AND OPERATIONS—FRACTIONS

*Use the following information to answer the next question.*

Clint drew the following diagram. He then shaded parts of the diagram to represent a pair of equivalent fractions.

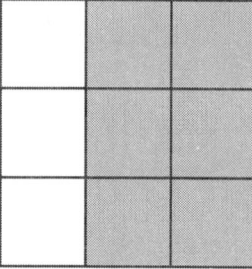

104. Which of the following pairs of equivalent fractions are represented by the shaded part of the diagram Clint drew?

A. $\frac{1}{3}$ and $\frac{6}{9}$

B. $\frac{1}{3}$ and $\frac{3}{9}$

C. $\frac{2}{3}$ and $\frac{3}{9}$

D. $\frac{2}{3}$ and $\frac{6}{9}$

*Use the following information to answer the next question.*

Stanley bought a box of candy. There were 16 pieces of candy in the box. He wanted to share them with his friends. He gave 9 pieces to his friend Chad and 4 pieces to his friend Katie, and kept 5 for himself.

105. Who has a fraction of candy that is equivalent to $\frac{1}{4}$?

A. Chad

B. Katie

C. Chad and Katie

D. Stanley and Chad

*Use the following information to answer the next question.*

Kevin is using fraction strips to find equivalent fractions.

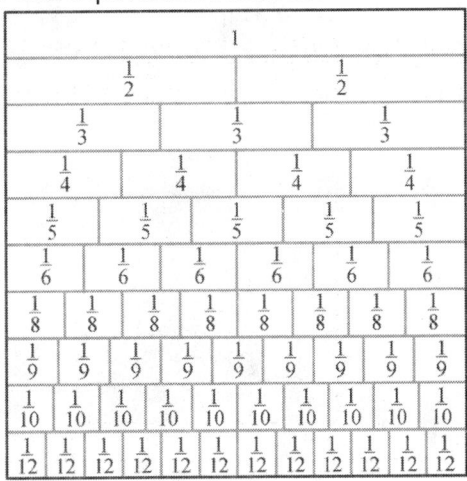

106. Which of the following fractions is equivalent to $\frac{1}{4}$?

   A. $\frac{1}{8}$

   B. $\frac{2}{6}$

   C. $\frac{3}{8}$

   D. $\frac{3}{12}$

*Use the following information to answer the next question.*

Trudi wants to compare the fractions $\frac{1}{3}$, $\frac{2}{3}$, $\frac{1}{6}$, and $\frac{5}{6}$.

107. Which of the following comparisons is **true**?

   A. $\frac{1}{6} > \frac{1}{3}$

   B. $\frac{1}{3} < \frac{5}{6}$

   C. $\frac{2}{3} < \frac{1}{6}$

   D. $\frac{2}{3} > \frac{5}{6}$

*Use the following information to answer the next question.*

The given number lines show three different fractions.

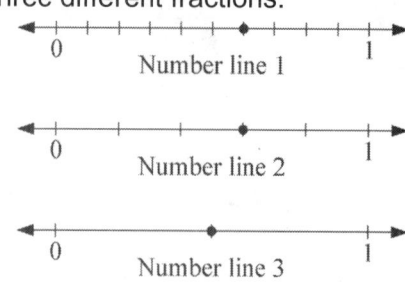

108. Which of the following statements about these given fractions is **true**?

   A. The fraction $\frac{1}{2}$ is equal to $\frac{3}{5}$.

   B. The fraction $\frac{3}{5}$ is less than $\frac{1}{2}$.

   C. The fraction $\frac{6}{10}$ is equal to $\frac{3}{5}$.

   D. The fraction $\frac{6}{10}$ is less than $\frac{1}{2}$.

*Use the following information to answer the next question.*

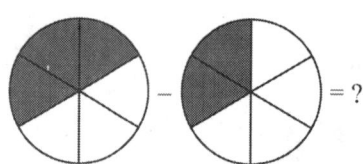 = ?

A fraction problem is given.

109. Which of the following fraction circles represents the solution to this problem?

A.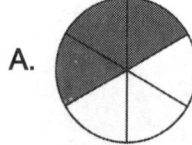

B.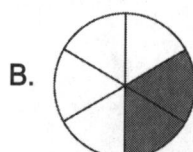

C.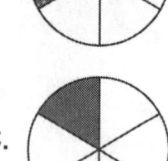

D.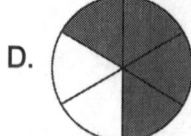

Exercise #2          Castle Rock Research

Use the following information to answer the next question.

A fraction problem is given.

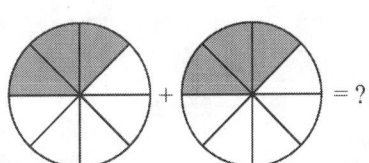

110. Which of the following fraction circles represents the solution to this problem?

A.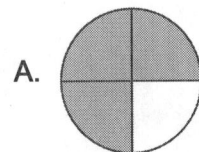

B. (circle with 1/4 shaded)

C.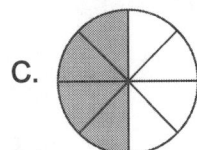

D. (circle with 8 sections, 3 shaded)

111. What is the sum of $\frac{2}{7} + \frac{4}{7}$?

A. $\frac{6}{7}$

B. $\frac{8}{7}$

C. $\frac{6}{14}$

D. $\frac{8}{14}$

112. When $\frac{1}{5}$ is subtracted from $\frac{3}{5}$, the difference is

A. $\frac{1}{2}$

B. $\frac{2}{5}$

C. $\frac{3}{5}$

D. $\frac{4}{5}$

113. Which of the following addition sentences is equal to $\frac{4}{5}$?

A. $\frac{1}{4} + \frac{1}{4} + \frac{1}{4} + \frac{1}{4}$

B. $\frac{1}{5} + \frac{1}{5} + \frac{1}{5} + \frac{1}{5}$

C. $\frac{1}{4} + \frac{1}{4} + \frac{1}{4} + \frac{1}{4} + \frac{1}{4}$

D. $\frac{1}{5} + \frac{1}{5} + \frac{1}{5} + \frac{1}{5} + \frac{1}{5}$

*Use the following information to answer the next question.*

Pencils come in packages of 6.

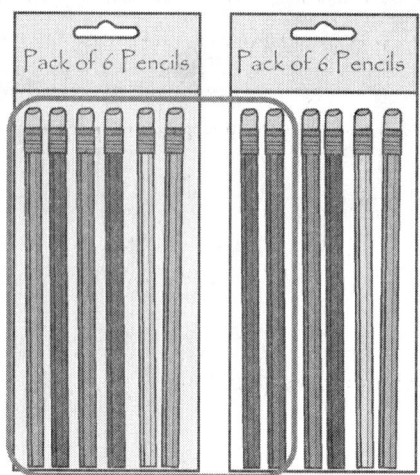

114. How many packages are circled?

   A. $\frac{6}{8}$
   B. $\frac{8}{12}$
   C. $1\frac{2}{6}$
   D. $1\frac{4}{6}$

115. What is $2\frac{1}{3} + 3\frac{2}{3}$?

   A. 5
   B. $5\frac{4}{3}$
   C. 6
   D. $6\frac{3}{3}$

116. What is $2\frac{1}{8} - \frac{3}{8}$?

   A. $1\frac{2}{8}$
   B. $1\frac{6}{8}$
   C. $2\frac{2}{8}$
   D. $2\frac{6}{8}$

*Use the following information to answer the next question.*

Kate bought a cake to share with her friends. The cake was cut into 20 equal pieces. Kate ate 4 pieces, and her friends ate 15 pieces.

117. In fraction form, how much more cake did Kate's friends eat than Kate?

   A. $\frac{4}{20}$
   B. $\frac{4}{15}$
   C. $\frac{11}{20}$
   D. $\frac{11}{15}$

*Use the following information to answer the next question.*

> Samia wants to finish her homework early so she can go to play at her friend's house. She does $\frac{1}{5}$ of her homework during class and another $\frac{3}{5}$ on the bus.

118. How much of Samia's homework is already finished when she arrives at home?

   A. $\frac{2}{5}$
   B. $\frac{2}{10}$
   C. $\frac{4}{5}$
   D. $\frac{4}{10}$

119. Which of the following expressions shows $\frac{2}{5} \times 4$ as repeated addition?

   A. $\frac{2}{5} + 4$
   B. $\frac{2}{5} + \frac{2}{5}$
   C. $\frac{2}{5} + \frac{2}{5} + 4$
   D. $\frac{2}{5} + \frac{2}{5} + \frac{2}{5} + \frac{2}{5}$

*Use the following information to answer the next question.*

> An area model is given.
>
>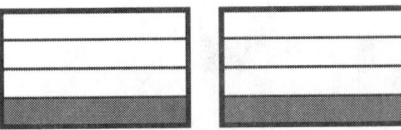

120. Which of the following number sentences represents this area model?

   A. $\frac{3}{4} \times 1$
   B. $\frac{3}{8} \times 1$
   C. $\frac{1}{4} \times 2$
   D. $\frac{1}{8} \times 2$

*Use the following information to answer the next question.*

> Tyrone needs to write a book report that is 2 pages long. He writes $\frac{1}{3}$ of it during class time.

121. How much has Tyrone already written?

   A. $\frac{1}{2}$ of a page
   B. $\frac{2}{3}$ of a page
   C. 1 page
   D. 2 pages

122. Written with the lowest common denominator, $\frac{1}{2}$ and $\frac{2}{3}$ are equal to the fractions

   A. $\frac{1}{6}$ and $\frac{2}{6}$
   B. $\frac{3}{6}$ and $\frac{4}{6}$
   C. $\frac{1}{12}$ and $\frac{2}{12}$
   D. $\frac{6}{12}$ and $\frac{8}{12}$

123. What is the sum of $\frac{3}{12} + \frac{2}{3}$?

   A. $\frac{11}{12}$
   B. $\frac{9}{12}$
   C. $\frac{6}{12}$
   D. $\frac{5}{12}$

124. Which of the following decimals represents the fraction $\frac{67}{100}$?

   A. 0.067
   B. 0.67
   C. 6.7
   D. 67

125. Which of the following fractions represents the decimal 0.2?

   A. $\frac{1}{2}$
   B. $\frac{2}{10}$
   C. $\frac{20}{10}$
   D. $\frac{2}{100}$

Use the following information to answer the next question.

The given circle is divided into ten equal parts with some of the parts shaded and some of the parts not shaded.

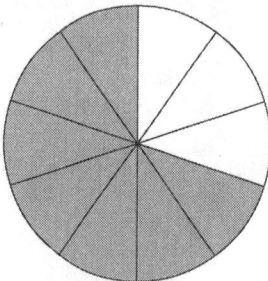

126. The shaded part of the circle can be represented by the decimal number
   A. 0.07
   B. 0.7
   C. 3.7
   D. 7.0

127. Written as a fraction, 0.04 is

   A. $\frac{4}{1}$

   B. $\frac{4}{10}$

   C. $\frac{4}{100}$

   D. $\frac{4}{1,000}$

*Use the following information to answer the next question.*

A number line is given.

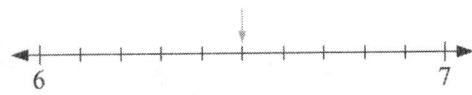

128. What number is the arrow pointing to? _____

129. Which of the following sets of numbers is arranged in **ascending order**?

   A. 5,321 < 5,321.245 < 5,321.45 < 5,321.5 < 5,322
   B. 5.32 < 5,321.5 < 5,321.45 < 5,321.24 < 5,322
   C. 5,322 < 5.32 < 5,321.5 < 5,321.45 < 5,321.24
   D. 5,321.24 < 5,321.45 < 5,321.5 < 5.32 < 5,322

*Use the following information to answer the next question.*

Zach's teacher wrote the given decimal numbers on the board. She asked Zach to place the decimal numbers in order.

2.8, 3.3, 2.5, 3.6

130. Which of the following lists shows the decimal numbers in order from the **least** to **greatest** value?

   A. 3.6, 3.3, 2.8, 2.5
   B. 2.8, 3.6, 2.5, 3.3
   C. 2.8, 2.5, 3.6, 3.3
   D. 2.5, 2.8, 3.3, 3.6

# EXERCISE #2—NUMBER AND OPERATIONS—FRACTIONS
## ANSWERS AND SOLUTIONS

| 104. D | 111. A | 118. C | 125. B |
| 105. B | 112. B | 119. D | 126. B |
| 106. D | 113. B | 120. C | 127. C |
| 107. B | 114. C | 121. B | 128. 6.5 |
| 108. C | 115. C | 122. B | 129. A |
| 109. C | 116. B | 123. A | 130. D |
| 110. A | 117. C | 124. B | |

**104. D**

Choice D is correct. The pair of equivalent fractions $\frac{2}{3}$ and $\frac{6}{9}$ are represented by the shaded parts of the diagram Clint drew.

**105. B**

Step 1
Determine what fractions of candy Stanley and his friends received.

- Chad received $\frac{9}{16}$.
- Katie received $\frac{4}{16}$.
- Stanley received $\frac{5}{16}$.

Step 2
Determine which of the fractions is equivalent to $\frac{1}{4}$.

The fractions $\frac{9}{16}$ and $\frac{5}{16}$ are already in lowest terms, so they are not equal to $\frac{1}{4}$.

The fraction $\frac{4}{16}$ can be reduced.

$\frac{4}{16} \div 4 = \frac{1}{4}$

Therefore, Katie's fraction of candy is equivalent to $\frac{1}{4}$.

**106. D**

Draw a line that extends down from the right edge of $\frac{1}{4}$.

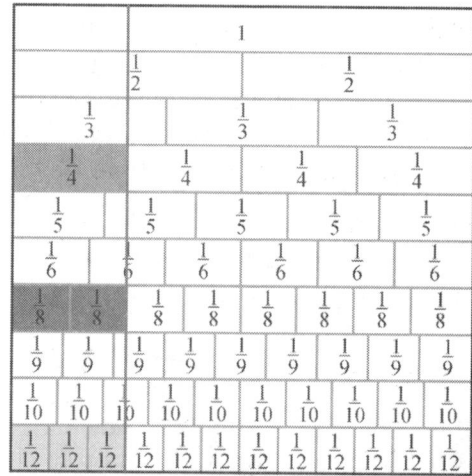

The fractions that have their right edges exactly on the line are $\frac{2}{8}$ and $\frac{3}{12}$. These fractions are both equivalent to $\frac{1}{4}$.

The fractions $\frac{1}{8}$, $\frac{2}{6}$, and $\frac{3}{8}$ are not equivalent to $\frac{1}{4}$.

## 107. B

**Step 1**
Rewrite the fractions with a common denominator.

- Factors of 3 are 3, 6, and 9.
- Factors of 6 are 6, 12, and 18.

The lowest common denominator is 6.

The fractions $\frac{1}{6}$ and $\frac{5}{6}$ already have denominators of 6. Write $\frac{1}{3}$ and $\frac{2}{3}$ with a denominator of 6.

$$\frac{1}{3} = \frac{1 \times 2}{3 \times 2} = \frac{2}{6}$$
$$\frac{2}{3} = \frac{2 \times 2}{3 \times 2} = \frac{4}{6}$$

**Step 2**
Compare the fractions.
When the denominators are the same, the fraction with the smaller numerator is less than the fraction with the bigger numerator:

- The number 1 is less than 2, so $\frac{1}{6} < \frac{2}{6}$.

  This means that $\frac{1}{6} < \frac{1}{3}$.

- The number 2 is less than 5, so $\frac{2}{6} < \frac{5}{6}$.

  This means that $\frac{1}{3} < \frac{5}{6}$.

- The number 4 is greater than 1, so $\frac{4}{6} > \frac{1}{6}$.

  This means that $\frac{2}{3} > \frac{1}{6}$.

- The number 4 is less than 5, so $\frac{4}{6} < \frac{5}{6}$.

  This means that $\frac{2}{3} < \frac{5}{6}$.

The only true comparison is $\frac{1}{3} < \frac{5}{6}$.

## 108. C

**Step 1**
Find out what fraction the first number line shows.

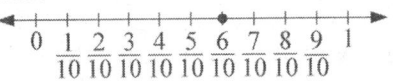

The number line is broken into 10 parts. This means that the denominator of the unknown fraction will be 10.
The dot on the number line is 6 ticks over from the left. This means the number line is showing the fraction $\frac{6}{10}$.

**Step 2**
Find out what fraction the second number line shows.

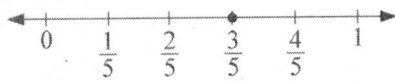

The number line is broken into 5 parts. This means that the denominator of the unknown fraction will be 5.
The dot on the number line is 3 ticks over from the left. This means the number line is showing the fraction $\frac{3}{5}$.

**Step 3**
Find out what fraction the third number line shows.

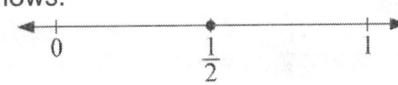

The number line is broken up into 2 equal parts. This means that the denominator of the unknown fraction will be 2.
The dot on the number line is 1 tick over from the left. This means the number line is showing the fraction $\frac{1}{2}$.

### Step 4
Compare the fractions by lining up the number lines.
It is important to make sure the number lines are the same size when you are comparing fractions with unlike denominators.

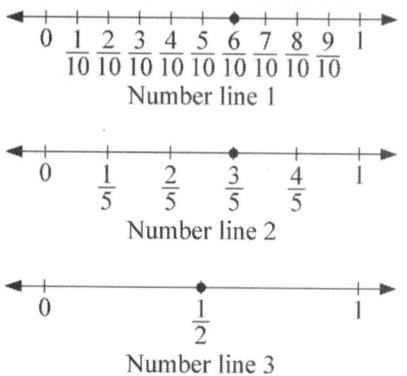

When comparing the number lines, you can see that the fractions $\frac{6}{10}$ and $\frac{3}{5}$ are equal because they are lined up exactly above each other.
They are both greater than $\frac{1}{2}$ because they are closer to 1 on the number lines.
The only true statement is that $\frac{6}{10}$ is equal to $\frac{3}{5}$.

### 109. C
#### Step 1
Determine the equation.
Both fractions have 6 parts that make a whole. The denominator of both fractions is 6.
The first fraction has 3 shaded areas, so the fraction is $\frac{3}{6}$.
The second fraction has 2 shaded areas, so the fraction is $\frac{2}{6}$.
$\frac{3}{6} - \frac{2}{6} = ?$

#### Step 2
Determine the solution.
Because the fractions have the same denominator, the numerators can be subtracted.
$\frac{3}{6} - \frac{2}{6} = \frac{1}{6}$

#### Step 3
Model the solution.
The denominator 6 means there are 6 parts in total that make the fraction whole.
The numerator 1 means that only 1 part of the 6 is shaded.

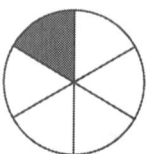

### 110. A
#### Step 1
Determine the equation.
Both fractions have 8 parts that make a whole. Therefore, the denominator of both fractions is 8.
The first fraction has 3 shaded areas, so the fraction is $\frac{3}{8}$.
The second fraction has 3 shaded areas, so the fraction is $\frac{3}{8}$.
$\frac{3}{8} + \frac{3}{8} = \square$

#### Step 2
Determine the solution, and reduce if possible.
Because the fractions have the same denominator, the numerators can be added together.
$\frac{3}{8} + \frac{3}{8} = \frac{6}{8}$
The fraction $\frac{6}{8}$ can be reduced to $\frac{3}{4}$.

**Step 3**

Model the solution.

The denominator 4 means there are 4 parts in total that make the fraction whole.

The numerator 3 means 3 of the 4 parts are shaded.

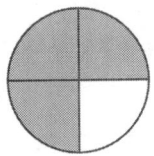

**111. A**

**Step 1**

Add the numerators of the fractions, but keep the denominators the same.

$\frac{2}{7} + \frac{4}{7} = \frac{2+4}{7} = \frac{6}{7}$

**Step 2**

Reduce the resulting fraction to lowest terms.

The fraction is already in lowest terms, so there is no need to reduce the fraction.

The sum of $\frac{2}{7} + \frac{4}{7}$ is $\frac{6}{7}$.

**112. B**

Subtract the numerators of the fractions while keeping the denominators the same.

$\frac{3}{5} - \frac{1}{5} = \frac{3-1}{5} = \frac{2}{5}$

**113. B**

In the fraction $\frac{4}{5}$, the number 5 shows that the fraction is split into 5 parts. Each of those parts is $\frac{1}{5}$.

If you have 4 of those parts, you need to add $\frac{1}{5}$ four times.

$\frac{1}{5} + \frac{1}{5} + \frac{1}{5} + \frac{1}{5}$

**114. C**

One whole package is circled, and part of another package is also circled. The number of circled packages will be a mixed number.

**Step 1**

Count the number of wholes.

There is 1 whole package circled.

**Step 2**

Decide what the fraction is.

Look at the package with only some circled pencils. Only 2 out of the 6 pencils are circled. That means that the fraction is $\frac{2}{6}$.

**Step 3**

Put the whole and the part together. Write the whole first, then the fraction.

There are $1\frac{2}{6}$ circled packages of pencils.

**115. C**

**Method 1**

Use pictures.

Draw a picture of each fraction.

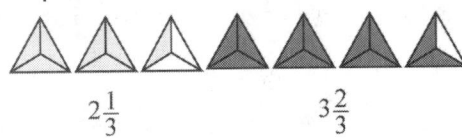

Put the two fractions together. $2\frac{1}{3} + 3\frac{2}{3} = 6$

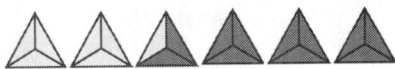

**Method 2**

Use a number line.

Label $2\frac{1}{3}$ on a number line divided into thirds.

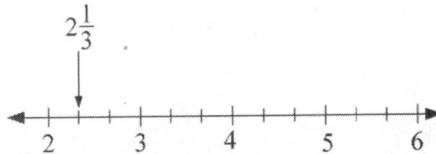

Count up 3 wholes and 2 thirds. To make the counting easier, start by counting the 2 thirds to reach 3. Then, count up the 3 wholes.

$2\frac{1}{3} + 3\frac{2}{3} = 6$

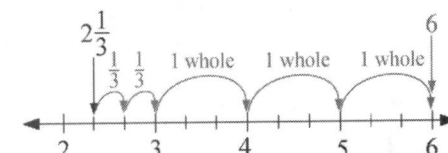

**Method 3**
Use number sense.
Add the wholes.
$2 + 3 = 5$
Add the fractions.
$\frac{1}{3} + \frac{2}{3} = \frac{3}{3}$

The answer is $5\frac{3}{3}$. The fraction part of a mixed number always has to be a proper fraction, with a numerator smaller than the denominator.

Try writing $5\frac{3}{3}$ a different way. $2\frac{1}{3} + 3\frac{2}{3} = 6$

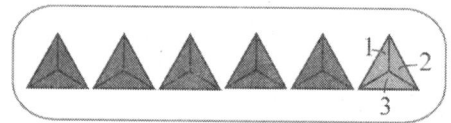

6 wholes

**116. B**

**Method 1**
Use pictures.

Draw a picture of $2\frac{1}{8}$.

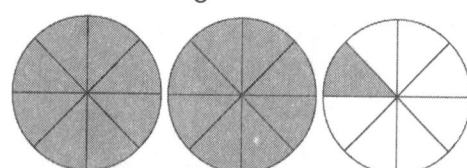

Cross out 3 eighths.

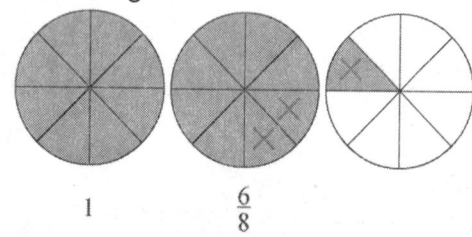

There is 1 whole and 6 eighths left over.
$2\frac{1}{8} - \frac{3}{8} = 1\frac{6}{8}$

**Method 2**
Use a number line.

Label $2\frac{1}{8}$ on a number line divided into eighths.

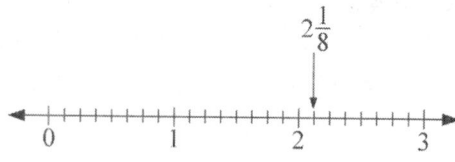

Count back 3 eighths.

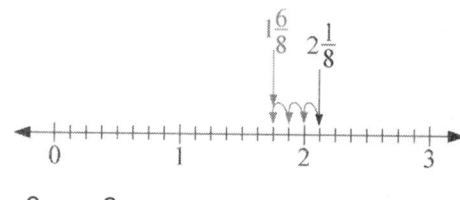

$2\frac{1}{8} - \frac{3}{8} = 1\frac{6}{8}$

**Method 3**
Use number sense.

Subtract the whole numbers, and subtract the fractions. The problem with $2\frac{1}{8} - \frac{3}{8}$ is that you cannot subtract $\frac{1}{8} - \frac{3}{8}$. Try rewriting $2\frac{1}{8}$ a different way.

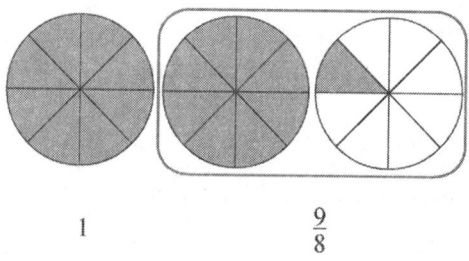

1        $\frac{9}{8}$

The mixed number $2\frac{1}{8}$ is the same as $1\frac{9}{8}$. Now you can find the solution. The new subtraction sentence is $1\frac{9}{8} - \frac{3}{8}$.

Subtract the wholes. The second fraction does not have any wholes.
$1 - 0 = 1$

Subtract the fractions.
$\frac{9}{8} - \frac{3}{8} = \frac{6}{8}$

Put the wholes and the fractions back together.
$2\frac{1}{8} - \frac{3}{8} = 1\frac{6}{8}$

117. C

**Step 1**
Identify the fractions in the problem.
The denominator of the fraction is 20 because the cake was cut into 20 equal pieces.
Kate's friends ate 15 pieces of the 20-piece cake, so the fraction of cake that they ate is $\frac{15}{20}$.
Kate ate 4 out of 20 pieces of cake, so the fraction of the cake she ate is $\frac{4}{20}$.

**Step 2**
Subtract the numerators.
15 − 4 = 11

**Step 3**
Put the difference over the like denominator.
The denominator stays the same.
The difference is 11, and the like denominator is 20, so the fraction is $\frac{11}{20}$.
Kate's friends ate $\frac{11}{20}$ more of the cake than she did.

118. C

Samia finished $\frac{1}{5}$ of her homework in class and $\frac{3}{5}$ on the bus. To find out how much she has finished in total, add the fractions.
$\frac{1}{5} + \frac{3}{5} = \frac{1+3}{5} = \frac{4}{5}$

Samia has already finished $\frac{4}{5}$ of her homework by the time she arrives at home.

119. D

**Step 1**
Decide how many times you need to add the fraction.
The expression $\frac{2}{5} \times 4$ means that there are 4 groups of $\frac{2}{5}$. You should add the fraction 4 times.

**Step 2**
Write the addition sentence.
$\frac{2}{5} + \frac{2}{5} + \frac{2}{5} + \frac{2}{5}$
If you want to solve the multiplication problem, you can add the fractions.
$\frac{2}{5} \times 4 = \frac{2}{5} + \frac{2}{5} + \frac{2}{5} + \frac{2}{5}$
$= \frac{2+2+2+2}{5}$
$= \frac{8}{5}$

120. C

**Step 1**
Figure out the whole number.
The large rectangles represent the whole number.
There are 2 large rectangles, so the whole number is 2.

**Step 2**
Figure out the fraction that is multiplied by the whole number.
The denominator of the fraction is equal to the number of parts in which each rectangle is divided. The denominator is 4 because each rectangle is divided into 4 parts.

$\frac{\phantom{1}}{4}$

The numerator of the fraction will be equal to the number of shaded parts. The numerator is 1 because 1 part of each rectangle is shaded.
$\frac{1}{4}$

**Step 3**
Figure out the number sentence.
The expression represented by the area model is $\frac{1}{4} \times 2$.
To find the product, count the total number of shaded parts and put it over the denominator (4).
$\frac{1}{4} \times 2 = \frac{2}{4}$

## 121. B

The question is asking for $\frac{1}{3}$ of 2 pages. To find out the number of pages Tyrone has written, you need to multiply 2 by $\frac{1}{3}$. Convert 2 into a fraction, and then multiply the numerator by the numerator and the denominator by the denominator.

$$2 \times \frac{1}{3} = \frac{2}{1} \times \frac{1}{3}$$
$$= \frac{2 \times 1}{1 \times 3}$$
$$= \frac{2}{3}$$

Tyrone has already written $\frac{2}{3}$ of a page.

## 122. B

**Step 1**
Choose a common denominator.
The denominator of $\frac{1}{2}$ is 2. The denominator of $\frac{2}{3}$ is 3. Find a number that is a multiple of both 2 and 3:

- Multiples of 2 include 2, 4, 6, 8, and 10.
- Multiples of 3 include 3, 6, 9, 12, and 15.

The number 6 is the lowest common multiple of both 2 and 3. Use this as the common denominator.

**Step 2**
Write the first fraction with a denominator of 6.
$$\frac{1}{2} = \frac{?}{6}$$
To go from a denominator of 2 to a denominator of 6, you need to multiply by 3. Multiply the numerator and denominator by 3.
$$\frac{1}{2} = \frac{1 \times 3}{2 \times 3} = \frac{3}{6}$$

**Step 3**
Write the second fraction with a denominator of 6.
$$\frac{2}{3} = \frac{?}{6}$$
To go from a denominator of 3 to a denominator of 6, you need to multiply by 2. Multiply the numerator and denominator by 2.
$$\frac{2}{3} = \frac{2 \times 2}{3 \times 2} = \frac{4}{6}$$
The fractions $\frac{1}{2}$ and $\frac{2}{3}$ are equal to $\frac{3}{6}$ and $\frac{4}{6}$.

## 123. A

**Step 1**
Create equivalent fractions.
The denominators are multiples of each other, so look at the fraction with the smaller denominator. The fraction with the smaller denominator is $\frac{2}{3}$.
$$\frac{2}{3} = \frac{4}{6} = \frac{6}{9} = \frac{8}{12}$$

**Step 2**
Add the fractions.
$$\frac{3}{12} + \frac{2}{3} = \frac{3}{12} + \frac{8}{12}$$
$$= \frac{3 + 8}{12}$$
$$= \frac{11}{12}$$

## 124. B

**Step 1**
Determine the place value of the decimal.
The fraction has a denominator of 100. This means that the decimal will have its last digit in the hundredths place.

**Step 2**
Determine the digits in the decimal.
The digits in the numerator will be the digits of the decimal. The number 67 represents the digits in the numerator.
Since the last digit must be in the hundredths place, 6 will be in the tenths place, and 7 will be in the hundredths place.

### Step 3
Write the decimal.

The fraction $\frac{67}{100}$ written as a decimal is 0.67.

### 125. B

#### Step 1
Determine the denominator.
Use the place value of the last digit in the decimal number as the denominator of the fraction.
The 2 in the decimal is in the tenths place, so the denominator is represented as $\frac{?}{10}$.

#### Step 2
Determine the numerator.
Remove the decimal point. The digits to the right of the decimal become the numerator. When the decimal is removed from 0.2, the 2 is left. This number becomes the numerator.

The fraction will now be $\frac{2}{10}$.

The fraction $\frac{2}{10}$ represents the decimal 0.2.

### 126. B

The shaded part of the circle can be represented by the decimal number 0.7.

Since there are ten parts to the circle, the decimal will be in the tenths place. There are 7 parts that are shaded, so the decimal number is written as 0.7.

### 127. C

#### Step 1
Figure out the denominator.
The place value of the last digit of the decimal is the same as the denominator of the fraction. The last digit of 0.04 is 4, and it is in the hundredths place. The denominator of the fraction is 100.

$\frac{?}{100}$

### Step 2
Figure out the numerator.
The digits in the decimal will be the numerator of the fraction.

The digits in 0.04 are 0, 0, and 4. Drop the zeros at the beginning of the decimal, and write 4 as the numerator.

The fraction is $\frac{4}{100}$.

### 128. 6.5

The number line shows the numbers between 6 and 7. The line is divided into tenths, and the arrow is pointing to the number that is 5 tenths greater than 6.

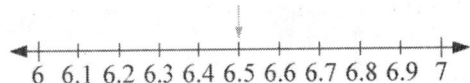

The number is 6.5.

### 129. A

When numbers are in ascending order they are arranged from least value to greatest value.

On a number line, the portion from 5,321 to 5,322 can be divided into 10 equal parts.

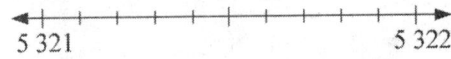

Place the numbers 5,321.45, 5,321.245, and 5,321.5 on the number line.

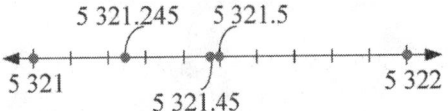

Since the numbers increase from left to right on a number line, it can be concluded that 5,321 < 5,321.245 < 5,321.45 < 5,321.5 < 5,322.

### 130. D

Choice D is correct. From least to greatest value, the decimal numbers are 2.5, 2.8, 3.3, 3.6.

Start by ordering the whole numbers that have the least value.
Since 2 < 3, 2.5 and 2.8 will come before 3.3 and 3.6.

To order 2.3 and 2.5, look at the digits in the tenths places.
Since 3 < 5, 2.3 is less than 2.5.

To order 3.3 and 3.6, look at the digits in the tenths places.
Since 3 < 6, 3.3 is less than 3.6.

Measurement and Data

# MEASUREMENT AND DATA

## Table of Correlations

| Standard | | Concepts | Exercise #1 | Exercise #2 |
|---|---|---|---|---|
| 4.MD | Measurement and Data | | | |
| 4.MD.1 | Know relative sizes of measurement units within one system of units including km, m, cm; kg, g; lb, oz.; l, ml; hr, min, sec. Within a single system of measurement, express measurements in a larger unit in terms of a smaller unit. Record measurement equivalents in a twocolumn table. | Select and Justify Choice of Appropriate Unit to Measure Mass | 131 | 166 |
| | | Providing Referents for Centimeters and Meters | 132 | 165 |
| | | Providing Referents for Liters and Milliliters | 133 | 164 |
| | | Performing Simple Unit Conversions within a System of Measurement | 134 | 163 |
| | | Selecting Appropriate Customary Units of Weight | 135 | 162 |
| | | Understanding Unit Conversion | | |
| 4.MD.2 | Use the four operations to solve word problems involving distances, intervals of time, liquid volumes, masses of objects, and money, including problems involving simple fractions or decimals, and problems that require expressing measurements given in a larger unit in terms of a smaller unit. Represent measurement quantities using diagrams such as number line diagrams that feature a measurement scale. | Solving Problems Involving the Subtraction of Fractions with Like Denominators | 90 | 117 |
| | | Solving Problems Involving the Addition of Fractions with Like Denominators | 91 | 118 |
| | | Solving Problems Involving Capacity | 136 | 167 |
| | | Solving Problems about Elapsed Time | 137 | 168 |
| | | Solving Length Problems | 138 | 169 |
| | | Solving Problems Involving Mass | 139 | 170, 173 |
| | | Solving Problems Involving Length | 140 | 171 |
| | | Solving Problems Involving Converting Customary Units of Mass | 141 | 172 |
| | | Solving Problems Involving Mass | 142 | 173 |
| | | Solving Problems with Money | 143 | 174 |
| 4.MD.3 | Apply the area and perimeter formulas for rectangles in real world and mathematical problems. | Measure and Record Areas of Rectangles | 144 | 175 |
| | | Solving Problems Involving the Perimeter of Rectangles | 145 | 176 |
| | | Solve Problems Involving the Areas of Rectangles | 151 | 177 |
| | | Using Formulas to Find the Perimeter | 146, 147, 148, 150 | 178, 179, 180, 181 |
| | | Calculating the Perimeter of a Square | 147 | 181 |
| | | Calculating the Unknown Side of a Rectangle | 149 | 182 |
| | | Finding an Unknown Side of a Rectangle | 152 | 183 |
| | | Formulas for the Perimeter of Rectangles | | |
| 4.MD.4 | Make a line plot to display a data set of measurements in fractions of a unit (1/2, 1/4, 1/8). Solve problems involving addition and subtraction of fractions by using information presented in line plots. | Organizing Collected Data using Line Plots | 153 | 184 |
| | | Measuring Lengths to the Nearest $\frac{1}{4}$, $\frac{1}{2}$, $\frac{3}{4}$, or Whole Inch | 154 | 185 |

| | | Drawing Conclusions from a Line Plot | 155 | 186 |
|---|---|---|---|---|
| 4.MD. 5A | Recognize angles as geometric shapes that are formed wherever two rays share a common endpoint, and understand concepts of angle measurement: An angle is measured with reference to a circle with its center at the common endpoint of the rays, by considering the fraction of the circular arc between the points where the two rays intersect the circle. An angle that turns through 1/360 of a circle is called a "one-degree angle," and can be used to measure angles. | Measuring Angles | 156 | 187 |
| | | Constructing Angles | 157 | 188 |
| 4.MD. 5B | Recognize angles as geometric shapes that are formed wherever two rays share a common endpoint, and understand concepts of angle measurement: An angle that turns through n one–degree angles is said to have an angle measure of n degrees. | Measuring Angles | 156 | 187 |
| | | Constructing Angles | 157 | 188 |
| 4.MD. 6 | Measure angles in whole–number degrees using a protractor. Sketch angles of specified measure. | Measuring Angles | 156 | 187 |
| | | Constructing Angles | 157 | 188 |
| | | Relate Measures of Benchmark Angles to Degrees | 158 | 189 |
| | | Estimating the Size of an Angle by Comparing with Benchmark Angles | 159 | 190 |
| 4.MD. 7 | Recognize angle measure as additive. When an angle is decomposed into non–overlapping parts, the angle measure of the whole is the sum of the angle measures of the parts. Solve addition and subtraction problems to find unknown angles on a diagram in real world and mathematical problems. | Angles on Straight Lines | 160 | 191 |
| | | Finding Missing Angles in Circles | 161 | 192 |

*4.MD.1*  *Know relative sizes of measurement units within one system of units including km, m, cm; kg, g; lb, oz.; l, ml; hr, min, sec. Within a single system of measurement, express measurements in a larger unit in terms of a smaller unit. Record measurement equivalents in a twocolumn table.*

## SELECT AND JUSTIFY CHOICE OF APPROPRIATE UNIT TO MEASURE MASS

**Mass** is a measure of how much matter is in an object.

The metric system of units includes these common units for measuring mass:

- Milligrams (mg): Milligrams are used to measure very light objects, such as feathers.
- Grams (g): Grams are used to measure objects that have medium weight, such as small toys or food.
- Kilograms (kg): Kilograms are used to measure heavier objects, such as people.

*Example*

Which unit of measure is **most appropriate** for measuring the weight of a full pop can?

*Solution*

A full pop can should be measured in grams. The weights of smaller, lighter objects are often measured in milligrams. Kilograms are usually used to measure the weights of heavier objects.

---

## PROVIDING REFERENTS FOR CENTIMETERS AND METERS

When you want to estimate the length of something, the easiest way is to use a **referent**. A referent is a shape or object that has about the same size as the measure that you are using. You can use that shape or object to help you estimate the length, width, or height of an object or a distance between objects.

A centimeter (cm) is about the width of your fingernail. You can use your fingernail as a referent to help you estimate the length of a small object like a glue stick.

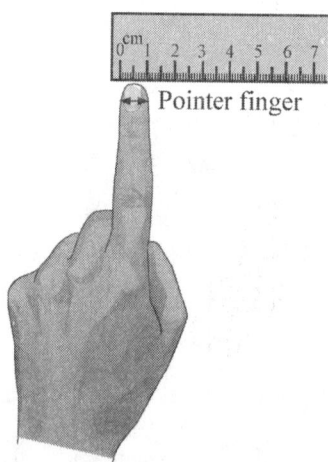

Some other common referents that are about 1 cm include the length or width of a number cube and the length or width of a sugar cube.

A meter (m) has 100 cm. It is about the length of a giant step. You can use a giant step as a referent to help you estimate larger objects, like the width of your classroom.

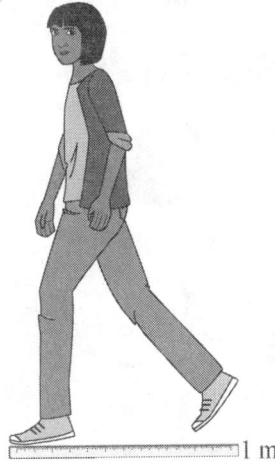

Some common referents that are about the size of 1 m include the distance from fingertip to fingertip when your arms are spread wide, the distance from the floor to the doorknob, and the height of a desk.

When you are choosing a referent, be sure to use something that makes sense to you. If you cannot really remember how big a sugar cube is, do not use that as a referent for 1 cm.

Different referents are good in different situations. A giant step is a good referent to use for 1 m when you are estimating the distance from your classroom to the gym. But if you need to estimate the height of the ceiling, it is hard to imagine walking up the side of the wall. It might be easier to look at the distance from the floor to the doorknob.

## Providing Referents for Liters and Milliliters

When you want to estimate the capacity of something, the easiest way is to use a **referent**. A referent is an object or container that has about the same capacity as the measure that you are using. You can use that object to help you estimate the capacity of a container.

A milliliter is a very small amount of liquid; 1 mL is only a few drops of water. Some medicine droppers can measure 1 mL.

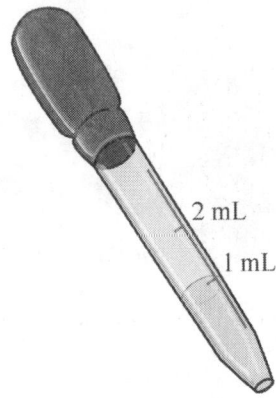

It is very difficult to imagine 1 mL because it is so small. A more useful referent for milliliters might be a teaspoon. A teaspoon from a measuring spoon set holds exactly 5 mL, but a regular teaspoon like the kind you might use to eat your breakfast cereal also holds about 5 mL.

Since you see this kind of spoon so often, you probably know about how much liquid it can hold. This is a good referent for 5 mL.

There are many common containers that hold 1 L. One example is a juice carton.

Other common referents for 1 L are a 1 L water bottle or a 1 L measuring cup.

Make sure that you choose a referent that makes sense to you. If you always drink water from the tap or from an individual-sized water bottle, then you may not have a clear idea of the size of a 1 L water bottle. In that case, maybe using the juice carton makes more sense.

## PERFORMING SIMPLE UNIT CONVERSIONS WITHIN A SYSTEM OF MEASUREMENT

There are many times when you need to change one unit into another unit to solve a problem. For example, you may be asked to make the following conversions:

- Feet (ft) into inches (in)
- Ounces (oz) into cups (c)
- Days into weeks
- Grams (g) into kilograms (kg)
- Centimeters (cm) into meters (m)

Not for Reproduction

In order to convert into different units, you must understand the relationship between the units. To convert inches into feet, you need to know that there are 12 in in 1 ft.

Once you know how the units are related, you can make the conversion by using a picture or a chart.

*Example*

Each student in Mr. Gordon's class needs 1 oz of water for an experiment. There are 24 students in the class.

How many cups of water will the students need in total?

*Solution*

**Step 1**

Determine the units to convert.

Since each student needs 1 oz of water and there are 24 students, a total of 24 oz of water is needed.

You need to know how many cups are equal to 24 oz.

**Step 2**

Find the relationship between the units.

The relationship is that 8 oz = 1 c.

**Step 3**

Convert 24 oz to cups.

One way to do this is to draw a picture. You can draw 24 cups with 1 oz in each cup, which is 24 oz. You know that there are 8 oz in 1 c, so you can circle groups of 8 oz to find out how many cups there are.

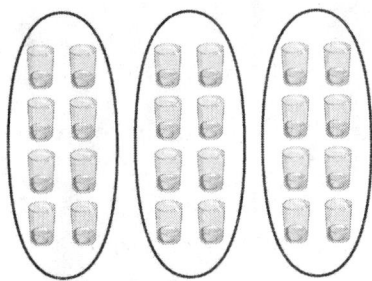

There are three sets of 8 oz.

The students will need 3 c of water for the experiment.

---

*Example*

Robert is making puppets for a puppet show. He needs 40 cm of ribbon to make one puppet. He will be making a total of 10 puppets.

How many meters of ribbon does Robert need to make all of the puppets?

*Solution*

**Step 1**

Determine the units that need to be converted.

Robert needs 40 cm of ribbon to make one puppet, and he is going to make 10 puppets. In total, that is 400 cm of ribbon. You need to find out how many meters are equal to 400 cm.

**Step 2**

Find the relationship between the units. The relationship is that 100 cm = 1 m.

**Step 3**

Convert 400 cm into meters.

Make a chart to determine the number of meters.

| m | cm |
|---|---|
| 1 | 100 |
| 2 | 200 |
| 3 | 300 |
| 4 | 400 |

In the chart, 400 cm = 4 m.

Robert needs 4 m of ribbon to make all 10 puppets.

---

## SELECTING APPROPRIATE CUSTOMARY UNITS OF WEIGHT

Weight measures how heavy an object is, or how much gravity is pulling on an object. Common customary units of weight are tons, pounds, and ounces.

An ounce (oz) is the unit used to weigh light objects. A strawberry weighs about 1 oz. You should use ounces to measure the weight of lighter objects, such as a pencil case or a paperback book.

A pound (lb) is the same as 16 oz. A pineapple might weigh about 1 lb. Use pounds to measure the weight of heavier objects, such as your backpack or a desk.

A ton (T) is the same as 2,000 lb. A car weighs about 1 T. Use tons to measure the weight of very heavy objects, such as cars and whales.

When you want to measure the weight of an object, you need to choose which unit to use. If you measure the weight of your car in ounces or a strawberry in tons, it will be very difficult to understand the measurement.

*Example*

For homework, Colin has to pick five things in his house to weigh. He chooses the objects and writes them in the given list:

- A camera
- A large sack of potatoes
- A box of crackers
- A hot tub full of water
- His little sister

Make a table to show which customary unit Colin should use to find the weight of each object in his list.

*Solution*

**Step 1**

Decide which unit Colin should use for each object.

- A camera is very light. Colin should use ounces.
- A large sack of potatoes is too heavy to measure in ounces. Colin should use pounds.
- A box of crackers is very light. Colin should use ounces.
- A hot tub full of water is very heavy. Colin should use tons.
- His little sister is too heavy to measure in ounces. Colin should use pounds.

### Step 2
Make the table, and place the objects in the columns.
The following table shows the objects placed with the appropriate units used for weighing them.

| Ounces | Pounds | Tons |
|---|---|---|
| Camera | Potatoes | Hot tub |
| Crackers | Sister | |

## Understanding Unit Conversion

You use units whenever you measure anything. For example, you can use centimeters or feet and inches to measure your height. If you measure your weight, you can use kilograms or pounds.

Sometimes, it can be helpful to convert between units:

- If you are comparing objects measured in different units, you need to convert all of the measurements into the same unit.
- When the unit you used to measure is too big or too small, it might make more sense if you gave it a different unit.
- Sometimes you might use a measuring tool that has a different unit than what you need.

When you convert from one unit into another, you need to know the relationship between the units. For example, if you want to convert a time from minutes into hours, you need to know that there are 60 minutes in an hour.

## Units of Time

This table shows the relationship between common units of time:

| Time | |
|---|---|
| 1 minute | 60 seconds |
| 1 hour | 60 minutes |
| 1 day | 24 hours |
| 1 week | 7 days |

## Customary Units

Customary Units are used in the United States. They are also sometimes used in other countries, such as Canada and the United Kingdom.

These tables show the relationships between common customary units:

| Length | |
|---|---|
| 1 ft | 12 in |
| 1 yd | 3 ft |
| 1 yd | 36 in |
| 1 mi | 1,760 yd |
| Mass | |
| 1 lb | 16 oz |
| 1 T | 2,000 lb |

| Capacity | |
|---|---|
| 1 c | 8 oz |
| 1 pt | 2 c |
| 1 qt | 2 pt |
| 1 qt | 4 c |
| 1 gal | 4 qt |

## Metric Units

Metric units are used in nearly every country in the world.

These tables show the relationships between common metric units:

| Length | |
|---|---|
| 1 cm | 10 mm |
| 1 m | 100 cm |
| 1 km | 1,000 m |

| Mass | |
|---|---|
| 1 kg | 1,000 g |
| 1 t | 1,000 kg |

| Capacity | |
|---|---|
| 1 L | 1,000 mL |

*4.MD.2* Use the four operations to solve word problems involving distances, intervals of time, liquid volumes, masses of objects, and money, including problems involving simple fractions or decimals, and problems that require expressing measurements given in a larger unit in terms of a smaller unit. Represent measurement quantities using diagrams such as number line diagrams that feature a measurement scale.

## Solving Problems Involving Capacity

When you have a word problem that is about capacity, read the question carefully to decide if you need to add, subtract, multiply, or divide. Sometimes, keywords can help you:

- For addition, some of the keywords are *total*, *more*, *altogether*, and *sum*.
- For subtraction, some of the keywords are *difference*, *more than*, *less than*, and *fewer*.
- For multiplication, some of the keywords are *groups*, *times*, *product*, and *total*.
- For division, some of the keywords are *groups*, *share*, *split*, and *quotient*.

*Example*

Jodie always brings a large bottle of water with her to school. She drinks 125 mL of water at recess and another 275 mL of water at lunch.

How much more water does she drink at lunch than at recess?

*Solution*

### Step 1
Read the question carefully, and decide which operation to use.
The question asks how much more water she drinks at lunch. To compare the two amounts, you need to subtract.

### Step 2
Solve the problem by subtracting.

```
  275
- 125
  150
```

Jodie drinks 150 mL more water at lunch than she does at recess.

---

*Example*

Diego, Sophie, and Sandra decide to have a lemonade stand. Diego brings 4 L of lemonade, Sophie brings 3 L, and Sandra brings 2 L. They take turns selling the lemonade. Each of the children sells the same amount of lemonade during their turn.

If they sell all the lemonade that they brought, what is the amount of lemonade each of them sold?

*Solution*

### Step 1
Read the question carefully, and decide which operations to use.
First, you will need to find the total amount of lemonade that the children brought. To do this, you will have to add the amounts together.
Each of the children sold the same amount of lemonade. To split something into equal groups, you need to divide.

### Step 2
Add the amounts together.
$4 + 3 + 2 = 9$
They brought a total of 9 L of lemonade.

### Step 3
Divide.
There are 3 children, so divide by 3.
$9 \div 3 = 3$
Each of the children sold 3 L of lemonade.

# Solving Problems about Elapsed Time

You can use your knowledge about measuring time to solve a wide variety of real-world problems. Whenever you have a problem you need to solve, you should follow a four-step problem-solving process:

1. Read the question carefully, and understand what the question is asking.
2. Make a plan. Decide if you need to add, subtract, multiply, or divide, and in which order.
3. Solve the problem. Follow your plan.
4. Decide if your answer is reasonable. Use estimation to check your answer and see if your answer makes sense.

Keep the following ideas in mind when reading the problem. They can help you better understand the problem and assist you when solving the problem:

- Look for key words.
- Decide what information is important.
- Pay close attention to the numbers given in the question.
- Draw a picture or diagram of the question.
- Make predictions about what your answer will look like. Will the number be big or small? Will it be a money amount? A length? A unit of time?
- Think about the operation you are using. For example, if you are multiplying, you know that your answer will be larger than the numbers by which you are multiplying.
- Check your answer with your predictions to see if your answer is reasonable.

*Example*

Raya wakes up at 7:20 A.M. It takes her 20 min to shower and brush her teeth and another 15 min to eat breakfast. It takes 3 min for Raya to walk to the bus stop, and the bus arrives at school after another 14 min.

If school starts at 8:30 A.M., how much time will Raya have at school before her first class starts?

*Solution*

### Step 1
Determine what is being asked.
The important information is that the things that Raya needs to do before school take her 20 min, 15 min, 3 min, and 14 min. She wakes up at 7:20 A.M., and school starts at 8:30 A.M.
Use this information to decide how many minutes before her first class Raya arrives at school.
The answer will be a number of minutes, and it will probably be a small amount of time because there is only just over an hour between the time Raya wakes up and the time school starts.

### Step 2
Make a plan.
Start by finding out what time Raya arrives at school. Do this by adding up the time it takes her to do each of her morning activities or by using a number line.
Find out how much time is left before school starts by subtracting the time she arrives at school from 8:30 A.M. or by using a number line.

**Step 3**

Solve the problem.

1. Find out what time Raya arrives at school. Add up the time it takes her to do each of her activities.
$$\begin{pmatrix} 20 \text{ min} + 15 \text{ min} \\ + 3 \text{ min} + 14 \text{ min} \end{pmatrix} = 52 \text{ min}$$
Adding 52 min to 7:20 A.M. gives the time 8:12 A.M.

It is also possible to find out what time Raya arrives at school by using a number line. Draw a number line from 7:20 A.M., and then add each morning activity, marking the time that each one is complete.

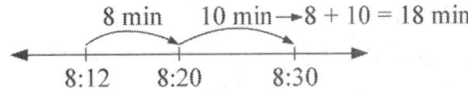

2. Find out how much time is left before school starts. Subtract 8:12 A.M. from 8:30 A.M.

   8:30
   − 8:12  It is also possible to use a time line to count up from 8:12 A.M. to 8:30 A.M.
   0:18

**Step 4**

Decide if the answer is reasonable.

The answer is a number of minutes, and it is a short amount of time, which is what was predicted in step 1. It is also quite reasonable to arrive at school 18 min early, so this answer is reasonable.

Raya has 18 min before her first class.

---

## SOLVING LENGTH PROBLEMS

When you solve problems involving length, the units of measure must be the same. If they are not the same, you must convert them before solving the problem.

The given chart is a review of measurement relationships that will help you when you convert units.

| Unit | Equivalent Unit |
|------|-----------------|
| 1 cm | 10 mm |
| 1 m | 100 cm |
| 1 km | 1,000 m |

When you convert a large unit into a smaller unit, the answer will be a larger number.
large unit → smaller unit = larger number

To convert a large unit to a smaller unit, use multiplication.

For example, to convert 5 meters into centimeters, multiply 5 m by 100.
5 × 100 = 500
   5 m = 500 cm

When you convert a small unit to a larger unit, the answer will be a smaller number.
small unit → larger unit = smaller number

When you convert from a small unit to a larger unit, use division.

For example, to convert 4,000 meters to kilometers, divide 4,000 m by 1,000.
4,000 ÷ 1,000 = 4
4,000 m = 4 km

*Example*

Lucy's parents are putting new trim on her bedroom wall. The bedroom wall measures 2 m in length. They have 300 cm of trim to use.

Once the wall is completely trimmed, how many meters of trim will be left over?

*Solution*

**Step 1**
Convert the 300 cm of trim into meters.

Because you are converting a small unit (centimeters) to a larger unit (meters), use division.
100 cm ÷ 100 = 1 m
300 cm ÷ 100 = 3 m

Lucy's parents have 3 m of trim to use.

**Step 2**
Determine how many meters of trim will be left over.

Subtract 3 m of trim from 2 m of wall.
3 m – 2 m = 1 m

Once the new trim is on Lucy's bedroom wall, there will be 1 m of trim left over.

## SOLVING PROBLEMS INVOLVING MASS

To solve problems that involve mass, you need to make sure that all the units are the same before comparing them.

To convert measurements, you need to know the relationship between grams and kilograms. There are 1,000 g in 1 kg. That means that one gram is one thousandth of a kilogram.

When you change from a larger unit, such as kilograms, to a smaller unit, such as grams, the number of grams will be larger than the number of kilograms. That means you should multiply the number of kilograms by 1,000 to find the number of equal grams.

When you change from a smaller unit, such as grams, to a larger unit, such as kilograms, the number of kilograms will be smaller than the number of grams. That means you should divide the number of grams by 1,000 to find the number of equal kilograms.

*Example*

Mike bought a bag of sugar and a bag of flour. The bag of sugar was marked as weighing 4 kg, and the flour was marked as weighing 3,000 g.

Determine how much less the bag of flour weighs in kilograms.

*Solution*

**Step 1**
Identify the important information.

The bag of sugar has a mass of 4 kg, and the bag of flour has a mass of 3,000 g.

### Step 2
Determine which operation to use.

The words *how much less* indicate subtraction, because they are asking for the difference between the two masses.

### Step 3
Convert grams into kilograms.
$$1,000 \text{ g} = 1 \text{ kg}$$
$$3,000 \text{ g} \div 1,000 = 3 \text{ kg}$$
The bag of flour weighs 3 kg.

### Step 4
Find the difference in weight between the sugar and flour.
$$4 \text{ kg} - 3 \text{ kg} = 1 \text{ kg}$$
The flour weighs 1 kg less than the sugar.

---

## SOLVING PROBLEMS INVOLVING LENGTH

You can use your knowledge about measuring length to solve a wide variety of real-world problems. When you are solving these problems, follow these steps:

1. Determine what is being asked.
2. Decide which operations you need to use.
3. Solve the problem.

*Example*

Murray was putting new carpet in his living room and bedroom. He bought a roll of carpet that was 10 m long. The living room is 7 m long, and the bedroom is 4 m long.

Is Murray's carpet roll long enough to stretch the length of both rooms?

*Solution*

### Step 1
Determine what is being asked.

You need to find out if the roll of carpet is enough for the length of two rooms.

### Step 2
Decide what operations to use.

You will need to use addition to find the total length of the two rooms.

### Step 3
Solve the problem.
$$7 \text{ m} + 4 \text{ m} = 11 \text{ m}$$
Since Murray's carpet roll is only 10 m, he will not have enough carpet because the total length of the two rooms is 11 m.

SOLVING PROBLEMS INVOLVING CONVERTING CUSTOMARY UNITS OF MASS

In the customary system of measurement, mass is measured in tons (T), pounds (lb), and ounces (oz). The given table shows the relationships among these units.

| Unit | Conversion |
| --- | --- |
| 1 T | 2,000 lb |
| 1 lb | 16 oz |

When converting from a smaller unit to a larger unit, such as pounds to tons, use division for the conversion. When converting from a larger unit to a smaller unit, such as pounds to ounces, use multiplication for the conversion.

*Example*

Maureen is shopping for fruit at the grocery store. She can buy 3 lb of peaches for $5, but the scale at the grocery store only measures in ounces.

How many ounces are in 3 lb of peaches?

*Solution*

**Step 1**
Determine what operation to use.

When converting from pounds to ounces, you are converting a larger to a smaller unit. Use multiplication.

**Step 2**
Perform the conversion.

There are 16 oz in 1 lb. To find out how many ounces are in 3 lb, multiply 3 by 16.
1 lb = 16 oz
3 × 16 = 48
There are 48 oz in 3 lb of peaches.

---

*Example*

Jane was researching facts about hippos for a report she was writing. She read that the average mass of a male hippo is about 4,000 lb.

What is the hippo's mass in tons?

*Solution*

**Step 1**
Determine what operation to use.

When converting from pounds to tons, you are converting a smaller to a larger unit. Use division.

**Step 2**
Perform the conversion.

There are 2,000 lb in 1 T. To find out how many tons are in 4,000 lb, divide 4,000 by 2,000.
2,000 lb = 1 T
4,000 ÷ 2,000 = 2
There are 2 T in 4,000 lb. The mass of the hippo is 2 T.

## SOLVING PROBLEMS INVOLVING MASS

Mass can be measured using *grams* and *kilograms*. The following keywords will help you identify what operation to use when you are working on a mass problem:

- Addition—sum, total, equal, greater than, plus
- Subtraction—difference, less than, reduced, minus
- Multiplication—times, multiply, product
- Division—groups, quotient, each, divide

To solve problems involving mass, follow these steps:

1. Determine what the problem is asking by identifying the important information.
2. Determine which operation to use.
3. Solve the problem.

*Example*

Jake and his brothers Billy and Jon need to help carry firewood at their grandparents' farm. They need to carry a total of 27 kg of firewood.

If the 3 boys divide the total mass equally, how many kilograms of firewood does each boy need to carry?

*Solution*

**Step 1**
Determine what the problem is asking by identifying the important information.
The question is asking you to divide the total mass equally between the 3 boys.

**Step 2**
Determine which operation to use.
Use division to find the amount in kilograms that each boy will have to carry.

**Step 3**
Solve the problem.
Divide the total mass of firewood (27 kg) by 3.
$27 \div 3 = 9$
The total mass of firewood each boy will have to carry is 9 kg.

---

## SOLVING PROBLEMS WITH MONEY

Many children start to have their own money when they begin to get an allowance from their parents. Some children get money as gifts for special occasions. Other children earn their own money by doing chores around the house.

If you have your own money, you need to plan how you are going to use it. You can spend all of your money as soon as you get it, or you can save it up to buy larger things. You can use the four operations to solve problems that are related to money.

*Example*

Aiden earns money in the summer by mowing the lawn. Every time he mows the lawn, he gets $4.00.

If Aiden mows the lawn 3 times, how much money will he earn?

*Solution*

Every time Aiden mows the lawn, he earns $4.00. To find out how much he gets if he mows the lawn 3 times, multiply 4 by 3.
4 × 3 = 12

Aiden will earn $12.00.

---

*Example*

Carrie earned $15.00 by helping clean the house. She wants to buy a CD that costs $9.00.

If Carrie buys the CD, how much money will she have left over?

*Solution*

Carrie starts with $15.00 and then spends $9.00 of it. You need to use subtraction.
15 − 9 = 6

If Carrie buys the CD, she will have $6.00 left.

---

*4.MD.3 Apply the area and perimeter formulas for rectangles in real world and mathematical problems.*

## MEASURE AND RECORD AREAS OF RECTANGLES

**Area** is how much space a shape covers. The area of a shape is expressed as the number of square units, such as square **inches** ($in^2$), square **yards** ($yd^2$), square **centimeters** ($cm^2$), square **meters** ($m^2$).

For example, one square inch, or $1\ in^2$, has a width of 1 in and a length of 1 in. This area is written as $1\ in^2$ to show the two dimensions. You read $in^2$ as *square inches* or *inches squared*.

To find the area of a rectangle, multiply the length by the width.

Area = length × width
$A = l \times w$
$A = units^2$

*Example*

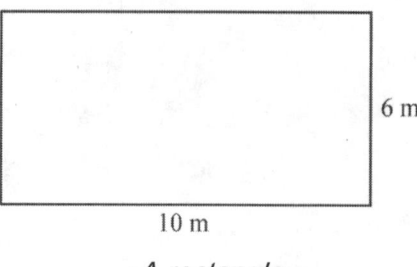

*A rectangle*

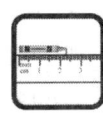

Find the **area** of the given rectangle. Be sure to include the correct unit of measure in your answer.

Solution

$A = l \times w$
$A = 10 \text{ m} \times 6 \text{ m}$
$A = 60 \text{ m}^2$

---

Example

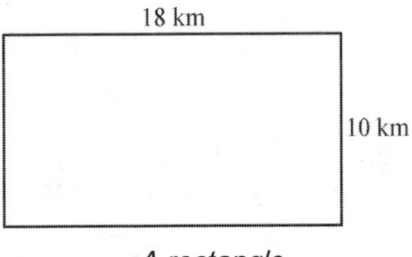

A rectangle

Find the **area** of the given rectangle. Be sure to include the correct unit of measure in your answer.

Solution

$A = l \times w$
$A = 18 \text{ km} \times 10 \text{ km}$
$A = 180 \text{ km}^2$

---

## SOLVING PROBLEMS INVOLVING THE PERIMETER OF RECTANGLES

To solve a problem requiring the perimeter of a rectangle, use one of the following formulas:
Perimeter = side + side + side + side, perimeter = 2(*l* × *w*), or perimeter = 2*l* + 2*w*.

Example

Mrs. Sanders loves fresh vegetables. She decides to make a **rectangular** garden in her backyard. Her garden is 34 ft long and 19 ft wide. She needs to build a fence around her garden so that her dog cannot get in and dig up all her vegetables. To find out how much fencing she should order, Mrs. Sanders needs to find the **perimeter** of her garden plot.

What is the perimeter of Mrs. Sanders's garden plot?

Solution

**Step 1**
Draw the garden plot with its dimensions.

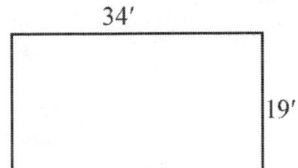

**Step 2**

Calculate the perimeter of the garden plot.

Use one of the perimeter formulas to find the perimeter of the garden plot.

Perimeter = $2l + 2w$
= $(2 \times 34) + (2 \times 19)$
= $(68) + (38)$
= $106$

The exact perimeter of the garden plot is 106 ft.

---

## SOLVE PROBLEMS INVOLVING THE AREAS OF RECTANGLES

To solve a problem requiring the area of a rectangle, use the formula area = length × width.

*Example*

Callie is thinking about buying a certain carpet for the front entrance of her house. She wants to know if the carpet will fit in the front entrance. The entrance has an area of 25 ft$^2$.

If the rectangular carpet is 6 ft long and 4 ft wide, what is its **area**?

*Solution*

**Step 1**

Calculate the area of the carpet.

The length of the carpet is 6 ft. The width of the carpet is 4 ft.

$A = 6 \times 4$
  = $24$

The area of the carpet is 24 ft$^2$.

**Step 2**

Determine if the carpet will fit in Callie's entrance way.

The entrance has an area of 25 ft$^2$. The carpet has an area of 24 ft$^2$. The carpet will fit.

---

## USING FORMULAS TO FIND THE PERIMETER

**Perimeter** is the distance around the outside of a shape. There are several different formulas that can be used to find the perimeter of a polygon.

- For any polygon, use the formula $P = s_1 + s_2 + ... + s_n$, where $n$ is the number of sides of the polygon.
- For regular polygons, use $P = s \times n$, where $s$ is the length of one side and $n$ is the number of sides.
- For rectangles, use $P = 2l + 2w$ or $P = 2(l + w)$, where $l$ is the length and $w$ is the width of the rectangle.
- For squares, use $P = 4s$, where $s$ is the length of one side.

To find the perimeter of a polygon, follow these steps:

1. Decide which formula to use.
2. Apply the formula.

*Example*

Maryam has a patio and a swimming pool in her backyard.

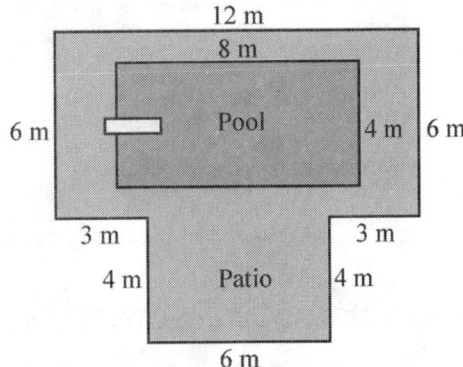

What is the perimeter of the patio?

*Solution*

**Step 1**
Decide which formula to use.
The patio is an irregular polygon with eight sides, so you will use the formula
$P = s_1 + s_2 + s_3 + s_4 + s_5 + s_6 + s_7 + s_8$.

**Step 2**
Apply the formula.
$P = s_1 + s_2 + s_3 + s_4 + s_5 + s_6 + s_7 + s_8$
$= 12 + 6 + 3 + 4 + 6 + 4 + 3 + 6$
$= 44$

Remember to include the unit when you write your answer.
The patio has a perimeter of 44 m.

What is the perimeter of the swimming pool?

*Solution*

**Step 1**
Decide which formula to use.
The swimming pool is a rectangle, so you can use $P = 2l + 2w$ or $P = 2(l + w)$.
Try $P = 2(l + w)$.

**Step 2**
Apply the formula.
The length of the pool is 8 m, and the width is 4 m. Solve inside the parentheses first.
$P = 2(l + w)$
$= 2(8 + 4)$
$= 2(12)$
$= 24$

Notice that 2(12) is another way to write 2 × 12.

Remember to include the unit when you write your answer.
The perimeter of the pool is 24 m.

*Example*

A square stamp has sides that are 3 cm long.

What is the perimeter of the stamp?

*Solution*

**Step 1**

Decide which formula to use.

The stamp is a square, so the formula $P = 4s$ can be used.

**Step 2**

Apply the formula.

$P = 4s$
$\phantom{P} = 4 \times 3$
$\phantom{P} = 12$

Remember to include the unit in the final answer.

The perimeter of the stamp is 12 cm.

---

*Example*

A stop sign has sides that are each 25 cm long.

What is the perimeter of the stop sign?

*Solution*

**Step 1**

Decide which formula to use.

The stop sign is a regular polygon because all the sides are the same length.

You should use the formula for a regular polygon.

$P = s \times n$

**Step 2**

Apply the formula.

There are eight sides, so $n = 8$. Each side is 25 cm long, so $s = 25$.

$P = s \times n$
$\phantom{P} = 25 \times 8$
$\phantom{P} = 200$

Remember to include the unit when you write your answer.

The perimeter of the stop sign is 200 cm.

---

## CALCULATING THE PERIMETER OF A SQUARE

The perimeter of any polygon is the total distance around the outside of the shape.

For any polygon, including a square, the perimeter is the sum of the side lengths and widths.

Since a square has four sides, the perimeter of a square can be calculated by adding the lengths of the four sides, as expressed in the formula $P = $ side 1 + side 2 + side 3 + side 4.

However, since all four sides of a square are the same length, the perimeter of a square can also be calculated by multiplying the side length by 4, as expressed in the formula $P = 4 \times$ side.

*Example*

A square is shown. Each side is 4 cm long.

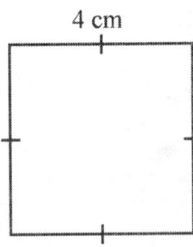

4 cm

What is the perimeter of the given square? _____ cm

*Solution*

To find the perimeter of a polygon, measure the length of each side, and add the lengths together.

Since each side of the given square is 4 cm long, add the four lengths together.

4 cm + 4 cm + 4 cm + 4 cm = 16 cm

Since the shape is a square and all four sides are the same length, you can also multiply to find the perimeter.

$4 \times 4 = 16$

The perimeter of the given square is 16 cm.

*Example*

A square stamp has sides that are 3 cm long.

What is the perimeter of the stamp?

*Solution*

**Step 1**
Decide which formula to use.
The stamp is a square, so the formula $P = 4s$ can be used.

**Step 2**
Apply the formula.
$P = 4s$
  $= 4 \times 3$
  $= 12$
Remember to include the unit in the final answer.
The perimeter of the stamp is 12 cm.

---

*Example*

A square classroom is 49 m². 

What is its perimeter?

*Solution*

**Step 1**
Calculate the measure of one side length.
$\sqrt{49} = 7$
Each side is 7 m long.

**Step 2**
Calculate the perimeter.
Perimeter is the distance around the outside of an object. Each side is 7 m long, and there are four sides.
$P_{square} = 4s$
  $= 4 \times 7$
  $= 28$ m
The perimeter of the classroom is 28 m.

## CALCULATING THE UNKNOWN SIDE OF A RECTANGLE

To calculate the unknown side length of a rectangle when the area and the other side length are given, use the following formula:

$$\frac{\text{area}}{\text{given side length}} = \text{unknown side length}$$

*Example*

If the area of a rectangle is 30 cm² and one of the side lengths is 5 cm, what is the length of the other side?

*Solution*

To find the missing side length, use the formula

$$\frac{\text{area}}{\text{given side length}} = \text{unknown side length}$$

Substitute 30 cm² for the area and 5 cm for the given side length.

$$\frac{30 \text{ cm}^2}{5 \text{ cm}} = 6 \text{ cm}$$

The missing side length is 6 cm.

---

## FINDING AN UNKNOWN SIDE OF A RECTANGLE

Sometimes, you are given the perimeter of a rectangle and the length of one side, and you need to find the length of the missing side.

To calculate the length of the missing side, use the following steps:

1. Find the total length of the known sides.
2. Subtract the total from the perimeter.
3. Divide by 2 to find the unknown side.
4. Check your answer by calculating the perimeter using your answer for the unknown side.

*Example*

The perimeter of a rectangle is 18 cm. The length of the rectangle is 6 cm.

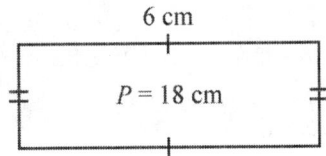

What is the width of the rectangle?

*Solution*

**Step 1**
Find the total length of the known sides.
Since the top and bottom lengths of the rectangle are the same, add the two lengths to find the total length of the known sides.
6 cm + 6 cm = 12 cm

**Step 2**
Subtract the total from the perimeter to find the total length of both missing sides.
18 cm − 12 cm = 6 cm

**Step 3**
Divide by 2 to find the width of the rectangle.
6 cm ÷ 2 = 3 cm

**Step 4**
Check your answer by calculating the perimeter using your answer for the unknown side.
perimeter = $l + w + l + w$
perimeter = 6 cm + 3 cm + 6 cm + 3 cm
perimeter = 18 cm
This is the same as the perimeter that was given. The answer is correct.
The width of the rectangle is 3 cm.

## FORMULAS FOR THE PERIMETER OF RECTANGLES

The distance around the outside of a shape is called the perimeter. If you have a rectangle that is drawn on a grid, you can count the number of squares around the outside to determine the perimeter.

*Example*
This rectangle has a perimeter of 16 squares.

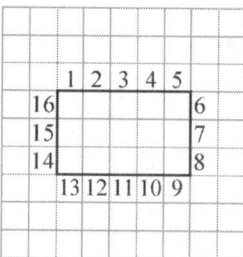

To find the perimeter of a rectangle more quickly, you can also use one of the following formulae:

- $P = l + w + l + w$
- $P = (2 \times l) + (2 \times w)$
- $P = 2 \times (l + w)$

All of these formulae will give you the same answer. You can decide which formula makes the most sense to you and always use that formula to find the perimeter of any given rectangle.

## FINDING THE PERIMETER BY ADDING THE SIDES

A rectangle has four sides. The top and bottom sides are the lengths of the rectangle. The other two sides are the widths of the rectangle.

Find the side lengths by counting the number of squares.

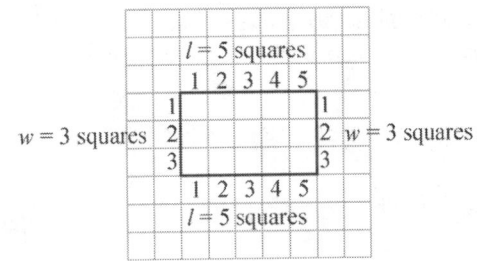

Add up the sides to find the perimeter.
$P = l + w + l + w$
$P = 5 + 3 + 5 + 3$
$P = 16$

## FINDING THE PERIMETER BY DOUBLING THE LENGTH AND DOUBLING THE WIDTH

Did you notice that the two lengths are the same and the two widths are the same?

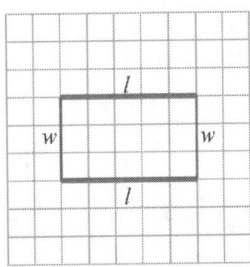

This means that you can multiply the length by 2 and multiply the width by 2. Then, add the results together to find the perimeter.
$P = (2 \times l) + (2 \times w)$
$P = (2 \times 5) + (2 \times 3)$
$P = 10 + 6$
$P = 16$

## FINDING THE PERIMETER BY DOUBLING THE LENGTH OF BOTH SIDES

In this rectangle, the bold section is the same length as the other section.

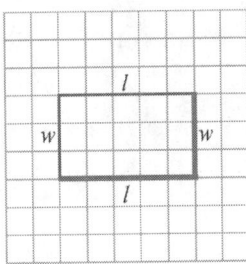

The bold section is equal to $l + w$. You can multiply this by 2 to find the perimeter.
$P = 2 \times (l + w)$
$P = 2 \times (5 + 3)$
$P = 2 \times 8$
$P = 16$

*4.MD.4  Make a line plot to display a data set of measurements in fractions of a unit (1/2, 1/4, 1/8). Solve problems involving addition and subtraction of fractions by using information presented in line plots.*

## ORGANIZING COLLECTED DATA USING LINE PLOTS

A **line plot** is a sketch of data in which a check mark, "X", or other symbol is drawn above a number line. It shows how often each result occurs.

To organize collected data on a line plot, follow these steps:

- Draw a horizontal line segment. Label all the possible outcomes under the line segment.
- Use a symbol to represent each time the outcome occurred.

*Example*

Bill performed a probability experiment with a die. He rolled the die 60 times and recorded the results.

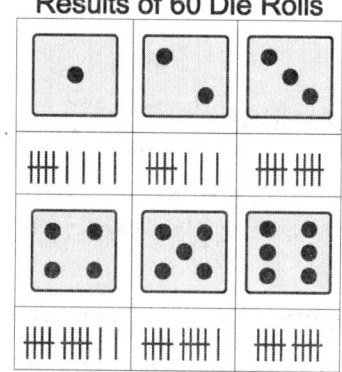

Results of 60 Die Rolls

Draw a **line plot** showing Bill's results.

*Solution*

**Step 1**
Create your line plot.
Draw a horizontal line. Write all the possible outcomes under the line.
Give your line plot a title.

**Results of 60 Die Rolls**

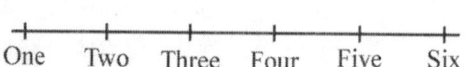

**Step 2**

Use a symbol to represent each time the outcome occurred.

In this case, draw Xs above the line to show Bill's results. Since he rolled one 9 times, you should make 9 Xs above the one heading. Record the number of times Bill rolled each number on the line plot.

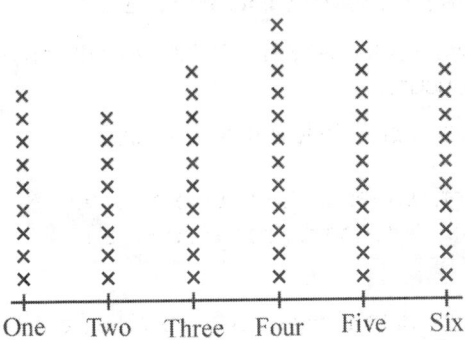

Results of 60 Die Rolls

---

# Measuring Lengths to the Nearest $\frac{1}{4}$, $\frac{1}{2}$, $\frac{3}{4}$, or Whole Inch

The inch (in) is a unit used to measure length. Rulers, measuring tapes, and yard sticks are some of the tools used to measure shorter lengths in inches. It is important to start measuring from the correct line at the beginning of the measuring tool.

Each line, or tick, on a measuring tool has a meaning. To measure the length of an object to the nearest $\frac{1}{4}$, $\frac{1}{2}$, or $\frac{3}{4}$ inch, you must understand what each of the lines means.

The longest black lines represent 1 inch. The medium lines in the middle represent $\frac{1}{2}$ an inch. The next smaller lines between those represent $\frac{1}{4}$ and $\frac{3}{4}$ of an inch. The smallest lines on this ruler each show $\frac{1}{8}$ of an inch.

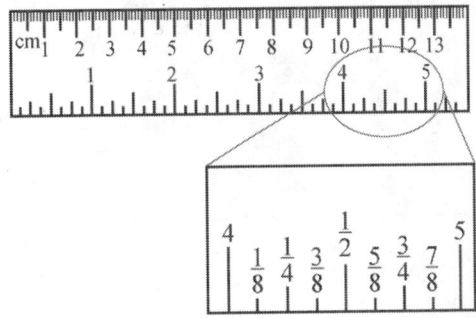

*Example*

Look at the black line below this ruler.

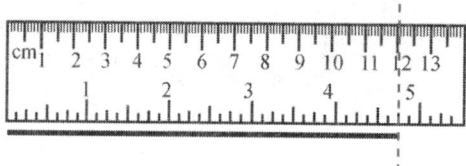

The line ends between the whole 4-inch and 5-inch marks. It ends on the $\frac{3}{4}$ in tick mark. Therefore, the line is $4\frac{3}{4}$ in long.

---

*Example*

Andy is measuring objects with a ruler. He wants to know how long his crayon is.

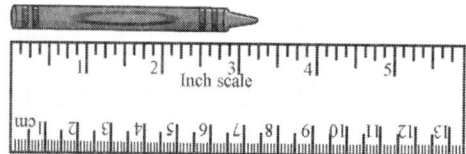

To the nearest $\frac{1}{4}$ in, find the length of Andy's crayon.

*Solution*

Look closely at where the tip of the crayon ends. The red dotted line marks the correct ending point.

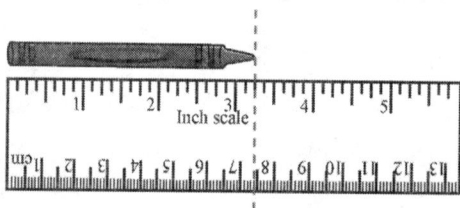

The crayon ends between the 3-inch and 4-inch marks on the ruler. It ends on the tick marking the $\frac{1}{4}$ in spot.

Therefore, Andy's crayon measures $3\frac{1}{4}$ in long.

# Drawing Conclusions from a Line Plot

A **line plot** is used to show data by making a mark, like an X, on a plot. This shows the frequency or how often those results occurred. When you look at a line plot, you can **draw conclusions** about all the information presented so you can identify patterns, make assumptions, or make predictions.

*Example*
The given line plot shows the results of a high jump event at a school's track and field day.

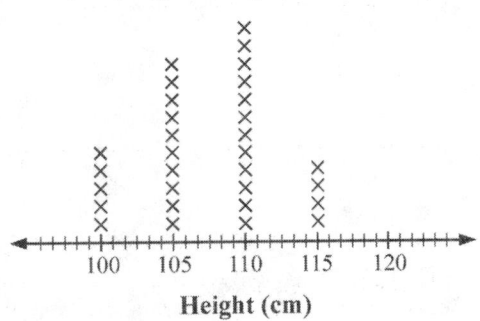

By looking at the line plot, you can conclude that the majority of the students were able to jump 110 cm. You can also conclude that none of the students were able to make the 120 cm mark. Finally, you can conclude that many more students can jump 105 cm than 100 cm.

*4.MD.5A Recognize angles as geometric shapes that are formed wherever two rays share a common endpoint, and understand concepts of angle measurement: An angle is measured with reference to a circle with its center at the common endpoint of the rays, by considering the fraction of the circular arc between the points where the two rays intersect the circle. An angle that turns through 1/360 of a circle is called a "one-degree angle," and can be used to measure angles.*

## MEASURING ANGLES

A **protractor** is an instrument for measuring angles. It is usually in the shape of a semicircle or circle and is marked around the edge in **degrees**.

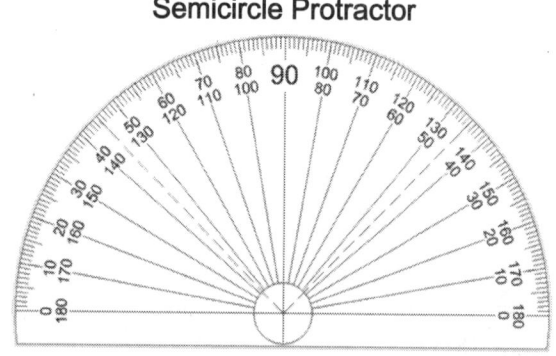

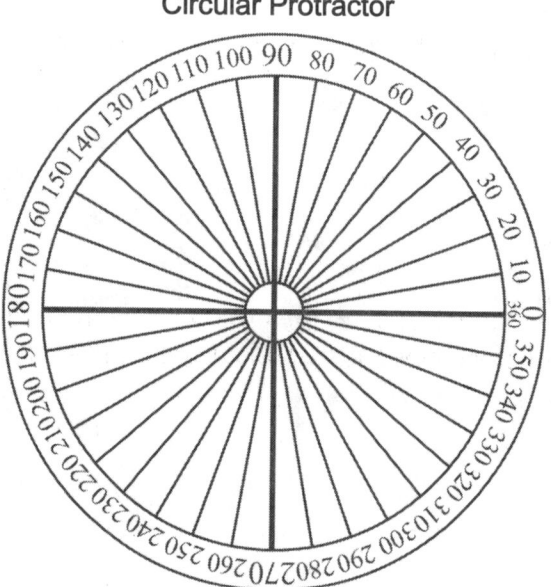

Measurement and Data

To find the measure of the following angle, you can use a semicircle protractor.

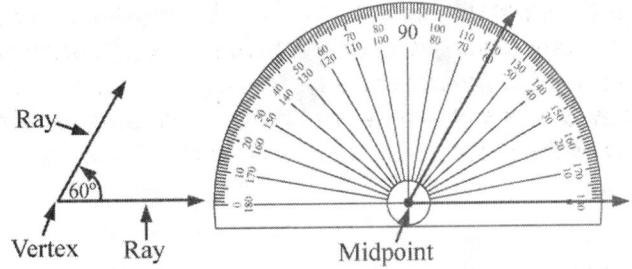

By counting the degrees between the two rays, you see that the measure of the angle is 60°.

*Example*
   Use a protractor to measure the size of the given angle.

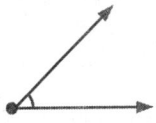

*Solution*
### Step 1
Place the midpoint of the protractor on the vertex of the angle. The 0° line on the right side of the protractor's inner scale should line up with the end of the bottom ray of the angle.

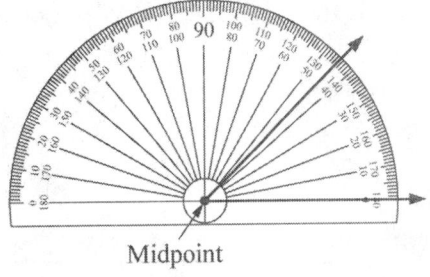

Start at the right side of the protractor's inner scale, at the 0° line, and count by tens until you reach the number of degrees closest to the upper ray without passing it.
10°, 20°, 30°, 40°

### Step 2
Count the individual ticks after 40° by ones until you reach the upper ray of the angle.
…41°, 42°, 43°, 44°, 45°

The measure of the given angle is 45°.

---

## CONSTRUCTING ANGLES

You can use either a semicircular or a circular protractor to construct angles.

To draw an angle using a protractor, follow these steps:

1. Draw a ray.
2. Place the protractor on the ray so that the midpoint of the protractor lines up with the end of the ray.
3. Starting at 0°, count the number of degrees needed to construct the angle.
4. Remove the protractor, and join the point that you marked and the endpoint of the ray that was drawn.

*Example*
Use a semicircular protractor to construct an angle of 145°.

*Solution*

**Step 1**
Draw a ray.

**Step 2**
Place the protractor on the ray so that the midpoint of the protractor lines up with the end of the ray.

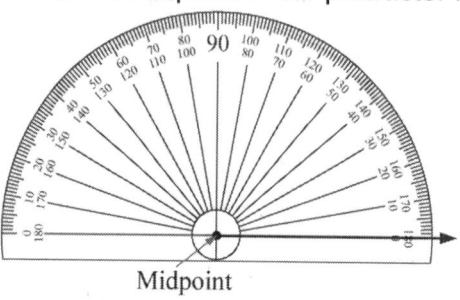

**Step 3**
Starting at 0°, count the number of degrees needed to construct the angle.
If the ray is pointing to the right, use the inside of the scale. If the ray is pointing to the left, use the outside scale. Always start measuring at 0°.
The angle needs to be 145°, so stop at 145. Using your pencil, mark the point that shows 145°.

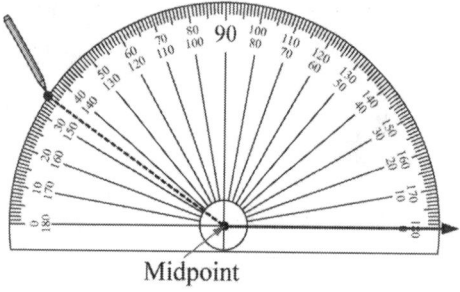

**Step 4**
Remove the protractor, and join the point that you marked and the endpoint of the ray that was drawn.

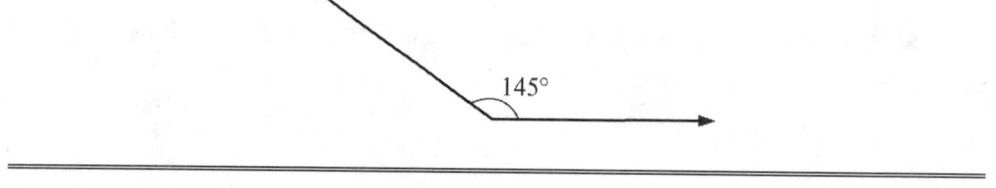

4.MD.6  *Measure angles in whole–number degrees using a protractor. Sketch angles of specified measure.*

## RELATE MEASURES OF BENCHMARK ANGLES TO DEGREES

Benchmark angles can be used to figure out a given angle's degree.

Angles are measured in units called **degrees** (°). The number of degrees tells how far one ray of the angle is from the other ray of the angle. Whenever you write the measure of an angle, you must write the degree symbol after the number.

The lengths of the rays do not affect the measure of the angle.

The measure of a right angle is 90°.

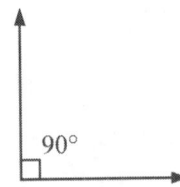

The measure of half a right angle is 45°. (90° ÷ 2 = 45°)

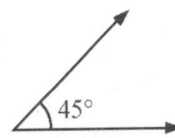

The measure of a straight angle is 180°. (90° + 90° = 180°)

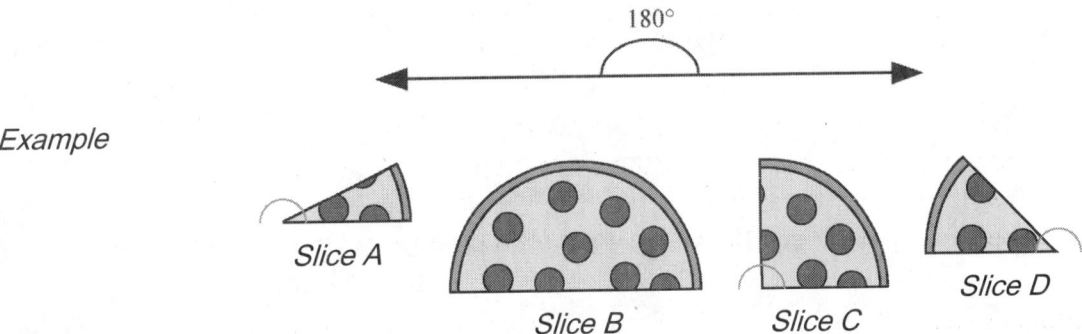

*Example*

Which slice of pizza shows an angle of 45 degrees?

*Solution*

**Step 1**
First identify the angle (or approximate angle) of each slice.

Using 90 degrees as a benchmark angle     you can see that Slice A is less than 90°.

Using 180 degrees as a benchmark angle     you can see that Slice B is a straight line, which is equal to 180°.

Using 90 degrees again as a benchmark angle     you can clearly see that Slice C is equal to 90° because it forms a square corner.

Finally we can see that Slice D is also less than a 90 degree angle. Slice D is actually exactly half of 90 degrees 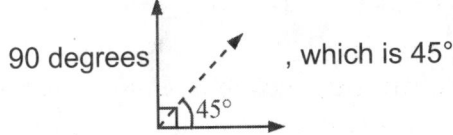, which is 45°.

**Step 2**
Slice D shows an angle of 45 degrees.

## ESTIMATING THE SIZE OF AN ANGLE BY COMPARING WITH BENCHMARK ANGLES

Angles that are easy to recognize are called **benchmark angles**.

Right angles and straight angles are both easy to recognize. They are examples of benchmark angles.

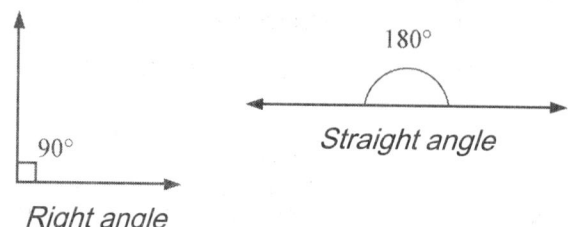

Another benchmark angle is a 45° angle. It is exactly half as big as a right angle.

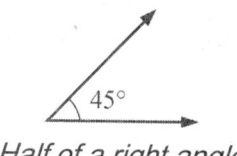

Half of a right angle

You can use benchmark angles to estimate the sizes of other angles:

- An angle that is bigger than a straight angle is greater than 180°.
- An angle that is between a right angle and a straight angle is between 90° and 180°.
- An angle that is between half a right angle and a right angle is between 45° and 90°.
- An angle that is less than half a right angle is less than 45°.

*Example*
Erik copies an angle from his textbook.

Use angle benchmarks to estimate the size of Erik's angle.

*Solution*
Compare Erik's angle with benchmark angles.

The angle is bigger than a right angle but smaller than a straight angle. That means it is between 90° and 180°.

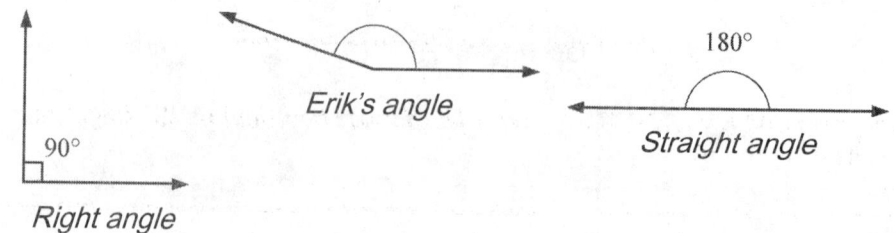

Erik's angle is almost as big as a straight angle. It is probably about 165°.

*4.MD.7 Recognize angle measure as additive. When an angle is decomposed into non–overlapping parts, the angle measure of the whole is the sum of the angle measures of the parts. Solve addition and subtraction problems to find unknown angles on a diagram in real world and mathematical problems.*

## ANGLES ON STRAIGHT LINES

A straight angle forms when two lines or rays meet in a straight line. There is no bend in the line. The angle is like a half circle from one side of the line to the other side.

You can form a straight angle by placing two index cards side by side.

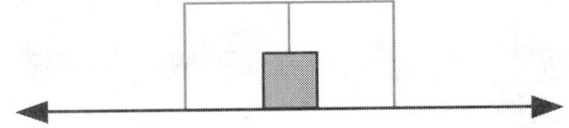

*The gray square shows where the corners of the two index cards meet to form a straight angle.*

**Supplementary angles** are two angles that add to 180°.

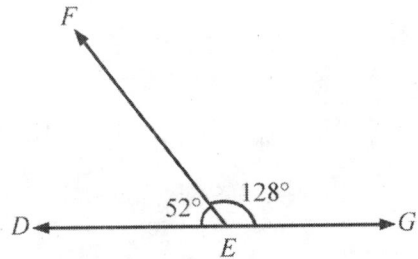

∠DEF + ∠FEG = 180°
52° + 128° = 180°

The two angles that make up the supplementary angles are called supplements. ∠DEF is a supplement to ∠FEG.

Lines can be split into more than two lines. All the angles on a straight line must add up to 180°.

*Example*
Angles AOF, FOD, and DOB are also angles on a straight line.

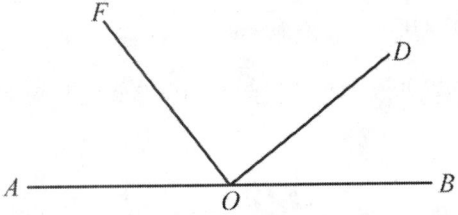

Angle AOF is 48°, and angle FOD is 93°. Angle DOB must be equal to 39° because 48° + 93° + 39° = 180°.

---

SOLARO Study Guide – Mathematics 4      Measurement and Data

# FINDING MISSING ANGLES IN CIRCLES

The angles surrounding a point in a circle will always add up to 360°.

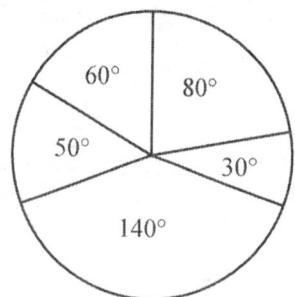

In this diagram, the point is surrounded by angles. The angles add up to 360°.
50° + 60° + 80° + 30° + 140° = 360°

If you are trying to find missing angles in a circle, follow these steps:

1. Calculate the total of the known angles.
2. Subtract the total of the known angles from 360°.

*Example*

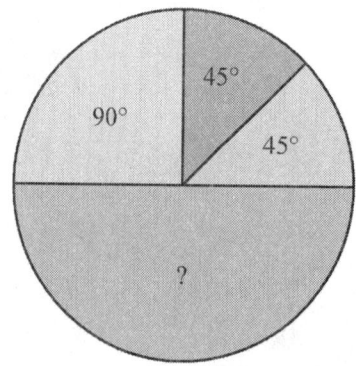

A circle is divided into sections with some given angles.

What is the missing angle in this circle?

*Solution*

**Step 1**
Calculate the total of the known angles.
90 + 45 + 45 = 180

**Step 2**
Subtract the total known angles from 360°.
360 − 180 = 180
The missing angle in the given circle is 180°.

Measurement and Data          Castle Rock Research

# EXERCISE #1—MEASUREMENT AND DATA

131. The mass of which of the following objects would be **best** measured in milligrams?
   A. one pear
   B. one grape
   C. one apple
   D. one banana

132. Which of the following referents is **most appropriate** for measuring the length of a centimeter?
   A. The width of your pointer finger
   B. The length of one giant step
   C. The thickness of a dime
   D. The length of a guitar

133. The **best** referent for 1 mL of water is
   A. a fish tank
   B. a tear drop
   C. an ice cube
   D. a small pond

*Use the following information to answer the next question.*

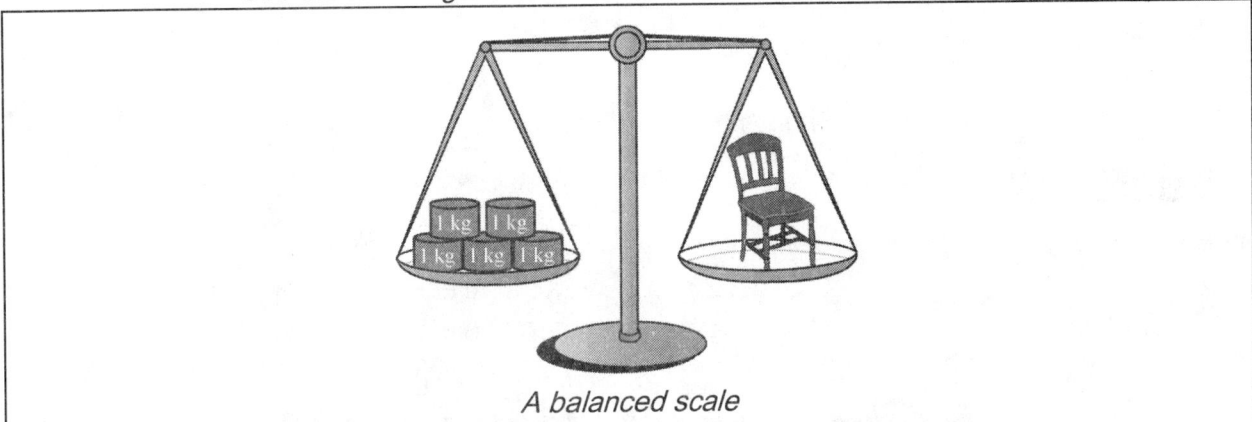

*A balanced scale*

134. What is the mass of the chair in grams?
   A. 5 g
   B. 50 g
   C. 500 g
   D. 5,000 g

135. Which of the following units is the **best** choice to measure the weight of a bucket of sand?
   A. Quarts
   B. Ounces
   C. Gallons
   D. Pounds

*Use the following information to answer the next question.*

David drinks 3 glasses of milk every day. Each glass contains 250 mL.

136. How much milk does David drink in a day?
   A. 500 mL
   B. 750 mL
   C. 800 mL
   D. 850 mL

*Use the following information to answer the next question.*

Anne and Tom went to see a new play. There are two acts in the play and a 30-minute break in between the acts. After the first act, Tom looked at the clock to check the time.

137. What time does the second act of the play start?
 A. 3:00
 B. 3:30
 C. 4:00
 D. 4:30

*Use the following information to answer the next question.*

Rhonda and Julie took a road trip. Their first stop was 51 km away.

138. How far away was their first stop in meters?
 A. 510 m
 B. 5,100 m
 C. 51,000 m
 D. 510,000 m

*Use the following information to answer the next question.*

Mark is packing boxes. One of the boxes has a mass of 8 kg, and the other box has a mass of 6 kg.

139. What is the total mass of the two boxes in grams?
 A. 14 g
 B. 1,400 g
 C. 14,000 g
 D. 140,000 g

*Use the following information to answer the next question.*

Lily is going on a cycling trip with her family. They are going to visit Lily's grandmother, who lives 65 km away. They decide that 65 km is too far to ride their bikes, so they drive the first 38 km and cycle the rest. They ride their bikes for 3 h.

140. How far did Lily's family ride their bikes each hour? _____ km

*Use the following information to answer the next question.*

Jasmine bought 3 lb of jellybeans to give out at her birthday party. She gave out all the jellybeans to 6 friends. Her friends all got the same amount of jellybeans.

141. How many ounces of jellybeans did each friend get? _____ oz

*Use the following information to answer the next question.*

Max and Kevin are helping their grandmother move. Max is carrying a box that has a mass of 925 g, and Kevin's box has a mass of 812 g.

142. What is the difference in mass between the box Max is carrying and the box Kevin is carrying?
 A. 275 g
 B. 203 g
 C. 155 g
 D. 113 g

*Use the following information to answer the next question.*

Seth earns money by walking dogs. He charges $4 per dog. In one week, he walked 9 dogs. During that same week, his parents paid him $15 for helping to clean the basement.

143. How much money in total did Seth earn that week? $_____

*Use the following information to answer the next question.*

144. Find the area of the shape.

*Use the following information to answer the next question.*

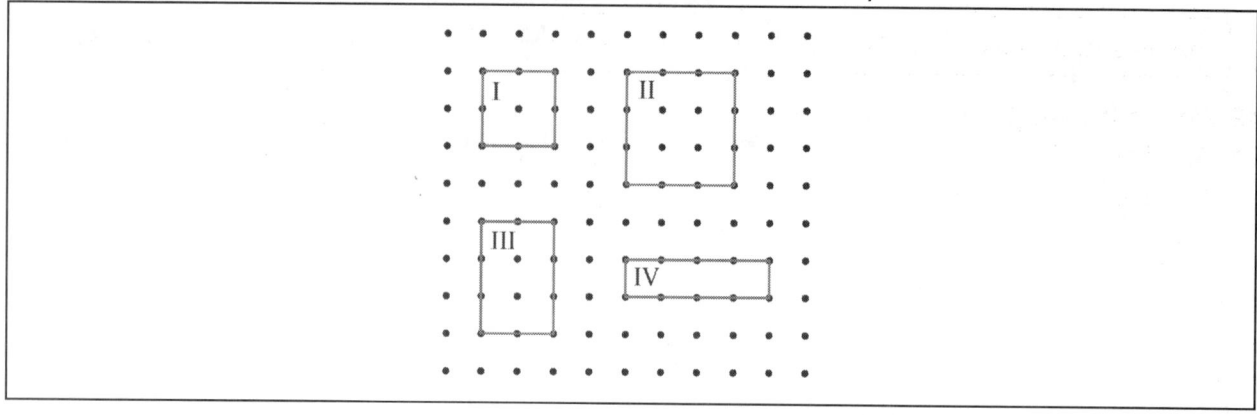

145. Which of the given rectangles have the same perimeter?
    A. Rectangles I and III
    B. Rectangles I and IV
    C. Rectangles II and III
    D. Rectangles III and IV

*Use the following information to answer the next question.*

Tina has a table with a rectangular top. The length and width are 40 in and 24 in, respectively. She wants to paste a ribbon around the edge of the table top. The cost of the ribbon is $0.10 per inch.

146. What is the total cost of the ribbon that is to be pasted around the boundary of the table top?
    A. 128 m
    B. $128
    C. 12.8 m
    D. $12.80

*Use the following information to answer the next question.*

Cecilia's mother is bringing a Christmas tree into her classroom, and Cecilia wants to use masking tape to mark off a square space for it.

147. If each side of the square is 1.5 m, how much tape does Cecilia need?
    A. 2.25 m
    B. 3 m
    C. 4.5 m
    D. 6 m

*Use the following information to answer the next question.*

The given diagram shows a quadrilateral.

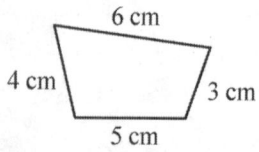

148. What is the perimeter of this quadrilateral?
    A. 10 cm
    B. 18 cm
    C. 22 cm
    D. 28 cm

Exercise #1     210     Castle Rock Research

Use the following information to answer the next question.

The area of a rectangle is 56 cm², and the length of one of the sides is 4 cm.

149. What is the length of the other side?
   A. 12 cm
   B. 14 cm
   C. 20 cm
   D. 24 cm

Use the following information to answer the next question.

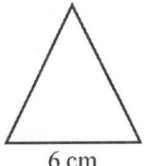

An equilateral triangle is given.

150. The perimeter of this triangle is _____ cm.

Use the following information to answer the next question.

Rectangle A has a length of 12 cm and a width of 4 cm. The length of rectangle B is twice that of rectangle A, and the width of rectangle B is twice that of rectangle A.

151. The area of rectangle B is _____ cm².

152. If the perimeter of a rectangle is 26 cm and one of the sides measures 7 cm, the length of the other side is _____ cm.

Use the following information to answer the next question.

Mrs. Morris used the following steps to teach her students how to organize their data using a line plot:

1. Use a scale from the smallest number to the largest number, using equal spacing in between. Include the numbers in between even if they do not appear in the data set.
2. Record the data by placing an X above each number. If a number appears more than once, then an additional X can be placed above the original X.
3. Identify the largest number and smallest number of the data set.
4. Draw a number line with the smallest number on the left and the largest number on the right.

153. What is the correct order of Mrs. Morris's steps?
   A. 3, 4, 1, 2
   B. 1, 2, 3, 4
   C. 2, 3, 1, 4
   D. 4, 3, 2, 1

*Use the following information to answer the next question.*

Michaela wants to know how long her gummy worm is. She places her gummy worm above a ruler.

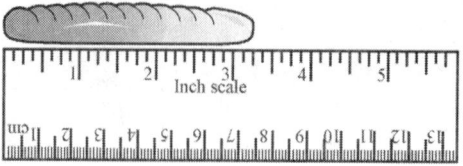

154. How long is Michaela's gummy worm?

   A. 3 in

   B. $3\frac{1}{4}$ in

   C. $3\frac{1}{2}$ in

   D. $3\frac{3}{4}$ in

*Use the following information to answer the next question.*

Ms. Brown's class decided to do a swim-a-thon to raise money for a new playground at their school. Students raised money based on the distance they swam. Ms. Brown made a line plot to show the number of students that swam each distance.

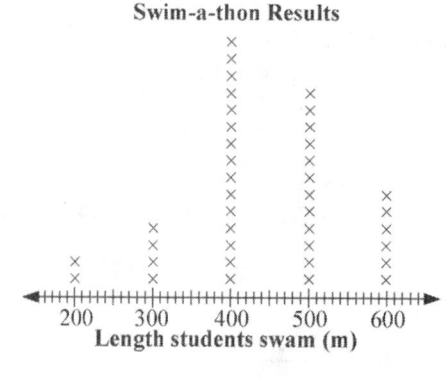

155. Which of the following statements about the given line plot is **false**?

   A. Most of the students swam 600 m.

   B. More students swam 400 m than 500 m.

   C. The smallest number of students swam 200 m.

   D. There were a total of 6 students who swam 200 m or 300 m.

156. Which of the following protractors shows an angle that measures 55°?

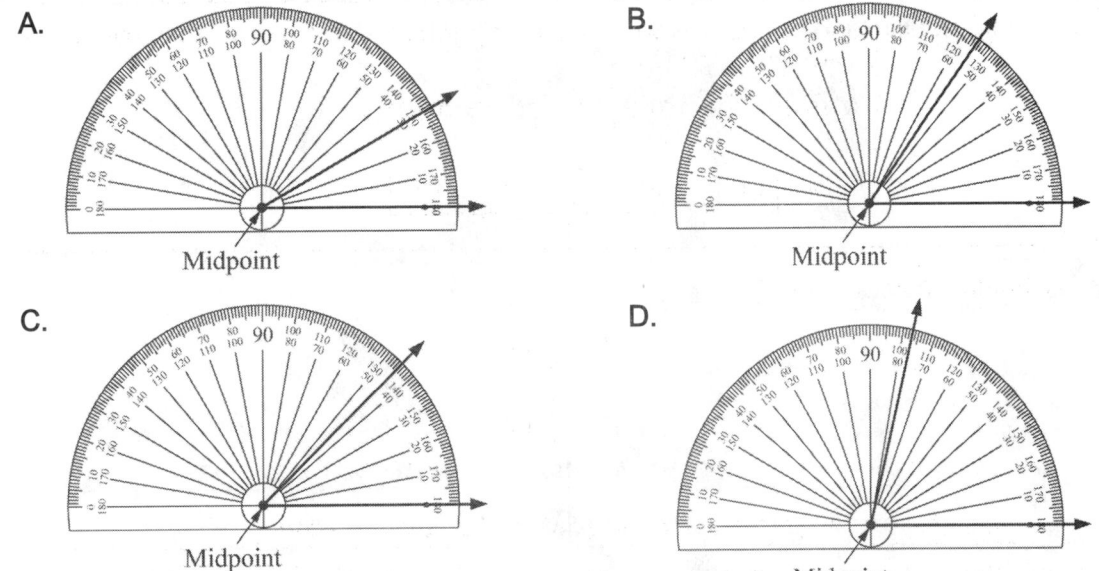

*Use the following information to answer the next question.*

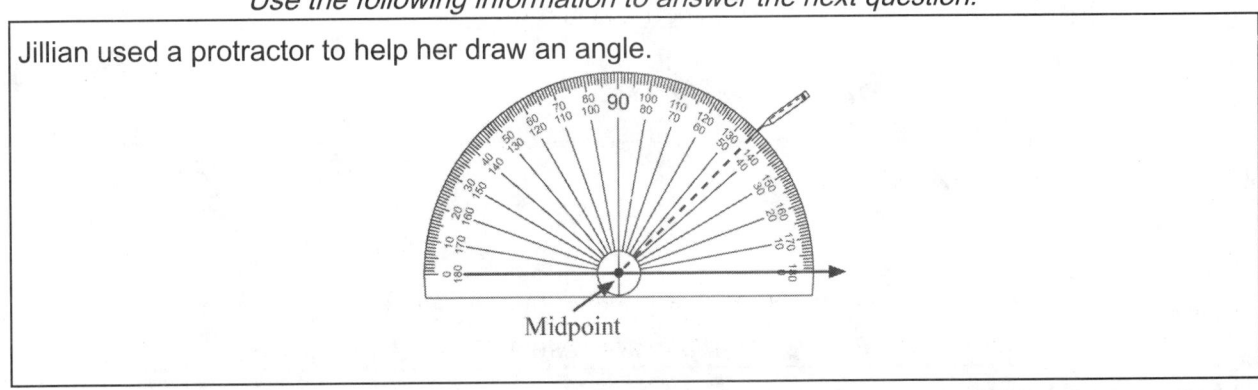

157. What is the measure of the angle Jillian drew? _____ °

158. Which of the following angles is greater than 90° but less than 180°?

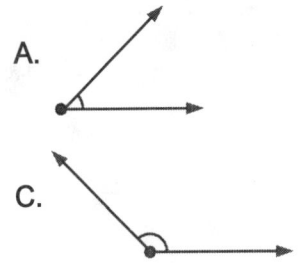
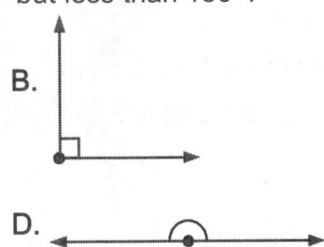

*Use the following information to answer the next question.*

Ellie draws a picture of a kite into her notebook.

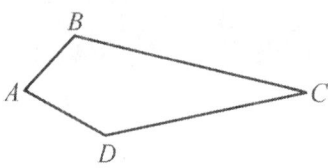

159. Which of the angles in the kite is closest to 80°?
   A. ∠A
   B. ∠B
   C. ∠C
   D. ∠D

*Use the following information to answer the next question.*

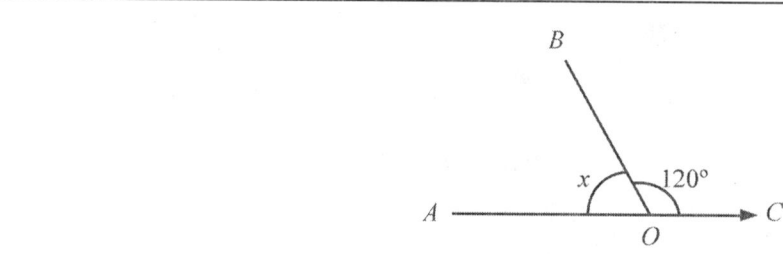

The given diagram shows ∠COB and ∠AOB.

160. What is the value of ∠AOB?
   A. 60°
   B. 70°
   C. 80°
   D. 90°

*Use the following information to answer the next question.*

A circle is split into sections with the given angles.

161. What is the missing angle in the given circle?
   A. 100°
   B. 110°
   C. 205°
   D. 215°

Not for Reproduction

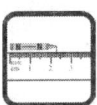

# EXERCISE #1—MEASUREMENT AND DATA  ANSWERS AND SOLUTIONS

| | | | |
|---|---|---|---|
| 131. B | 139. C | 147. D | 155. A |
| 132. A | 140. 9 | 148. B | 156. B |
| 133. B | 141. 8 | 149. B | 157. 45 |
| 134. D | 142. D | 150. 18 | 158. C |
| 135. D | 143. 51 | 151. 192 | 159. A |
| 136. B | 144. See solution | 152. 6 | 160. A |
| 137. C | 145. D | 153. A | 161. A |
| 138. C | 146. D | 154. B | |

### 131. B

One grape would be **best** measured in milligrams.

A milligram is a very small unit of measure and would be used to measure the mass of very small or light objects. One grape would be small and light.

### 132. A

The width of your pointer finger is the most appropriate referent because it is about the length of a centimeter.

The length of one giant step is about the same as a meter. The length of a guitar is much longer than a centimeter. The thickness of a dime is about the same as a millimeter.

### 133. B

The best referent for 1 mL is a tear drop.

Fish tanks and small ponds both hold several liters of water. An ice cube contains several teaspoons of water, and a teaspoon is larger than a milliliter.

### 134. D

**Step 1**
Determine the mass of the weights on the left side of the scale.

There are five weights, and each weight has a mass of 1 kg.
Add 1 kg + 1 kg + 1 kg + 1 kg + 1 kg = 5 kg, or multiply 1 kg × 5.

The mass of the five weights is 5 kg.

**Step 2**
Determine the mass of the chair.
Since the scale is balanced, the mass of the chair is the same as the mass of the five weights.
The mass of the chair is 5 kg.

**Step 3**
Change kilograms to grams.
1 kg = 1,000 g
Make a chart to help you determine the number of grams in 5 kg.

| Kilograms | Grams |
|---|---|
| 1 | 1,000 |
| 2 | 2,000 |
| 3 | 3,000 |
| 4 | 4,000 |
| 5 | 5,000 |

The chair has a mass of 5,000 g.

### 135. D

Quarts and gallons are both units of capacity. It is impossible to use them to measure weight. Ounces are used to measure the weight of things that are very light. A bucket of sand is much too heavy to be measured in ounces.

The best unit to measure the weight of a bucket of sand is pounds.

### 136. B

Each glass is 250 mL. Multiply by 3.
250 mL × 3 = 750 mL

The amount of milk in 3 glasses is 750 mL.

SOLARO Study Guide – Mathematics 4            215            Measurement and Data

**137.** C

When Tom looked at the clock after the first act, the time was 3:30.

To find out what time the second act starts, add 30 minutes to the time the first act ended.
  3:30
+0:30
  4:0

The second act of the play starts at 4:00.

**138.** C

Convert kilometers to meters to solve the problem.
 1 km = 1,000 m
51 km = 1,000 m × 51
51 km = 51,000 m

Rhonda and Julie's first stop was 51,000 m away.

**139.** C

**Step 1**
Find the total mass of the two boxes in kilograms.
8 kg + 6 kg = 14 kg
The total mass of the two boxes is 14 kg.

**Step 2**
Convert kilograms into grams.
      1 kg = 1,000 g
14 kg × 1,000 g = 140 g
The total mass of the two boxes is 14,000 g.

**140.** 9

**Step 1**
Determine what is being asked.
You need to find how far Lily's family travels on their bikes each hour.

**Step 2**
Make a plan.
You need to find out how far in total Lily and her family rode their bikes. Subtract the distance they drove from the total distance.
To find out how far they rode their bikes in 1 h, divide the distance they cycled by the number of hours they cycled.

**Step 3**
Solve the problem.
Subtract 38 from 65.
65 − 38 = 27
They cycled 27 km.
Divide 27 by 3.
27 ÷ 3 = 9
Lily and her family cycled 9 km each hour.

**141.** 8

**Step 1**
Convert the weight of the jellybeans from pounds to ounces.
There are 16 oz in 1 lb.
Use multiplication when you are converting from a larger unit to a smaller unit.
Multiply 16 by 3 to convert 3 lb to ounces.
16 × 3 = 48
Jasmine has 48 ounces of jellybeans.

**Step 2**
Jasmine split the jellybeans evenly among her 6 friends. You will need to use division.
48 ÷ 6 = 8
Each friend got 8 oz of jellybeans.

**142.** D

**Step 1**
Find out what the problem is asking by identifying the important information.
The question is asking the difference in mass between Max's and Kevin's boxes.

**Step 2**
Determine which operation to use.
To find the difference in mass of the two boxes, use subtraction.

### Step 3
Solve the problem.
Subtract the mass of Kevin's box from the mass of Max's box.
925 − 812 = 113
The difference in mass between the box Max is carrying and the box Kevin is carrying is 113 g.

### 143. 51
#### Step 1
Find out how much money Seth earned from walking the dogs.
Seth walked 9 dogs. He was paid $4 for each dog. Multiply 9 by 4.
9 × 4 = 36
Seth earned $36 from walking the dogs.

#### Step 2
Find out how much money Seth earned in total.
Add the money he earned from walking dogs to the money he earned by cleaning out the basement.
36 + 15 = 51
Seth earned a total of $51.

### 144.
#### Step 1
Determine the side lengths.
Count the number of squares on the length and the width.
$s$ = 7 units

#### Step 2
Substitute the known values into the area formula, and solve.
Since both the length and width measure 7 units, use the area formula for a square.
$A = s^2$
$= 7^2$
$= 7 × 7$
$= 49$ units$^2$

The area of the square is 49 units$^2$.

### 145. D
#### Step 1
Use the formula for perimeter to determine the perimeters of the rectangles in the given alternatives.
$P = l + w + l + w$
Perimeter of rectangle III:
$P = 3 + 2 + 3 + 2 = 10$ units

#### Step 2
Perimeter of rectangle IV:
$P = 4 + 1 + 4 + 1 = 10$ units

Rectangles III and IV have the same perimeter.

### 146. D
#### Step 1
Decide which formula to use.
The table top is a rectangle, so you can use $P = 2l + 2w$ or $P = 2(l + w)$.
Try $P = 2l + 2w$.

#### Step 2
Apply the formula:

- Length of the table = 40 in
- Width of the table = 24 in

$P = 2l + 2w$
$= 2 × 40 + 2 × 24$
$= 128$

#### Step 3
Calculate the total cost of the ribbon.
Multiply the total perimeter of the table top by the cost of 1 inch of ribbon.
128 × 0.10 = 12.80
The total cost of ribbon used to paste around the edge of the table top is $12.80.

### 147. D
#### Step 1
Decide which formula to use.
Use the formula for a square, $P = 4s$.

#### Step 2
Apply the formula.
$P = 4s$
$= 4 × 1.5$
$= 6$

Remember to include the unit when you write your answer.
Cecilia needs 6 m of tape.

### 148. B

**Step 1**
Decide which formula to use.
The quadrilateral is an irregular polygon with four sides, so you will use the formula
$P = s_1 + s_2 + s_3 + s_4$.

**Step 2**
Apply the formula.
$P = s_1 + s_2 + s_3 + s_4$
$P = 4 + 6 + 3 + 5$
$P = 18$
Remember to include the unit when you write your answer.
The perimeter of the quadrilateral is 18 cm.

### 149. B

To find the missing side length, use the formula
$\frac{\text{area}}{\text{given side length}} = \square$.
$\frac{56 \text{cm}^2}{4 \text{cm}} = 14 \text{cm}$
The missing side length is 14 cm.

### 150. 18

**Step 1**
Decide which formula to use.
This is an equilateral triangle, so you should use the formula for a regular polygon $P = s \times n$.

**Step 2**
Apply the formula.
There are three sides, so $n = 3$. Each side is 6 cm long, so $s = 6$.
$P = s \times n$
$\phantom{P} = 6 \times 3$
$\phantom{P} = 18$
Remember to include the unit when you write your answer.
The perimeter of the triangle is 18 cm.

### 151. 192

**Step 1**
To determine the length of rectangle $B$, double the length of rectangle $A$.
12 cm × 2 = 24 cm

**Step 2**
To determine the width of rectangle $B$, double the width of rectangle $A$.
4 cm × 2 = 8 cm

**Step 3**
To determine the area of rectangle $B$, multiply 24 by 8.
$A = l \times w$
$A = 24 \times 8$
$A = 192 \text{ cm}^2$

The area of rectangle $B$ is 192 cm².

### 152. 6

**Step 1**
Find the total length of the known sides.
You know that one of the side lengths of the rectangle is 7 cm. Since a rectangle has two sets of equal sides, you know that the other side length of the rectangle is also 7 cm.
The total length you know is 7 + 7 = 14.

**Step 2**
Find the total length of the unknown sides.
Subtract the total length of the known sides from the perimeter.
The total length of the known sides is 14 cm, and the perimeter is 26 cm.
26 − 14 = 12
The total length of the unknown sides is 12 cm.

**Step 3**
Find the width of the rectangle.
The total unknown length is 12 cm, and because there are two sets of equal sides in a rectangle, you need to divide the total by 2 to determine the length of the other side.
12 ÷ 2 = 6
The length of the other side is 6 cm.

**Step 4**
Check your answer by calculating the perimeter. Use your answer for the unknown side.
perimeter = $l + w + l + w$
perimeter = 7 + 6 + 7 + 6
perimeter = 26
This is the same as the perimeter that was given, so your answer is correct.
The length of the other side is 6 cm.

### 153. A

This is the order of steps for organizing data using a line plot:

- Identify the smallest number and largest number in the given data set.
- Draw a number line with the smallest number on the left and the largest number on the right.
- Use a scale from the smallest number to the largest number, using equal spacing in between. Include the numbers in between even if they do not appear in the data set.
- Record the data by placing an *X* above each number. If a number appears twice in a data set, then an additional *X* can be placed above the original X.

Therefore, the correct order of steps is 3, 4, 1, 2.

### 154. B

Look closely at the end of Michaela's gummy worm. The worm ends after the 3 in mark, on the second tick. This shows $\frac{1}{4}$ in.

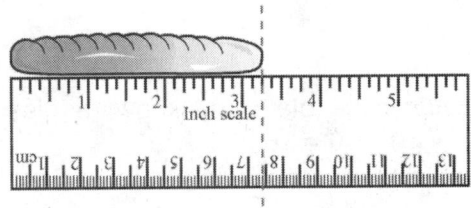

The gummy worm is $3\frac{1}{4}$ in long.

### 155. A

There were 2 students who swam 200 m, 4 students who swam 300 m, 15 students who swam 400 m, 12 students who swam 500 m, and 6 students who swam 600 m.

Only 6 students swam 600 m. There were more students who swam 400 m and 500 m. This conclusion is false.

Fifteen students swam 400 m, and 12 students swam 500 m. More students swam 400 m than 500 m.

Only 2 students swam 200 m. This is the smallest number.

Two students swam 200 m, and 4 students swam 300 m. That makes a total of 6 students who swam 200 m or 300 m.

### 156. B

The ray of the angle should pass through 55 on the protractor, with the other ray lining up with 0.

This protractor shows an angle that measures 55°.

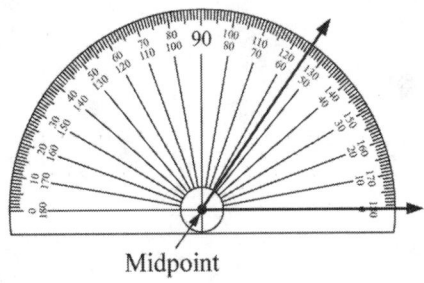

### 157. 45

**Step 1**
Starting at the 0° line, use the inner scale on the right side of the protractor, and count up the degrees by 10s to the number closest to the dotted line, but not crossing the line.
10°, 20°, 30°, 40°

**Step 2**
Since the dotted line is halfway between the 40° line and the 50° line, count the degrees by 1s to the halfway point, which is 45°.
41°, 42°, 43°, 44°, 45°

The measure of the angle Jillian drew is 45°.

### 158. C

An angle measuring 90° is a right angle.

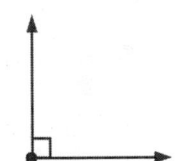

An angle measuring 180° is a straight angle.

This means that an angle greater than 90° but less than 180° must be between a right angle and a straight angle.

This angle is greater than a right angle but less than a straight angle.

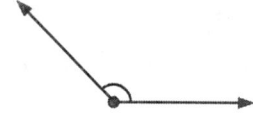

**159. A**

An 80° angle is bigger than 45° and smaller than 90°.

Angles B and D are both bigger than 90°.

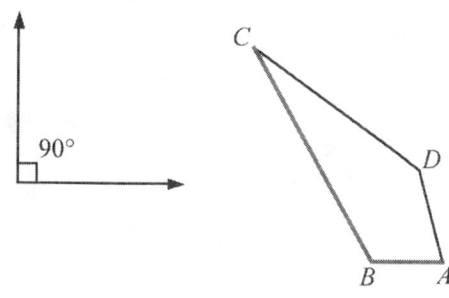

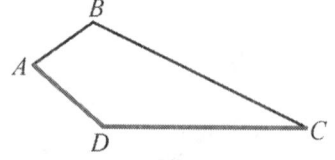

Angle C is smaller than 45°.

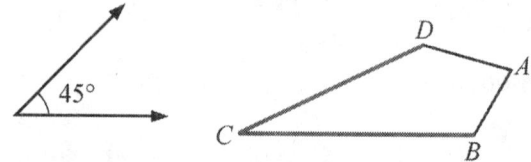

Angle A is bigger than 45° and smaller than 90°.

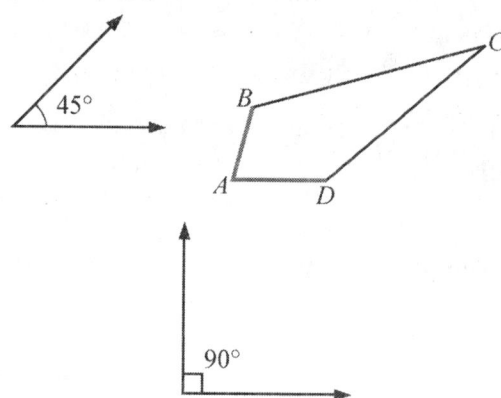

Angle A is closest to 80°.

**160. A**

Angles on a straight line add up to 180°. Two angles are supplementary when their sum is 180° on the line.

To find the value of the angle, subtract ∠COB from 180.
180 − 120 = 60
∠AOB = 60°

**161. A**

**Step 1**
Calculate the total of the known angles.
180 + 40 + 40 = 260

**Step 2**
Subtract the total of the known angles from 360.
360 − 260 = 100
The missing angle is 100°.

# EXERCISE #2—MEASUREMENT AND DATA

162. Which of the following objects is **best** measured in tons?
   A. Elephant
   B. Notebook
   C. Bag of flour
   D. Box of books

163. Mrs. Smith bought 3 kilograms of jellybeans for a party. How many grams of jellybeans did Mrs. Smith buy?
   A. 300 grams
   B. 330 grams
   C. 3,000 grams
   D. 3,300 grams

*Use the following information to answer the next question.*

Anson lines up these four containers.

164. Which of Anson's containers is the **best** referent for 1 L?

   A.
   B.
   C.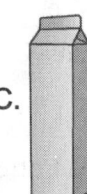
   D.

165. Which of the following referents is **most appropriate** for measuring the length of a meter?
   A. Length of a truck
   B. Length of a laptop
   C. Distance from a doorknob to the floor
   D. Distance from the tip to the base of your index finger

*Use the following information to answer the next question.*

Miranda made a list of items she found at the bottom of her book bag:

- plastic straw
- notebook
- apple
- paperclip
- gluestick

166. Which two items would have masses **best** measured in milligrams?
   A. gluestick and notebook
   B. notebook and paperclip
   C. plastic straw and apple
   D. plastic straw and paperclip

*Use the following information to answer the next question.*

Brad's dad fills the kettle with 12 cups of water. Each cup holds one-quarter liter of water.

167. How many liters of water does Brad's dad put into the kettle?
   A. 1 L
   B. 2 L
   C. 3 L
   D. 4 L

*Use the following information to answer the next question.*

Jason's parents are taking a three-day cooking course, and they ask him to babysit his little brother and sister. On Tuesday, Wednesday, and Thursday, his mom and dad leave the house at 3:55 P.M. and return at 6:15 P.M. They pay him $5.00/hr.

168. Rounded to the nearest dollar, how much money does Jason earn from babysitting? $_____

*Use the following information to answer the next question.*

Maria is putting new carpet in her house. She bought one roll that is 6 m long. She used 450 cm of it.

169. How much of the carpet is left?
   A. 1 m
   B. 1.5 m
   C. 2 m
   D. 2.5 m

*Use the following information to answer the next question.*

Kirsten is baking some cakes for her bakery. She needs 2,000 g of flour and 1,000 g of sugar.

170. What is the difference between the amount of flour and sugar needed in kilograms (kg)?
   A. 0.1 kg
   B. 1.0 kg
   C. 1.5 kg
   D. 2.0 kg

*Use the following information to answer the next question.*

Tracy is making macramé bracelets for her friends. She makes 6 bracelets that are each 9 cm long.

171. What is the total length of the bracelets that Tracy made? _____ cm

Exercise #2

*Use the following information to answer the next question.*

Jonah and Alexia want to bake 7 apple pies for the pie throwing contest at their school. Jonah brought 2 lb of apples, and Alexia brought 32 oz of apples.

172. How many pounds of apples do they have altogether?
　　A. 4 lb
　　B. 6 lb
　　C. 30 lb
　　D. 34 lb

*Use the following information to answer the next question.*

Shawn is reading a book about kangaroos. One picture shows 5 kangaroos that each have a mass of about 100 kg. Another picture shows 2 kangaroos that each have a mass of about 25 kg.

173. What is the total mass of all the kangaroos?
　　A. 500 kg
　　B. 525 kg
　　C. 550 kg
　　D. 600 kg

*Use the following information to answer the next question.*

Maya has $20 to spend at a garage sale. She sees several things she likes.

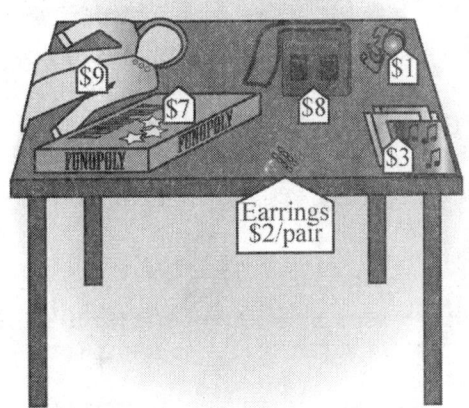

She does not have enough money to buy everything she wants, so she chooses three things. She pays with a $20 bill and does not get any change back.

174. What did Maya buy?
　　A. Jacket, game, and earrings
　　B. Purse, game, and yo-yo
　　C. Jacket, purse, and CD
　　D. Game, purse, and CD

*Use the following information to answer the next question.*

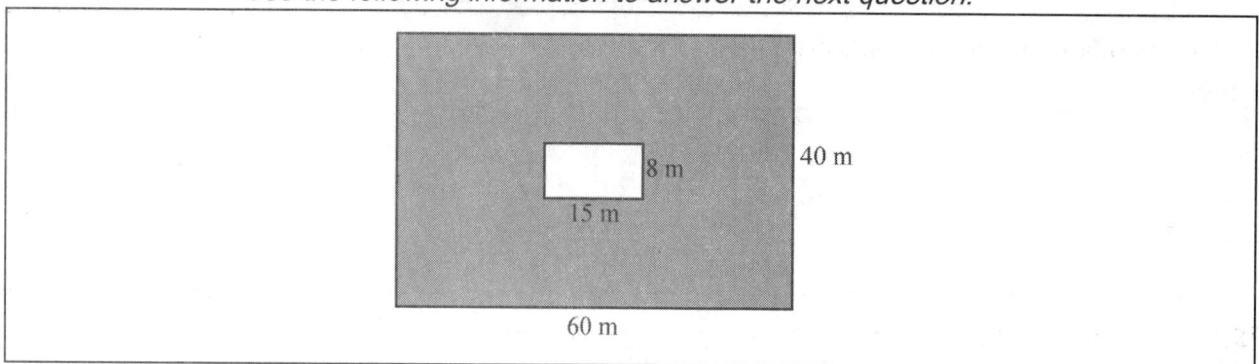

175. What is the area of the shaded part of the rectangle?
  A. 2,200 m²
  B. 2,280 m²
  C. 2,300 m²
  D. 2,400 m²

176. The length of a rectangle is twice its width. If the width of the rectangle is 5 m, then the perimeter of the rectangle is
  A. 15 m
  B. 25 m
  C. 30 m
  D. 45 m

*Use the following information to answer the next question.*

Using centimeter grid paper, Dai drew a rectangle with an area of 18 cm².

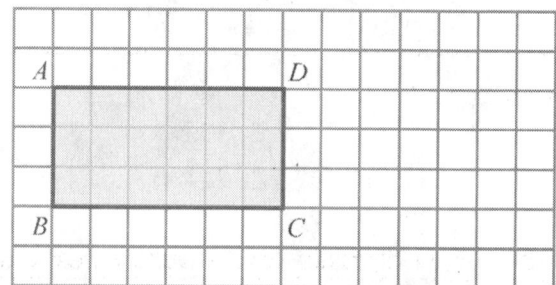

Dai then drew a second rectangle with lengths twice as long as the lengths of rectangle *ABCD*. Dai did not change the width of the second rectangle.

177. What was the area of the second rectangle?
  A. 2 times the original area
  B. 3 times the original area
  C. 4 times the original area
  D. 5 times the original area

Exercise #2

*Use the following information to answer the next question.*

This hexagon has sides measuring 7 m.

178. The perimeter of the given hexagon is _____ m.

179. The length of a rectangle is twice its width. If the width of the rectangle is 5 m, then the perimeter of the rectangle is
   A. 15 m
   B. 25 m
   C. 30 m
   D. 45 m

*Use the following information to answer the next question.*

A triangle is given.

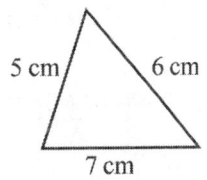

180. What is the perimeter of this triangle?
   A. 11 cm
   B. 13 cm
   C. 18 cm
   D. 22 cm

*Use the following information to answer the next question.*

Tran and his sister are helping to put a fence around their garden. The garden is a square with sides 6 m in length.

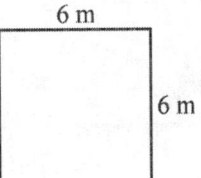

181. How much fence do they need?
   A. 12 m
   B. 18 m
   C. 24 m
   D. 36 m

*Use the following information to answer the next question.*

Lindy's classroom is 144 m².

182. If the length of her classroom is 12 m, what is the width?
  A. 11 m
  B. 12 m
  C. 13 m
  D. 14 m

*Use the following information to answer the next question.*

The perimeter of a rectangle is 32 cm. The width of the rectangle is 5 cm.

183. How long is the rectangle? _____ cm

*Use the following information to answer the next question.*

James surveyed some of his classmates to find out how many people were in each of their families. He wrote their answers on a piece of paper.

2, 4, 5, 7, 5, 2, 2, 4, 4, 7, 3, 4, 5, 4, 5

184. Which of the following line plots shows the data James collected?

A.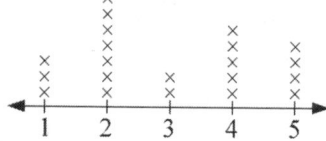

B.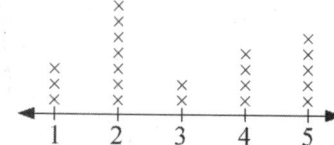

C.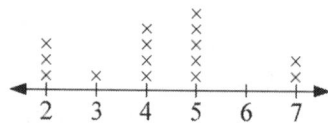

D.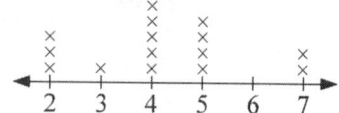

*Use the following information to answer the next question.*

Armin was measuring objects in his desk with his inch ruler. He measured his eraser, as shown in the given image.

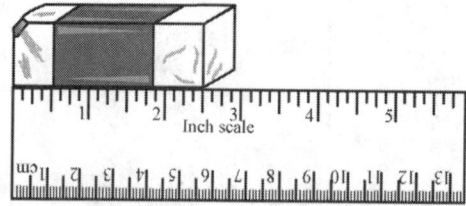

185. How long is Armin's eraser?
  A. 2 in
  B. $2\frac{1}{2}$ in
  C. $2\frac{3}{4}$ in
  D. 3 in

*Use the following information to answer the next question.*

Megan conducted an experiment by rolling a 6-sided number cube 22 times. She recorded the results on a line plot.

```
×
× ×         ×       ×
× ×         × ×     ×
× ×   ×     × ×     ×
× ×   ×     × ×     ×
―――――――――――――――――――――
1  2  3  4  5  6
```

186. Which of the following statements about the results of Megan's experiment is **true**?
   A. The number 1 was rolled the least.
   B. The number 3 was rolled the most.
   C. The numbers 4 and 6 were rolled the same number of times.
   D. The numbers 2 and 5 were rolled the same number of times.

*Use the following information to answer the next question.*

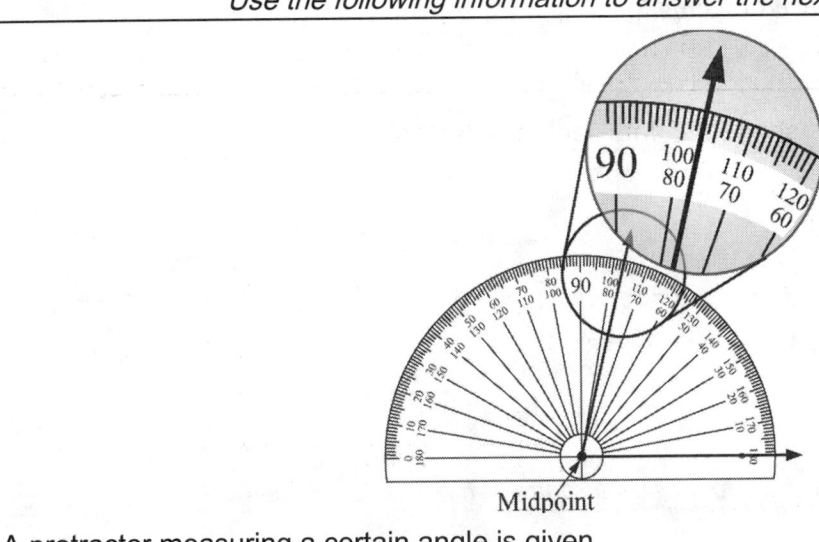

A protractor measuring a certain angle is given.

187. What angle is shown on this protractor?
   A. 82°            B. 80°
   C. 77°            D. 65°

188. Use a semicircular protractor to construct an angle of 145°.

189. Which of the following angle measures is greater than half a right angle measure and less than a right angle measure?
    A. 30°
    B. 45°
    C. 80°
    D. 90°

*Use the following information to answer the next question.*

Edwin, Wes, Liliana, and Abby each draw an angle.

190. Which of the children drew an angle that is **closest** to 110°?
    A. Wes
    B. Abby
    C. Edwin
    D. Liliana

*Use the following information to answer the next question.*

Triangle ABC is shown.

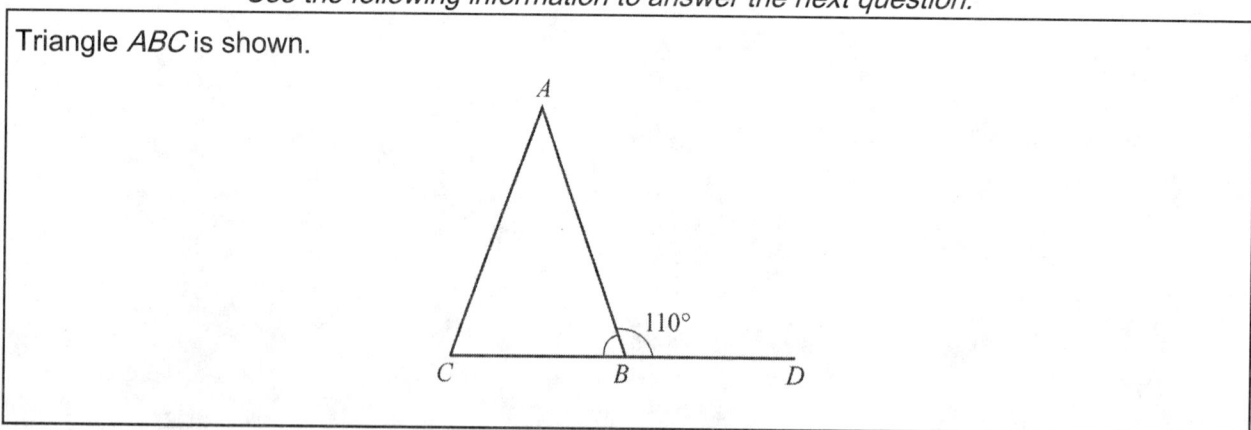

191. The measure of ∠ABC is _____°.

Exercise #2     228     Castle Rock Research

*Use the following information to answer the next question.*

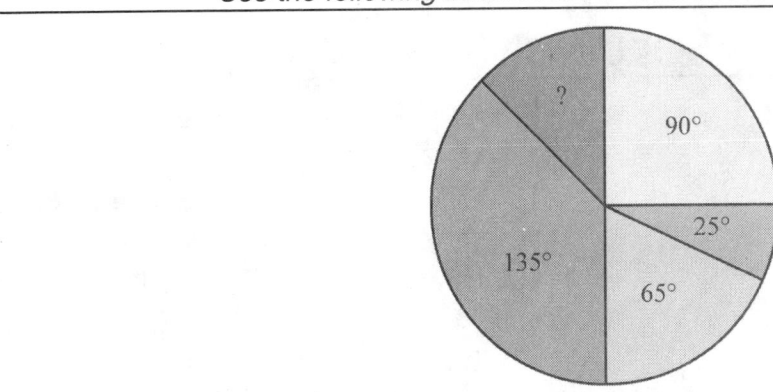

The point in the center of this circle is surrounded by the given angles.

192. What is the missing angle in the given circle?
    A. 45°
    B. 75°
    C. 150°
    D. 180°

# EXERCISE #2—MEASUREMENT AND DATA   ANSWERS AND SOLUTIONS

| 162. A | 170. B | 178. 42 | 186. C |
| --- | --- | --- | --- |
| 163. C | 171. 54 | 179. C | 187. C |
| 164. C | 172. A | 180. C | 188. See solution |
| 165. C | 173. C | 181. C | 189. C |
| 166. D | 174. C | 182. B | 190. D |
| 167. C | 175. B | 183. 11 | 191. 70 |
| 168. 35 | 176. C | 184. D | 192. A |
| 169. B | 177. A | 185. B | |

### 162. A

One ton is 2,000 lb. Tons are used to weigh objects that are very heavy. An elephant is heavy enough to measure in tons.

The notebook should be weighed in ounces, and the box of books and the bag of flour should be measured in pounds.

### 163. C

Choice C is correct. Mrs. Smith bought 3,000 grams of jellybeans.

Think:

1 kg = 1 0 g
2 kg = 2 0 g
3 kg = 3 0 g

### 164. C

The small cup would only hold a few spoonfuls of liquid. This is much less than a liter. The measuring cup is also too small to hold a liter. The jug would contain around 4 L.

The best referent for 1 L is the carton.

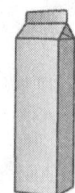

### 165. C

The best referent for measuring the length of a meter is the distance from a doorknob to the floor. This length is about 1 m.

The length of a truck is too large to be used as a referent for a meter. The distance from the tip to the base of your index finger and the length of a laptop are too small to be used as referents for a meter.

### 166. D

Choice D is correct. The plastic straw and paperclip would have masses best measured in milligrams.

All of the objects are light, but the masses of the plastic straw and paperclip would be extremely light. They would best be measured with the smallest unit, which is the milligram. The other items would best be measured in grams.

### 167. C

Choice C is correct. Brad's dad puts 3 L of water into the kettle.

There are four one-quarter liters in one liter, so 4 cups of water will equal 1 L.

Use repeated subtraction (12 – 4 = 8, 8 – 4 = 4, 4 – 4 = 0) or division (12 ÷ 4 = 3) to solve this problem.

### 168. 35

Step 1
Determine what is being asked.
The problem is to determine how much money Jason earns from babysitting.

**Step 2**
Make a plan.
First, find out how long Jason babysat each day. You can do this by using a timeline.
Next, find out how long Jason babysat in total. Multiply the amount of time he worked in one day by 3.
Finally, find out how much Jason earned in total. Multiply the number of hours by 5. The final answer should be in dollars.

**Step 3**
Solve the problem.
Find out how long Jason babysat each day. Make a timeline, and mark the start time, end time, and the hours in between. Then, add up the times on the timeline to see how long Jason babysat.

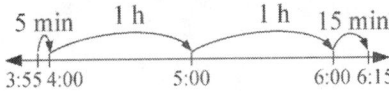

5 min + 1 hr + 1 hr + 15 min
= 2 hr and 20 min
Find out how long Jason babysat in three days.
  2 hr × 3 = 6 hr
20 min × 3 = 60 min = 1 hr
    6 + 1 = 7 hr
Find out how much Jason earns.
7 hr × $5.00 = $35.00
Jason earns $35.00 from babysitting.

**Step 4**
Decide if your answer is reasonable.
Since the question requires multiplication, the answer must be a larger number than the numbers being multiplied. The total (35) is larger than both 7 and 5, so the answer is reasonable.

**169. B**

**Step 1**
Convert the centimeter measurements to meter measurements.
1 m = 100 cm
The length of the carpet that was used is 450 cm, so divide 450 cm by 100 cm.
450 ÷ 100 = 4.5
Maria used 4.5 m of carpet.

**Step 2**
Use subtraction to determine how many meters of carpet are left.
6 m – 4.5 m = 1.5 m

**170. B**

**Step 1**
Find the difference in weight between the flour and sugar.
2,000 g – 1,000 g = 1,000 g
The difference between the flour and sugar is 1,000 g.

**Step 2**
Convert grams into kilograms.
1,000 g = 1 kg
The difference between the flour and sugar in kilograms is 1.0 kg.

**171. 54**

**Step 1**
Determine what is being asked.
You need to find the total length of 6 bracelets. Each bracelet is 9 cm long.

**Step 2**
Make a plan.
Multiply the length of each bracelet by the number of bracelets that Tracy made.

**Step 3**
Solve the problem.
Multiply 9 by 6.
9 × 6 = 54
In total, the length of Tracy's bracelets is 54 cm.

**172. A**

Before you can add the total amount of apples, they must have the same unit. The answer needs to be in pounds, so you should convert the number of apples Alexia brought from ounces to pounds.

**Step 1**
Determine what operation to use.
When converting from a smaller unit to a larger unit, such as ounces to pounds, use division for the conversion.

**Step 2**
Perform the conversion.
There are 16 oz in 1 lb. Divide 32 oz by 16.
32 ÷ 16 = 2
Alexia brought 2 lb of apples.

**Step 3**
Add the total amount of apples.
2 + 2 = 4
They have 4 lb of apples.

173. **C**

Choice C is correct. The total mass of all the kangaroos is 550 kg.

Count by 100s to find the mass of the 5 kangaroos.
100, 200, 300, 400, 500

The total mass of the 5 kangaroos is 500 kg.

Add (25 + 25 = 50) or count by 25s (25, 50) to find the total mass of the two lighter kangaroos.

Add the two totals together. 500 + 50 = 550

174. **C**

Find the total cost of each combination of items:

- The jacket costs $9, the game costs $7, and the earrings cost $2.
  9 + 7 + 2 = 18
- The game costs $7, the purse costs $8, and the CD costs $3.
  7 + 8 + 3 = 18
- The jacket costs $9, the purse costs $8, and the CD costs $3.
  9 + 8 + 3 = 20
- The purse costs $8, the game costs $7, and the yo-yo costs $1.
  8 + 7 + 1 = 16

Maya bought the jacket, purse, and CD.

175. **B**

**Step 1**
Determine the area of the large rectangle by substituting the appropriate numbers for the length (60 m) and the width (40 m) in the area formula.
$A = l \times w$
$A = 60 \times 40$
$A = 2,400 \text{ m}^2$

**Step 2**
Determine the area of the small (white) rectangle.
$A = l \times w$
$A = 15 \times 8$
$A = 120 \text{ m}^2$

**Step 3**
Subtract the two areas to determine the area of the shaded part.
$2,400 \text{ m}^2 - 120 \text{ m}^2 = 2,280 \text{ m}^2$
The area of the shaded part of the rectangle is $2,280 \text{ m}^2$.

176. **C**

Since the width of the rectangle is 5 m, the length is 10 m (twice the width: 2 × 5 = 10).

Since $P = l + w + l + w$, then
$P = 10 + 5 + 10 + 5 = 30$ m.

The perimeter of the rectangle is 30 m.

177. **A**

Choice A is correct. The area of the second rectangle was 2 times the original area.

The original area was $18 \text{ cm}^2$.

The measurements of the second rectangle are 3 cm (the width stays the same) and 12 cm (the length is twice as long).

$3 \times 12 = 36 \text{ cm}^2$

$36 \text{ cm}^2$ is two times greater than $18 \text{ cm}^2$ (18 × 2 = 36)

178. **42**

**Step 1**
Decide which formula to use.
The hexagon is a regular polygon because all the sides are the same length.
You should use the formula for a regular polygon $P = s \times n$.

**Step 2**
Apply the formula.
There are six sides, so $n = 6$. Each side is 7 m long, so $s = 7$.
$P = s \times n$
$\phantom{P} = 7 \times 6$
$\phantom{P} = 42$
Remember to include the unit when you write your answer.
The perimeter of the hexagon is 42 m.

179. **C**
**Step 1**
Calculate the length of the rectangle.
Since the width of the rectangle is 5 m, its length will be 10 (twice the width).
$2 \times 5 = 10$
**Step 2**
Decide which formula to use.
This is a rectangle, so you can use
$P = 2l + 2w$ or $P = 2(l + w)$.
Try $P = 2l + 2w$.
**Step 3**
Apply the formula.
The length of the rectangle is 10 m, and the width is 5 m.
$P = 2l + 2w$
$\phantom{P} = 2(10) + 2(5)$
$\phantom{P} = 20 + 10$
$\phantom{P} = 30$
Notice that $2(10)$ is another way to write $2 \times 10$.
Remember to include the unit when you write your answer.
The perimeter of the rectangle is 30 m.

180. **C**
**Step 1**
Decide which formula to use.
The triangle is an irregular polygon with three sides, so you will use the formula
$P = s_1 + s_2 + s_3$.

**Step 2**
Apply the formula.
$P = s_1 + s_2 + s_3$
$P = 5 + 6 + 7$
$P = 18$
Remember to include the unit when you write your answer.
The perimeter of the triangle is 18 cm.

181. **C**
**Step 1**
Decide which formula to use.
Since the garden is a square, the correct formula is $P = 4s$.
**Step 2**
Apply the formula.
$P = 4s$
$\phantom{P} = 4 \times 6$
$\phantom{P} = 24$
Remember to include the unit in the answer.
Tran and his sister need 24 m of fence.

182. **B**
To find the missing side length, use the formula
$$\frac{\text{area}}{\text{given side length}} = \frac{\text{unknown side}}{\text{length}}.$$
Substitute 144 m² for the area and 12 m for the given side length.
$$\frac{144 \text{ m}^2}{12 \text{ m}} = 12 \text{ m}$$
The width of Lindy's classroom is 12 m.

183. **11**
**Step 1**
Find the total length of the known sides.

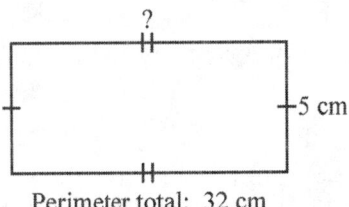

Perimeter total: 32 cm

One side is 5 cm long. This means the opposite side is also 5 cm. The total length of these two sides is 10 cm.
$5 + 5 = 10$ cm

### Step 2
Subtract the total length of the two known sides from the perimeter.
The perimeter is 32 cm.
32 − 10 = 22 cm

### Step 3
Divide 22 by 2 to find the length.
22 ÷ 2 = 11 cm

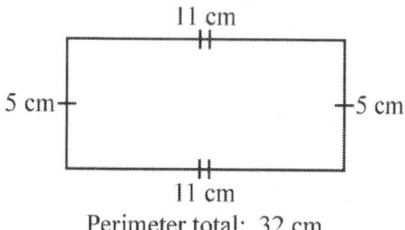
Perimeter total: 32 cm

The length of the rectangle is 11 cm.

### Step 4
To double-check that the answer is correct, add up all the sides of the rectangle. If the result is equal to the total perimeter (32 cm), it confirms the side measurements are correct.
perimeter = length + width + length + width
perimeter = 11 cm + 5 cm + 11 cm + 5 cm
perimeter = 32 cm
The side measurements are correct.

### 184. D

#### Step 1
Put the information in a frequency table.

| Number of Family Members | Number of Students |
|---|---|
| 2 | 3 |
| 3 | 1 |
| 4 | 5 |
| 5 | 4 |
| 6 | 0 |
| 7 | 2 |

#### Step 2
Draw a number line to show the number of family members.

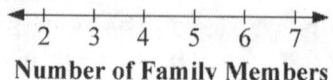
Number of Family Members

### Step 3
Put an X above each number to show how many students have that many people in their family.

- Three students have 2 family members. Draw 3 Xs above the 2.
- One student has 3 family members. Draw 1 X above the 3.
- Five students have 4 family members. Draw 5 Xs above the 4.
- Four students have 5 family members. Draw 4 Xs above the 5.
- Two students have 7 family members. Draw 2 Xs above the 7.

This line plot shows the data James collected.

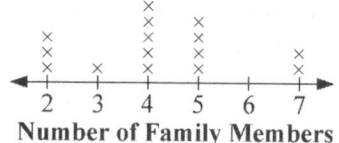
Number of Family Members

### 185. B
Look closely at where the eraser ends. It ends between the second and third whole inch tick, exactly at the $\frac{1}{2}$ inch mark. Armin's eraser is $2\frac{1}{2}$ in long.

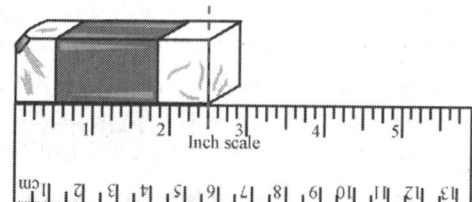

### 186. C
A conclusion that can be drawn from the data is that the numbers 4 and 6 were rolled the same number of times. Both these numbers have a frequency of 4. All the other given statements are false.

## 187. C

To determine the angle, you can count the little black ticks starting from 70.

The line on the protractor is 7 ticks from 70.
70 + 7 = 77

The angle on the protractor is 77°.

## 188.

**Step 1**
Draw a ray.

**Step 2**
Place the protractor on the ray so that the midpoint of the protractor lines up with the end of the ray.

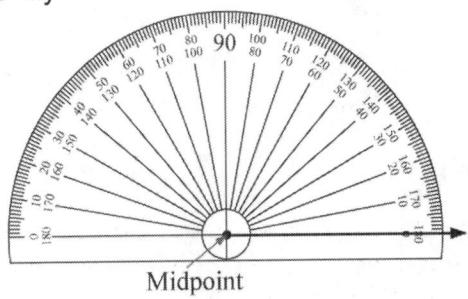

**Step 3**
Starting at 0°, count the number of degrees needed to construct the angle.

If the ray is pointing to the right, use the inside of the scale. If the ray is pointing to the left, use the outside scale. Always start measuring at 0°. The angle needs to be 145°, so stop at 145. Using your pencil, mark the point that shows 145°.

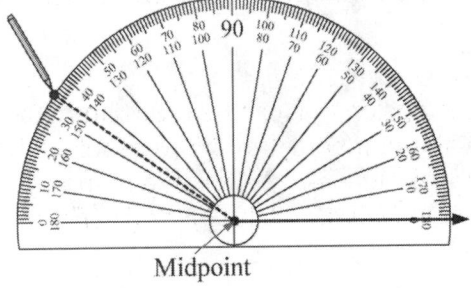

**Step 4**
Remove the protractor, and join the point that you marked and the endpoint of the ray that was drawn.

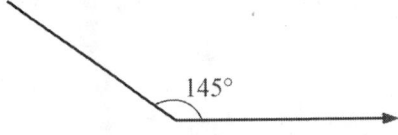

## 189. C

Choice C is correct. The measure is 80°.

The measure of half a right angle is 45°. The measure of a right angle is 90°.
The only given measure that is greater than 45° and less than 90° is 80°.

## 190. D

A 110° angle is bigger than 90° but smaller than 180°. That means it is bigger than a right angle but smaller than a straight angle.

Liliana's angle is the only angle that is bigger than a right angle but smaller than a straight angle.

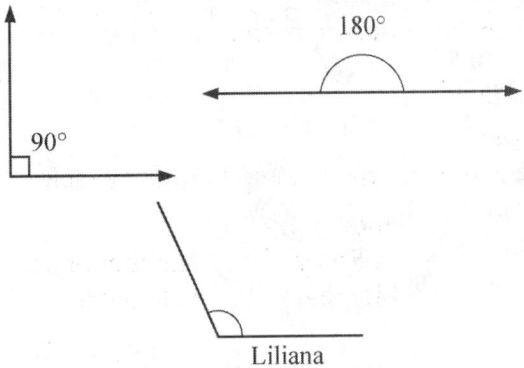

Edwin and Wes both drew angles that are smaller than right angles.

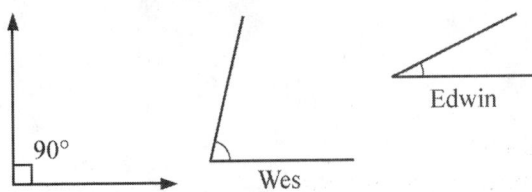

Abby's angle is bigger than a straight angle.

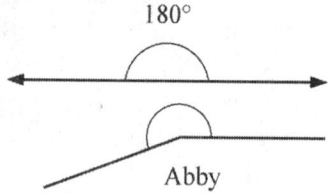

Liliana's angle is closest to 110°.

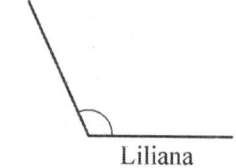

## 191. 70

Two angles on a straight line have a sum of 180°. Angles *ABD* and *ABC* make a straight line, so their sum is 180°.

The measure of ∠*ABD* is 110°, so ∠*ABC* is 180° − 110° = 70°.

## 192. A

There are 360° in a circle.

**Step 1**
Calculate the total of the known angles.
135 + 65 + 25 + 90 = 315°

**Step 2**
Subtract the total known angles from 360°.
360 − 315 = 45
The missing angle is 45°.

# Geometry

# GEOMETRY

## Table of Correlations

| Standard | | Concepts | Exercise #1 | Exercise #2 |
|---|---|---|---|---|
| **4.G** | Geometry | | | |
| 4.G.1 | Draw points, lines, line segments, rays, angles (right, acute, obtuse), and perpendicular and parallel lines. Identify these in two-dimensional figures. | Identifying Perpendicular Lines | 193 | 207 |
| | | Describing the Sides of a Two-Dimensional Shape | 195 | 208 |
| | | Identifying Intersecting Lines | 194 | 209 |
| | | Understanding Geometric Properties of Quadrilaterals | 195, 196, 197 | 210 |
| | | Identify Right Angles | 196 | 211 |
| | | Identifying Parallel Lines | 198 | 212 |
| | | Identifying Acute Angles | 199 | 213 |
| | | Identifying Obtuse Angles | 200 | 214 |
| | | Identifying Points, Line Segments, Lines, and Rays | 201 | 215 |
| 4.G.2 | Classify two-dimensional figures based on the presence or absence of parallel or perpendicular lines, or the presence or absence of angles of a specified size. Recognize right triangles as a category, and identify right triangles. | Relating Different Types of Quadrilaterals | 202 | 216 |
| | | Classifying Triangles According to Their Angles | 203 | 217 |
| | | Identifying Quadrilaterals | 204 | 218 |
| 4.G.3 | Recognize a line of symmetry for a two-dimensional figure as a line across the figure such that the figure can be folded along the line into matching parts. Identify line-symmetric figures and draw lines of symmetry. | Lines of Symmetry | 205 | 219 |
| | | Identifying Symmetrical Shapes | 206 | 220 |

*4.G.1* *Draw points, lines, line segments, rays, angles (right, acute, obtuse), and perpendicular and parallel lines. Identify these in two–dimensional figures.*

## IDENTIFYING PERPENDICULAR LINES

Perpendicular line segments are two segments in the same plane that intersect at 90° to form right angles. Right angles form square corners where the two rays meet at a vertex.

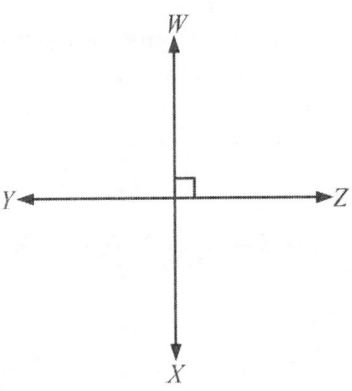

*Example*

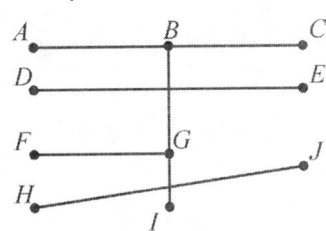

List the perpendicular line segments.

*Solution*

Perpendicular lines intersect at right angles (90°). Since line segment *BI* intersects line segments *AC*, *DE*, and *FG* at right angles, *BI* is perpendicular to *AC*, *DE*, and *FG*.

## DESCRIBING THE SIDES OF A TWO-DIMENSIONAL SHAPE

The sides of a two-dimensional (2-D) shape are called line segments. These sides, or line segments, can be described as horizontal, vertical, parallel, intersecting, or perpendicular.

# Horizontal Sides

The sides of a 2-D shape can be described as horizontal if they run straight across in a left-right manner.

*Example*

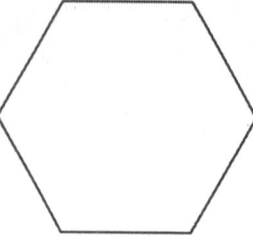

*A regular hexagon*

Determine how many horizontal sides a regular hexagon has, and verify your answer by placing an X on each horizontal side.

*Solution*

**Step 1**
Count the number of horizontal sides.
There are two horizontal sides in a regular hexagon.

**Step 2**
Verify your answer by placing an X on each horizontal side.
This hexagon shows the two horizontal sides marked with an X.

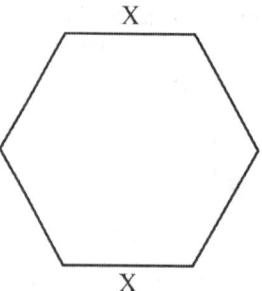

## VERTICAL SIDES

The sides of a 2-D shape can be described as vertical if they run straight up and down.

*Example*

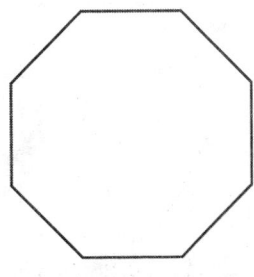

*A regular octagon*

Determine how many vertical sides a regular octagon has, and verify your answer by placing an X on each vertical side.

*Solution*

**Step 1**
Count the number of vertical sides.
There are two vertical sides in a regular octagon.

**Step 2**
Verify your answer by placing an X on each vertical side.
This octagon shows the two vertical sides marked with an X.

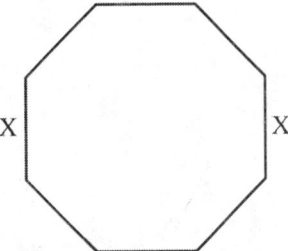

---

## PARALLEL SIDES

The sides of a 2-D shape can be described as parallel if they are opposite and exactly the same distance from each other. The sides may or may not be the same length.

*Example*
A regular hexagon is given.

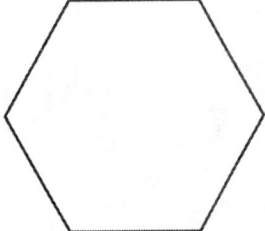

Determine how many pairs of parallel sides a regular hexagon has, and verify your answer by placing a different number of ticks on each pair of parallel sides.

Solution

**Step 1**

Count the number of pairs of parallel sides.
There are three pairs of parallel sides in a regular hexagon.

**Step 2**

Verify your answer by marking the pairs of sides.
Mark one pair of parallel sides with one tick, one pair of parallel sides with two ticks, and one pair of parallel sides with three ticks.
This hexagon shows the three pairs of parallel sides marked with ticks.

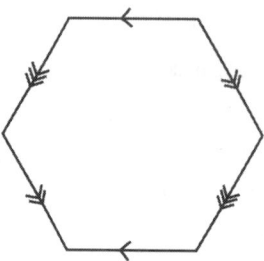

## INTERSECTING SIDES

The sides of a 2-D shape can be described as intersecting if they meet at a vertex.

Example
   Triangle ABC is given.

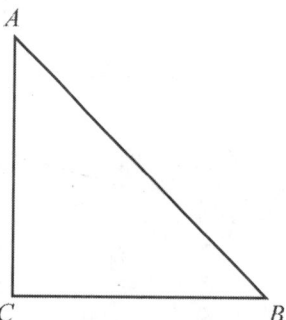

Determine how many pairs of intersecting sides triangle ABC has, and explain your answer by naming each pair of intersecting sides and its vertex.

Solution

**Step 1**

Determine how many pairs of intersecting sides there are in a triangle.
There are three pairs of intersecting sides.

**Step 2**

Describe the three pairs of intersecting sides.
Sides CA and AB intersect at vertex A, sides AB and BC intersect at vertex B, and sides BC and CA intersect at vertex C.

## PERPENDICULAR SIDES

The sides of a 2-D shape can be described as perpendicular if a horizontal side and a vertical side intersect to form a square corner, which is a 90° angle.

*Example*

A trapezoid is given.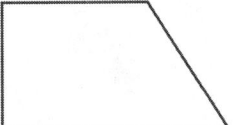

Determine how many pairs of perpendicular sides the given trapezoid has, and verify your answer by drawing square corners where the perpendicular sides meet.

*Solution*

**Step 1**
Determine how many pairs of perpendicular sides there are.
There are two pairs of perpendicular sides.
The top horizontal side and the left vertical side meet at a square corner, and the bottom horizontal side and the left vertical side meet at a square corner.

**Step 2**
Verify your answer by drawing squares where the perpendicular sides meet.
This trapezoid shows the square corners where the two pairs of perpendicular sides meet.

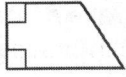

---

## IDENTIFYING INTERSECTING LINES

Intersecting lines are lines that cross each other and have exactly one point in common. The point where they cross is called the point of **intersection**.

*Example*

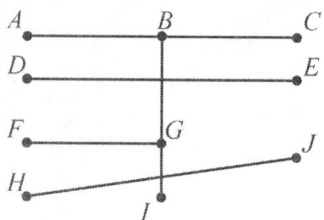

A group of line segments is shown.
List the intersecting line segments.

*Solution*

Intersecting lines are lines that cross each other and have exactly one point in common.

- Line segments *AC* and *BI* intersect.
- Line segments *DE* and *BI* intersect.
- Line segments *FG* and *BI* intersect.
- Line segments *HJ* and *BI* intersect.

## UNDERSTANDING GEOMETRIC PROPERTIES OF QUADRILATERALS

A **quadrilateral** is a special kind of polygon. They are closed shapes with four sides. Examples of regular quadrilaterals include **rectangles**, **squares**, **parallelograms**, **rhombuses**, and **trapezoids**.

Quadrilaterals can be defined by the following attributes:

- Number of parallel sides
- Number of equal-length sides
- Number of right angles
- Number of equal angles

## NUMBER OF PARALLEL SIDES

Quadrilaterals may have parallel sides.
For example, a rectangle has two sets of parallel sides.

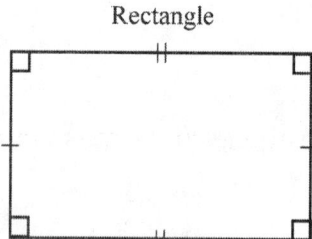

Rectangle

Other quadrilaterals may not have any parallel sides.
For example, the given quadrilateral does not have any parallel sides.

## NUMBER OF EQUAL-LENGTH SIDES

Quadrilaterals may have equal side lengths.

This rhombus has all four sides that are the same length.

Rhombus

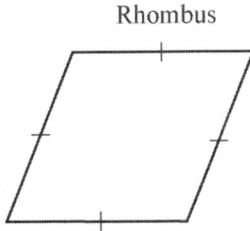

Quadrilaterals may not have equal side lengths

This quadrilateral does not have any sides that are equal.

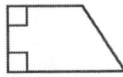

## NUMBER OF RIGHT ANGLES

A right angle is an angle that forms a square, like the corner of a book. It looks like this:

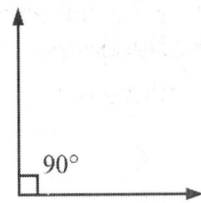

Different quadrilaterals have different numbers of right angles. For example, a square has four right angles.

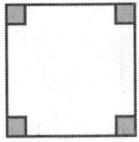

## NUMBER OF EQUAL ANGLES

Some quadrilaterals have angles that are equal. In the rhombus shown, you can see that the opposite angles are equal.

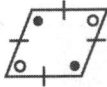

It is important to understand these properties because you can use them to describe quadrilaterals.

*Example*

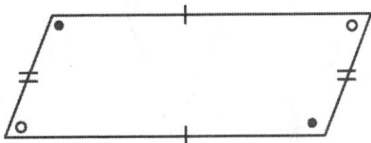

Describe the **geometric properties** of the quadrilateral.

*Solution*

**Step 1**
Describe the number of parallel sides.
This quadrilateral has two sets of parallel sides.

**Step 2**
Describe the equal side lengths.
This quadrilateral has opposite sides with the same lengths.

**Step 3**
Describe the number of right angles.
This quadrilateral does not have any right angles.

**Step 4**
Describe the number of equal angles.
This quadrilateral has opposite equal angles.

---

# IDENTIFY RIGHT ANGLES

An angle that forms a square corner, like the corner on a sheet of paper, is called a **right angle**.

Think about a square or a rectangle. All of the corners in a square and a rectangle are right angles. The right angles are shaded in the given diagrams to help you see how they make square corners.

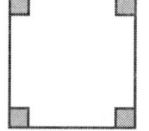

All of these objects have angles that are equal to right angles.

*Example*
Marc bent a pipe cleaner to make an angle.

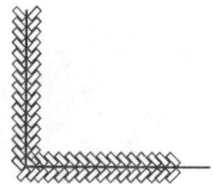

What kind of angle did Marc make?

*Solution*

The two sides of the angle meet at the *vertex* to form a square corner. This is a **right angle**.

Marc made a right angle.

## IDENTIFYING PARALLEL LINES

Parallel line segments are always the same distance away from each other. They never cross or intersect. The arrows along each of the lines indicate the lines are parallel.

*Example*

Carmen drew designs on four boxes.

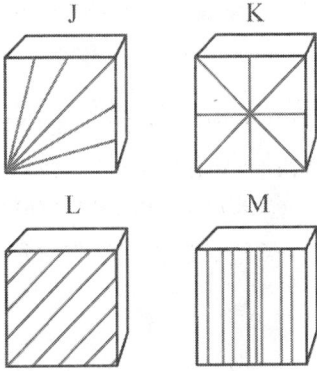

Which boxes are decorated with parallel lines?

*Solution*

Parallel lines are lines that are the same distance apart from each other at all points. Parallel line segments do not need to be the same length.

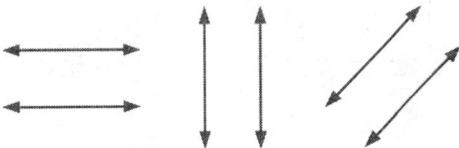

Boxes L and M are decorated with parallel lines. Box L is decorated with diagonal parallel lines. Box M is decorated with vertical parallel lines.

## IDENTIFYING ACUTE ANGLES

An acute angle has a measure that is greater than 0° and less than 90°. Acute angles are smaller than right angles.

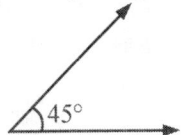

*Example*

Kendra draws the given angle.

Identify the given angle.

*Solution*

Compare the size of Kendra's angle with the benchmark angle of 90°, which forms a square corner at which the two rays meet.

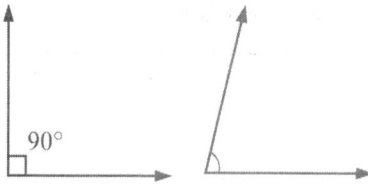

Since the given angle is less than 90°, it is an acute angle.

## IDENTIFYING OBTUSE ANGLES

An obtuse angle has a measure that is greater than 90° and less than 180°. Obtuse angles are larger than right angles and smaller than straight angles.

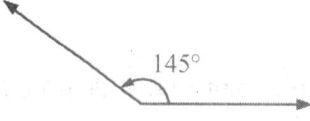

*Example*

A teacher draws the given angle on the board.

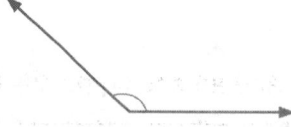

Identify this angle.

*Solution*

Compare the size of the given angle to the benchmark angles of 90° and 180°.

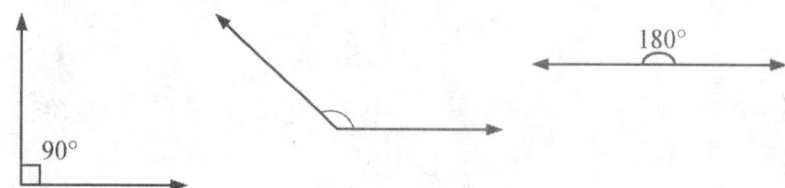

Since the given angle is more than 90° and less than 180°, it is an obtuse angle.

## IDENTIFYING POINTS, LINE SEGMENTS, LINES, AND RAYS

To identify points, line segments, lines, and rays, it is important to understand what each term means.

### POINTS

A point is a position in space.

D

C

Points can also be found in line segments. Points are usually named with a capital letter. For example, A, B, and C are points on this line segment.

*Example*

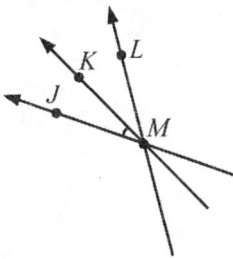

Identify the point that all the lines intersect at.

*Solution*

The point where the lines intersect is the point where all three of the lines cross each other. The name of the point where the lines cross is *M*.

### LINE SEGMENTS

A line segment has both a starting point and an ending point. This line segment is labeled as *AB*.

*Example*

Carrie draws this figure. She uses red, blue, and purple to color in the different parts of the figure.

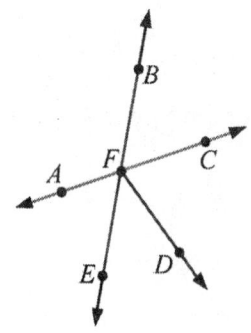

Which color shows a line segment?

*Solution*

A line segment has a starting point and an ending point. These points are labeled with capital letters.

The blue part is not a line segment because it continues forever in both directions. It is a line.

The purple part is not a line segment because it continues forever in one direction. It is a ray.

The line segment is the red part. It is called $\overline{BE}$ (line segment *BE*).

---

## LINES

A line has no beginning or end. It can be extended forever. It is straight with no turns or bends. A line contains all the points along it. A line is identified by arrows on either side to show that it continues in both directions.

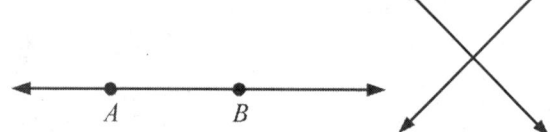

*Example*

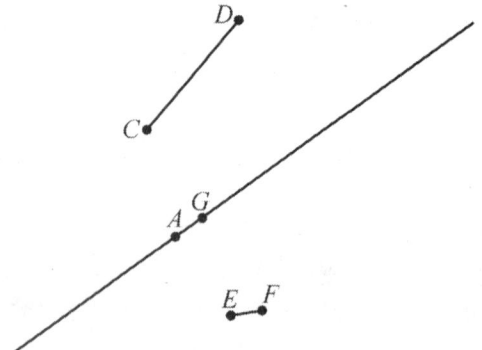

Identify the line in the given image.

*Solution*

A line has no beginning or end. It can be extended forever. In the given diagram, the line passes through points *A* and *G*.

A line segment has both a starting point and an ending point. In the given diagram, *EF* and *CD* are line segments.

---

## RAYS

A ray is a line with a starting point but no ending point. The arrowhead shows the direction in which the ray extends or continues.

When naming a ray, name it by the letter of its starting point and the letter it passes through. The names of these two rays are $\overrightarrow{IJ}$ and $\overrightarrow{FK}$.

*Example*

Identify the given image as a point, line, ray, or line segment.

*Solution*

A ray is a line with a starting point but no ending point. An arrowhead points in the direction that the ray will continue. The given image shows $\overrightarrow{AB}$.

---

4.G.2  *Classify two–dimensional figures based on the presence or absence of parallel or perpendicular lines, or the presence or absence of angles of a specified size. Recognize right triangles as a category, and identify right triangles.*

## RELATING DIFFERENT TYPES OF QUADRILATERALS

Quadrilaterals are closed four-sided figures. Some examples of regular quadrilaterals are parallelograms, rectangles, rhombuses, squares, and trapezoids.

You can compare quadrilaterals by describing the kinds of sides and angles they have. For example, a rectangle and a square both have four right angles.

A **parallelogram** has two sets of parallel lines. The opposite sides of a parallelogram are parallel. A regular parallelogram like the one shown has two angles greater than right angles and two angles less than right angles.

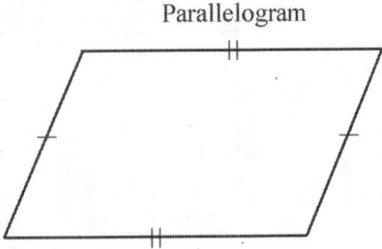

Parallelogram

A **rectangle** is a kind of parallelogram because it also has two sets of parallel lines that are opposite each other. A rectangle is different from a parallelogram because it has four right angles.

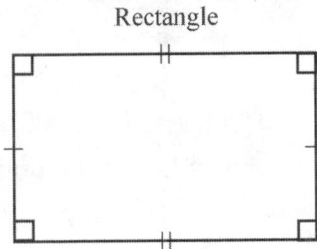

Rectangle

A **rhombus** is also a kind of parallelogram because it has two sets of parallel lines that are opposite each other. Also, it has two angles greater than right angles and two angles less than right angles. A rhombus has four sides of equal lengths. That makes it different from a regular parallelogram and a rectangle.

Rhombus

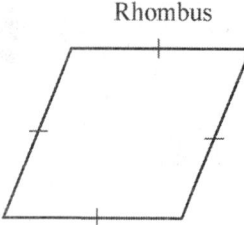

A **square** is a kind of parallelogram because it also has two sets of parallel sides that are opposite each other. A square is also a kind of rectangle because it has four right angles. It is also like a rhombus because it has four sides of equal lengths.

Square

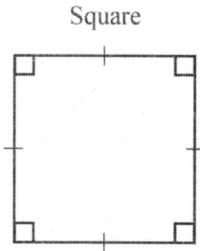

A **trapezoid** is different from any of the other shapes because it only has one set of parallel sides. It is like a parallelogram and a rhombus because it has two greater than right angles and two less than right angles.

Trapezoid

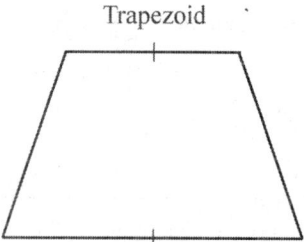

## CLASSIFYING TRIANGLES ACCORDING TO THEIR ANGLES

Angles are used to name and classify triangles. To classify triangles according to the measurement of their angles, you need to remember the definitions for acute, right, and obtuse angles.

- An acute angle measures less than 90°.
- A right angle measures exactly 90°.
- An obtuse angle measures greater than 90° but less than 180°.

Remember that if added together, the three angles that make up a triangle will equal 180°.

An **acute triangle** (acute-angled triangle) has three acute angles. Each angle must have a measure of less than 90 degrees. Following is an example of an acute triangle.

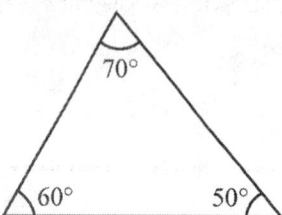

Geometry

An **equilateral triangle** is a special kind of acute triangle. An equilateral triangle is a triangle with three acute angles that are all equal.

Each angle in an equilateral triangle measures 60°. Following is an example of an equilateral triangle.

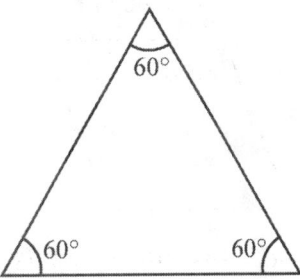

A **right triangle** (right-angled triangle) has one right angle. The right angle must have a measure of exactly 90 degrees (making a square corner). Following are two examples of right triangles.

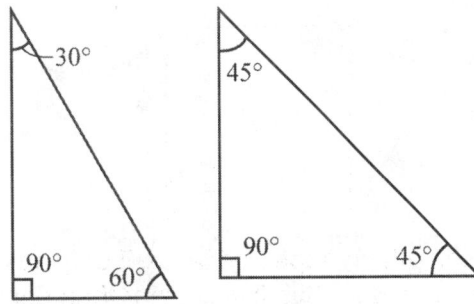

An **obtuse triangle** (obtuse-angled triangle) has one obtuse angle. The obtuse angle must be greater than 90° but less than 180°. Following is an example of an obtuse triangle.

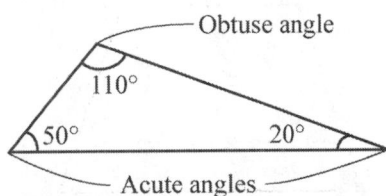

*Example*
   Which of the following triangles is an acute triangle?

*Solution*

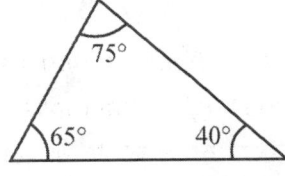

   This triangle is an acute triangle because each angle has a measure that is less than 90°.
   75° < 90°
   65° < 90°
   40° < 90°

# IDENTIFYING QUADRILATERALS

Quadrilaterals are a special kind of polygon. They are closed shapes with four sides. Examples of quadrilaterals include rectangles, squares, parallelograms, rhombuses, and trapezoids.

All quadrilaterals can be described based on these features:

- Number of parallel sides
- Number of equal-length sides
- Number of right angles
- Number of equal angles

A trapezoid only has one pair of parallel sides. Some trapezoids may have two right angles, but at least two of the angles are not right angles. Some trapezoids may also have two pairs of equal angles. This trapezoid does not have any right angles.

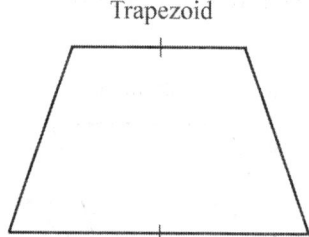
Trapezoid

A parallelogram has two pairs of sides that are opposite each other. They are parallel and the same length. The angles in the opposite corners of a parallelogram are always equal.

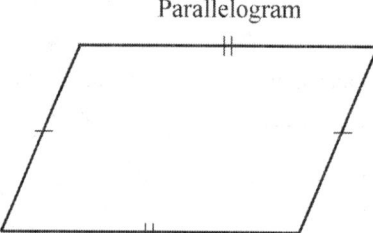
Parallelogram

A rectangle is a special parallelogram. It has two pairs of sides that are opposite each other. They are parallel and the same length. A rectangle is special because the angles in all four corners are equal. Each corner has a right angle, so a rectangle has four right angles.

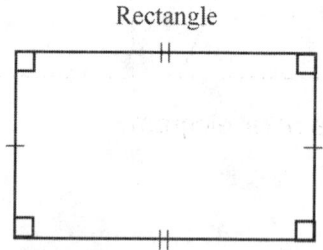
Rectangle

Geometry

A square is a special rectangle. It has two pairs of sides that are opposite each other. These sides are parallel and the same length. A square also four right angles. A square is different from a rectangle because all four sides of a square are the same length.

Square

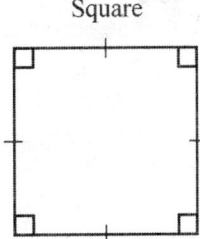

A rhombus is like a parallelogram, rectangle, and square. It has two pairs of sides that are opposite each other. They are parallel. Like a square, all four sides of a rhombus are equal in length. Like a parallelogram, angles in the opposite corners are always equal. The angles in a rhombus are not right angles.

Rhombus

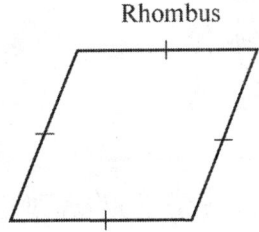

*Example*
Kyle draws four quadrilaterals.

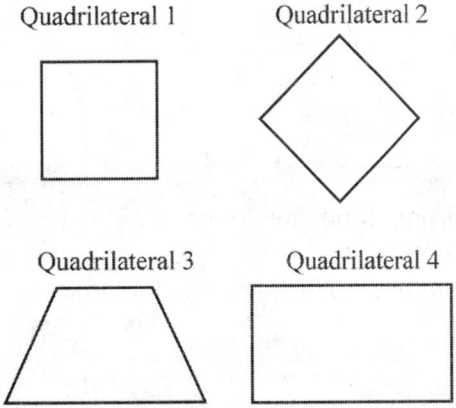

Which of Kyle's quadrilaterals is **not** a parallelogram?

*Solution*
**Step 1**
Think about the features of parallelograms.
A parallelogram has two pairs of sides that are opposite each other. They are parallel and the same length. The opposite angles in a parallelogram are always equal.

**Step 2**

Identify the features of each quadrilateral Kyle drew. Find the one that does not have the same features as the parallelogram.

Start with Quadrilateral 1. The opposite sides are equal. The opposite sides are also parallel and the same length. The opposite angles are equal. Quadrilateral 1 is a parallelogram.

Look at Quadrilateral 2. The opposite sides are equal, parallel, and the same length. The opposite angles are equal. Quadrilateral 2 is also a parallelogram.

Look at Quadrilateral 3. The two of the opposite sides are not equal. Two of the opposite sides are not parallel. Quadrilateral 3 cannot be a parallelogram.

Check Quadrilateral 4. The opposite sides are equal, parallel, and the same length. The opposite angles are equal. Quadrilateral 4 is parallelogram.

Quadrilateral 3 is not a parallelogram.

---

*4.G.3*  *Recognize a line of symmetry for a two-dimensional figure as a line across the figure such that the figure can be folded along the line into matching parts. Identify line–symmetric figures and draw lines of symmetry.*

## LINES OF SYMMETRY

A two-dimensional shape is symmetrical when half of the shape looks exactly like the other half.

When a shape is folded in half along a **line of symmetry**, both sides are exactly the same. You can think of a line of symmetry as a fold line.

*Example*

Shapes can be made symmetrical by horizontal, vertical, or diagonal lines of symmetry. These diagrams show symmetrical shapes by using these different lines.

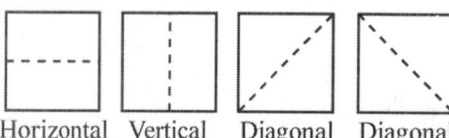

---

Some shapes do not have a line of symmetry. Some shapes have only one line of symmetry, and other shapes have more than one line of symmetry.

The following two-dimensional shapes are sorted according to the number of lines of symmetry they each have.

These shapes have no lines of symmetry.

These shapes have one line of symmetry.

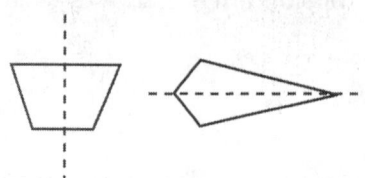

These shapes have two lines of symmetry.

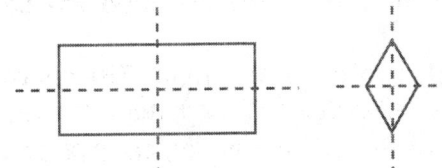

These shapes have more than two lines of symmetry.

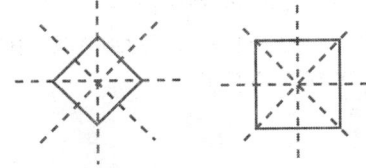

*Example*

How many lines of symmetry does a square have? _____

*Solution*

A square has 4 lines of symmetry:
One is vertical (line 1).
One is horizontal (line 3).
Two are diagonal (lines 2 and 4).

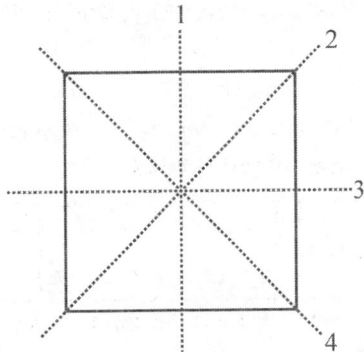

## IDENTIFYING SYMMETRICAL SHAPES

A two-dimensional shape is **symmetrical** when half the shape looks exactly like the other half. One way to know if a shape is symmetrical is to fold it in half. If the edges match exactly, the shape is symmetrical.

*Example*

This heart is symmetrical because both halves are the same when the shape is folded.

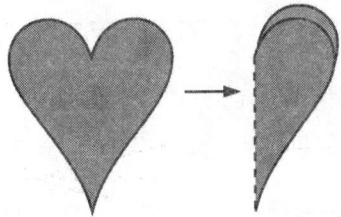

The place where the heart is folded makes a line. This line is called a **line of symmetry**. The part on one side of the line of symmetry is exactly the same size and shape as the part on the other side.

*This heart has one line of symmetry.*

*Example*

Eduardo draws these six shapes in his notebook.

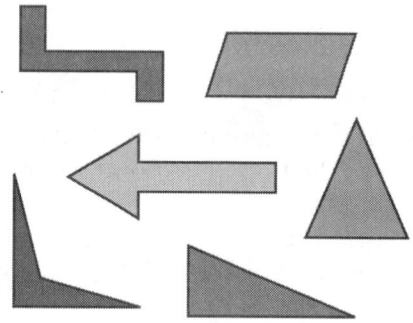

Sort the shapes according to whether they are symmetrical or not symmetrical.

*Solution*

**Step 1**

Decide which shapes are symmetrical.

The triangle has a vertical line of symmetry, so the triangle is symmetrical.

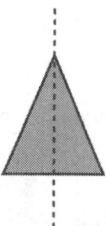

The arrow has a horizontal line of symmetry, so the arrow is symmetrical.

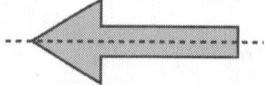

This airplane shape has a diagonal line of symmetry, so the airplane shape is symmetrical.

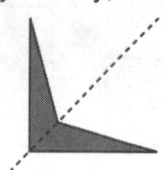

## Step 2
Decide which shapes are not symmetrical.

There is no way to fold the triangle so that the two halves are the same shape and size. This means the triangle is not symmetrical.

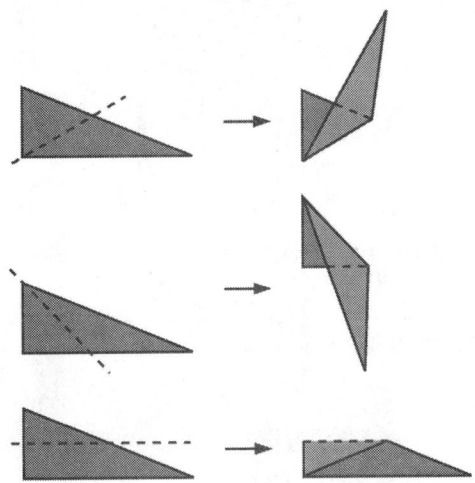

It is possible to fold the zigzag shape and the parallelogram so the two halves are the same shape and size. However, the edges do not line up. This means that the two shapes are not symmetrical.

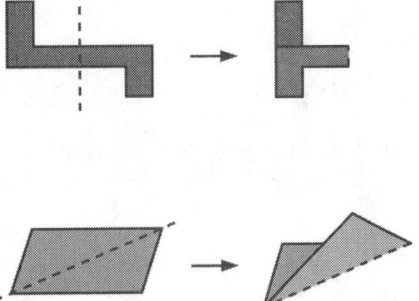

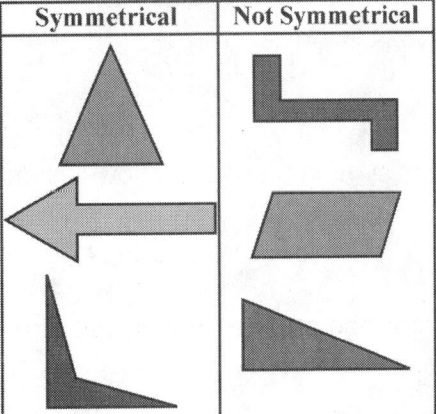

## Step 3
Sort the shapes.

This picture shows the shapes sorted correctly.

| Symmetrical | Not Symmetrical |
|---|---|
| triangle, arrow, boot shape | zigzag, parallelogram, right triangle |

# EXERCISE #1—GEOMETRY

*Use the following information to answer the next question.*

Two lines are shown.

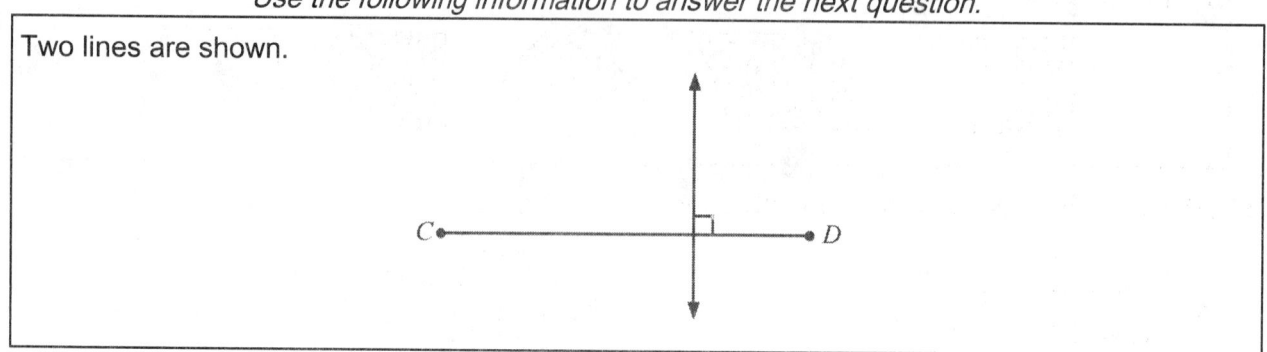

193. These lines are called
    A. vertical lines
    B. parallel lines
    C. horizontal lines
    D. perpendicular lines

*Use the following information to answer the next question.*

Jamal looks at four different kinds of fences.

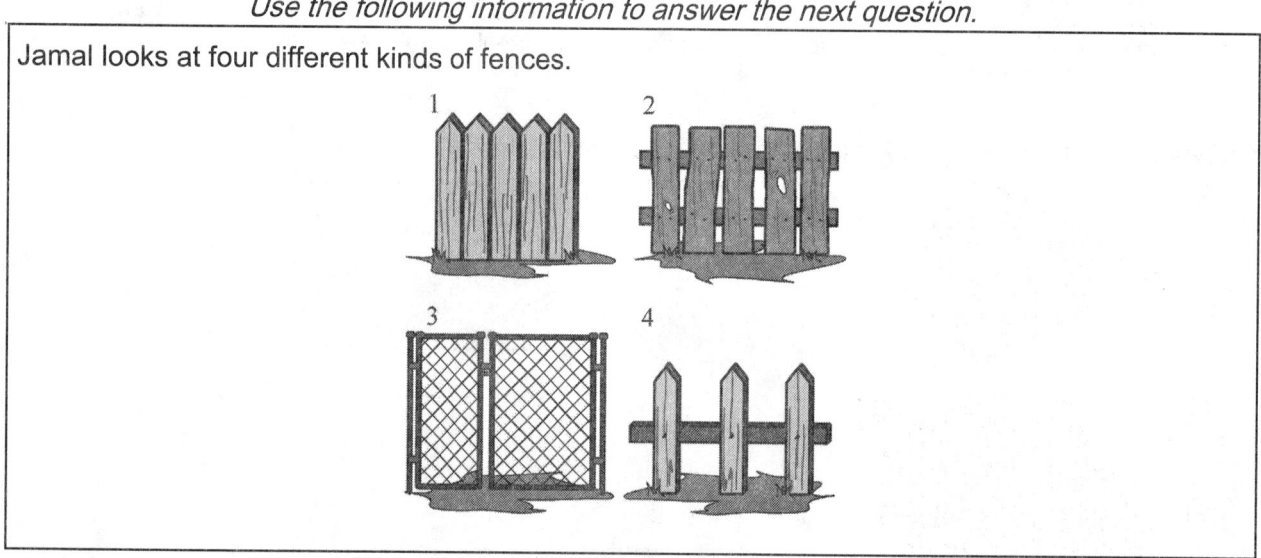

194. Which fence does **not** have intersecting lines?
    A. Fence 1
    B. Fence 2
    C. Fence 3
    D. Fence 4

*Use the following information to answer the next question.*

Jared has a set of quadrilaterals. He wants to sort them based on whether they have two pairs of parallel sides or not.

  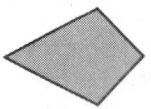  

195. Which of the following tables correctly sorts Jared's shapes?

A.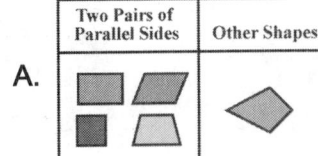

B.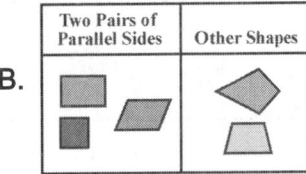

C.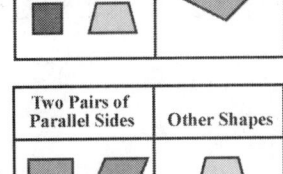

D.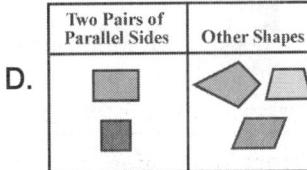

196. Which of the following shapes has exactly one right angle?

A.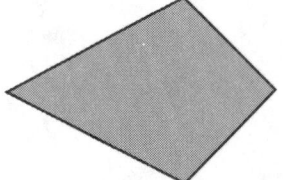

B.

C.

D.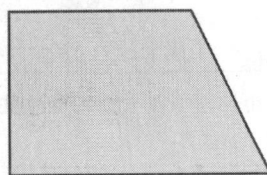

197. Which of the following shapes has exactly one pair of sides that are equal in length?

A.

B.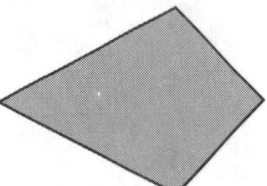

C.

D.

*Use the following information to answer the next question.*

Ben draws some lines.

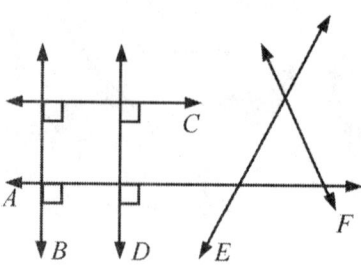

198. Which line is parallel to line *D*?
   A. Line *E*
   B. Line *A*
   C. Line *F*
   D. Line *B*

199. Which of the following angles is an acute angle?

A.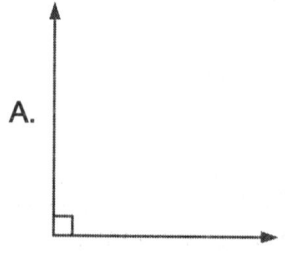

B.

C.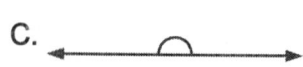

D.

*Use the following information to answer the next question.*

Harry used a protractor to draw these angles.

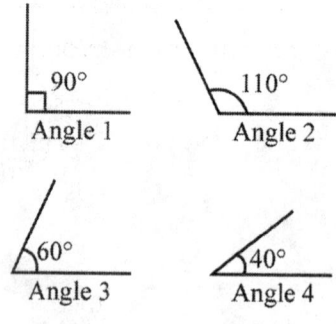

200. Which of the angles that Harry drew is an obtuse angle?
   A. Angle 1
   B. Angle 2
   C. Angle 3
   D. Angle 4

*Use the following information to answer the next question.*

A figure is shown.

201. Which of the following pairs of letters can be used to identify a line segment but **not** a ray or a line?
    A. BA
    B. BC
    C. EF
    D. FD

202. Which of the following statements about squares and rectangles is **true**?
    A. Squares and rectangles are trapezoids.
    B. Squares and rectangles are parallelograms.
    C. Squares have fewer right angles than rectangles.
    D. Squares have more parallel edges than rectangles.

*Use the following information to answer the next question.*

These triangles belong to the same group because they all share a common characteristic.

203. Which of the following triangles belongs to the same group as the given triangles?

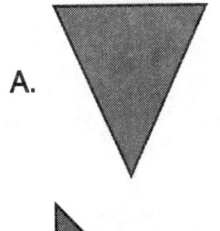
A.

B.

C.

D.

204. Which of the following quadrilaterals has four sides of equal length and no right angles?
    A. square
    B. rhombus
    C. rectangle
    D. trapezoid

205. Which of the following figures has correctly marked lines of symmetry?

    A.
    B.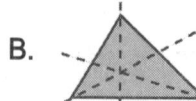
    C.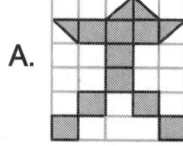
    D.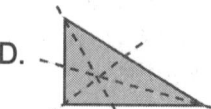

206. Which of the following diagrams has a symmetrical shape?

    A.
    B.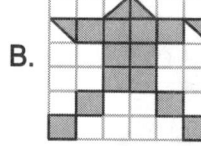
    C.
    D.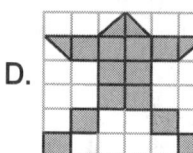

# EXERCISE #1—GEOMETRY ANSWERS AND SOLUTIONS

| 193. D | 197. C | 201. B | 205. A |
| 194. A | 198. D | 202. B | 206. D |
| 195. B | 199. B | 203. D | |
| 196. A | 200. B | 204. B | |

**193. D**

When lines cross at a right angle, they are perpendicular. The two lines shown form a right angle where they cross. This means the lines are perpendicular.

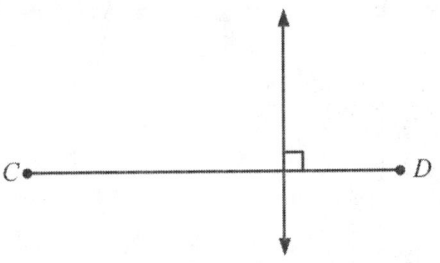

**194. A**

Intersecting lines are lines that cross at a common point. Fence 1 is the only fence without intersecting lines. All of the other fences show lines that have a common point. The lines in fence 2 and fence 4 intersect at 90°, which means they form perpendicular lines.

**195. B**

Step 1
Count the pairs of parallel sides on each shape. The square, the parallelogram, and the rectangle each have two pairs of parallel sides.

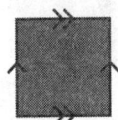  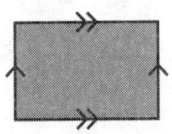

The trapezoid has only one pair of parallel sides.

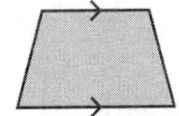

The kite does not have any parallel sides.

Step 2
Sort the shapes.

Shapes that have two pairs of parallel sides go in the first column. Those shapes are the square, the rectangle, and the parallelogram. Shapes that do not have two pairs of parallel sides go in the second column. Those shapes are the kite and the trapezoid.

| Two Pairs of Parallel Sides | Other Shapes |
|---|---|
| | |

**196. A**

Count the right angles on each of the shapes.

The kite has one right angle.

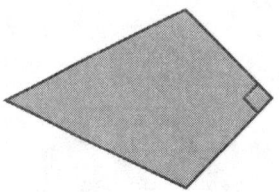

The rectangle has four right angles.

The parallelogram does not have any right angles.

The trapezoid has two right angles.

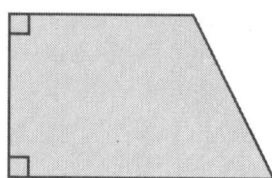

The only shape that has exactly one right angle is the kite.

### 197. C

Count the equal sides on each shape.

The rectangle, kite, and parallelogram all have two pairs of sides with equal lengths.

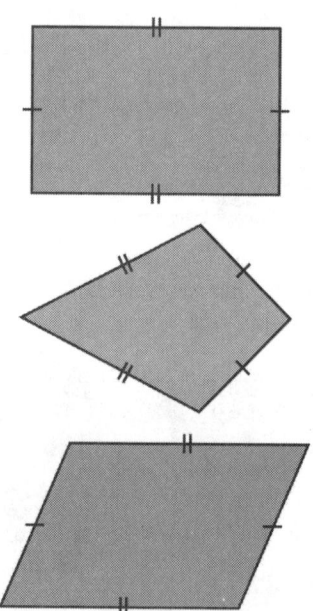

The trapezoid is the only shape that has one pair of sides with equal lengths.

### 198. D

Parallel lines are lines that run side by side. They never touch one another, and they are an equal distance apart.

Line *B* is parallel to line *D*. They never touch and are an equal distance apart.

Lines *A* and *C* form a right angle with line *D*. They are perpendicular lines. Lines *E* and *F* intersect with line *D*.

### 199. B

The measure of an acute angle is greater than 0° and less than 90°. Acute angles are smaller than right angles.

### 200. B

An obtuse angle is an angle that has a measure that is greater than 90° (a right angle) and less than a 180° angle (a straight line).
Angle 2 has a measure of 110°, which is *greater* than 90° and *less* than 180°.
90° < 110° < 180°

Angle 2 is an obtuse angle.

### 201. B

A line segment has a starting point and an ending point that are a set distance apart. These points are labeled with capital letters. A line segment does not extend forever. It does not curve or create an angle.

The letter pair *BA* can be used to identify a line segment that goes from point *B* to point *A*. It can also be used to identify a ray that starts at point *B* and continues past point *A*.

The letter pair *FD* can be used to identify a line segment that goes from point *F* to point *D*. It can also be used to identify a ray that starts at point *F* and continues past point *D*.

The letter pair *BC* can be used to identify a line segment that goes from point *B* to point *C*.

The letter pair *EF* is not a line segment, ray, or line because the points are not joined.

Line segment *BC* is formed by points *B* and *C*.

## 202. B

The relationships among the different types of quadrilaterals are shown in the given tree diagram.

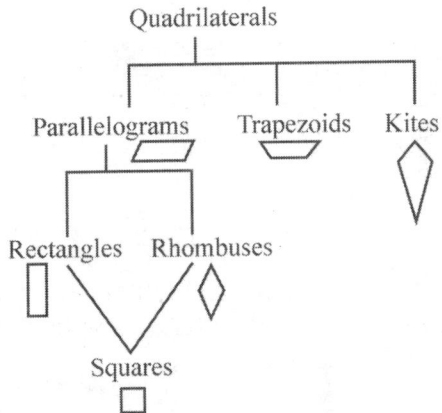

A rectangle is a parallelogram that has two pairs of parallel sides and four right angles.

A square is a parallelogram that also has two pairs of parallel sides and four right angles, but all four sides of a square are congruent.

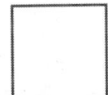

## 203. D

Determine the characteristic that makes the three given triangles belong to one group.

Since each of the three triangles has an obtuse angle (greater than 90° and less than 180°), the three triangles are all obtuse triangles.

To belong to the same group as the three given triangles, the triangle you select must also have an obtuse angle.

This triangle is an obtuse triangle and belongs to the same group as the given triangles.

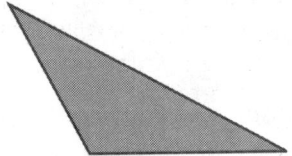

## 204. B

**Step 1**
Consider the characteristics of each given shape.

- A square has four sides of equal length and four right angles.
- A rhombus has four sides of equal length and no right angles.
- A rectangle has two sets of sides with equal side lengths and four right angles.
- A trapezoid may have one set of sides that are equal in length and may have one or two right angles, or no right angles.

**Step 2**
Identify the shape that matches the given characteristics.

A rhombus has four sides of equal length and has no right angles.

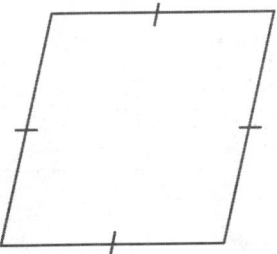

## 205. A

An object is symmetrical when one half of the object is a mirror image of the other half. A line of symmetry divides the object into two symmetrical halves.

The equilateral triangle has correctly marked lines of symmetry that divide the object into symmetrical halves.

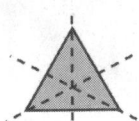

**206.** D

Diagram D has a symmetrical shape. If someone drew a vertical line right down the middle of the diagram, the two halves would be exactly the same size and shape.

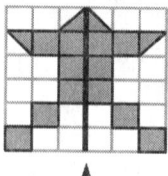

Line of symmetry

# EXERCISE #2—GEOMETRY

*Use the following information to answer the next question.*

A street map is shown.

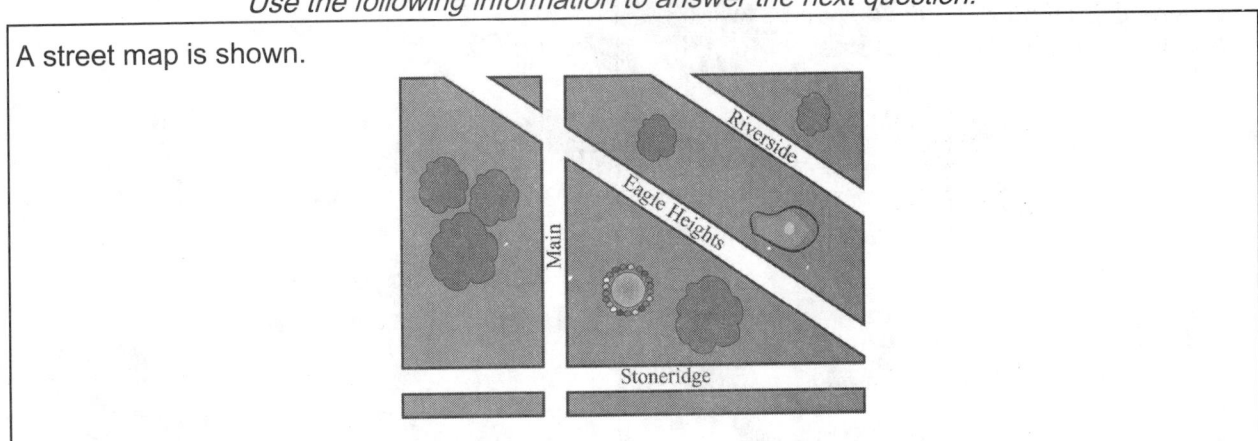

207. Which streets are perpendicular to each other?
   A. Main and Riverside
   B. Stoneridge and Main
   C. Riverside and Eagle Heights
   D. Eagle Heights and Stoneridge

*Use the following information to answer the next question.*

The teacher showed the class these four two-dimensional shapes.

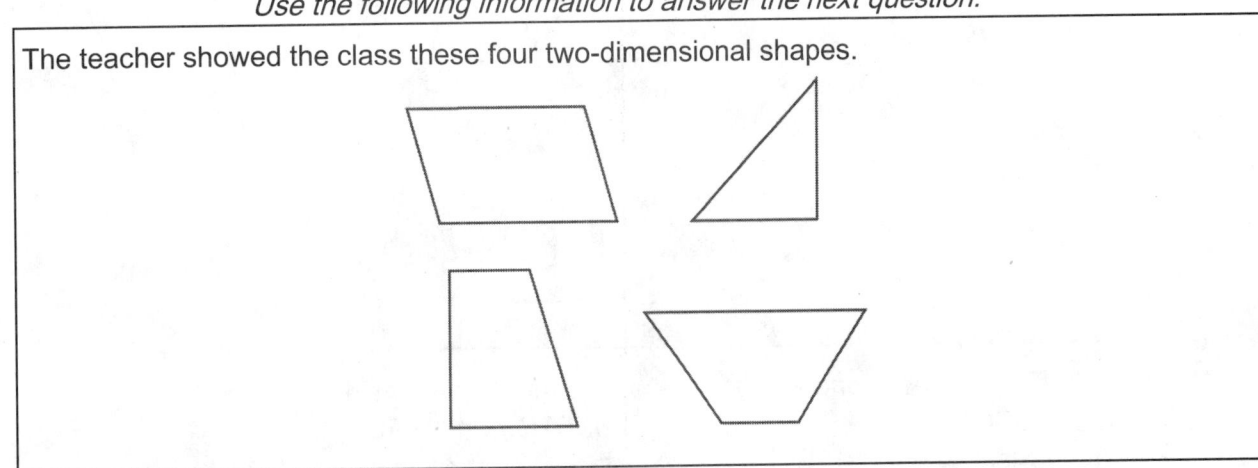

208. In the given shapes, how many pairs of perpendicular sides are there? _____

209. Which of the following letters of the alphabet contains a pair of intersecting lines?
   A. U
   B. X
   C. S
   D. C

*Use the following information to answer the next question.*

A quadrilateral is given.

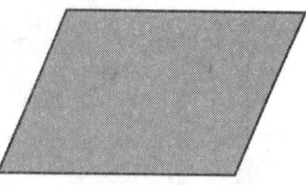

210. How many equal angles are there on the given quadrilateral?
    A. Zero equal angles
    B. Four equal angles
    C. One pair of equal angles
    D. Two pairs of equal angles

*Use the following information to answer the next question.*

A carpenter's square has a right angle.

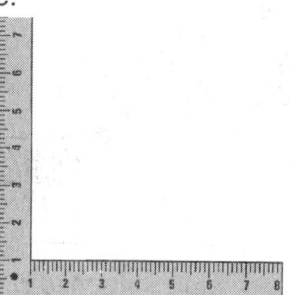

Four traffic signs are shown.

211. Which two traffic signs have angles that are equal to the carpenter's right angle?
    A. YIELD and STOP
    B. STOP and WALK
    C. YIELD and NO PARKING
    D. NO PARKING and WALK

212. Which of the following statements about parallel lines is **not** true?
    A. Parallel lines never intersect.
    B. The distance between parallel lines is constant.
    C. Parallel lines intersect each other at right angles.
    D. The two sides of a ruler represent parallel line segments.

*Use the following information to answer the next question.*

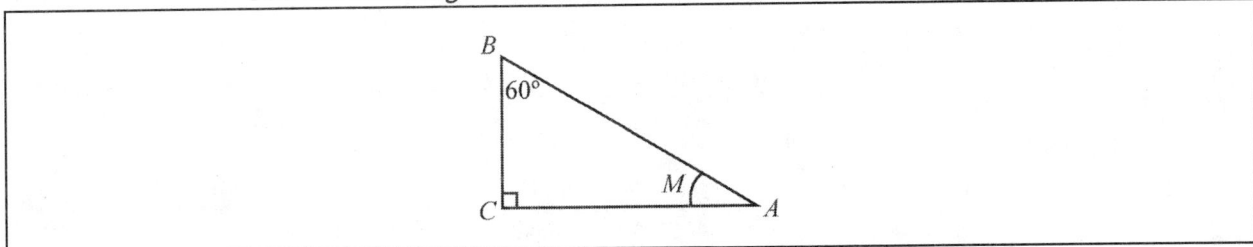

213. What type of angle is angle *M*?
   A. Straight angle
   B. Obtuse angle
   C. Acute angle
   D. Right angle

*Use the following information to answer the next question.*

214. As shown in the diagram, what type of angle is formed where the shaft of the hockey stick meets the blade?
   A. Right angle
   B. Acute angle
   C. Reflex angle
   D. Obtuse angle

*Use the following information to answer the next question.*

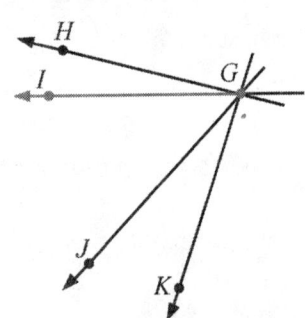

Gena draws some rays. She highlights one of the rays.

215. What is the name of the highlighted ray?
   A. $\overrightarrow{IH}$
   B. $\overrightarrow{GJ}$
   C. $\overrightarrow{GI}$
   D. $\overrightarrow{IG}$

Use the following information to answer the next question.

Kyle draws some quadrilaterals.

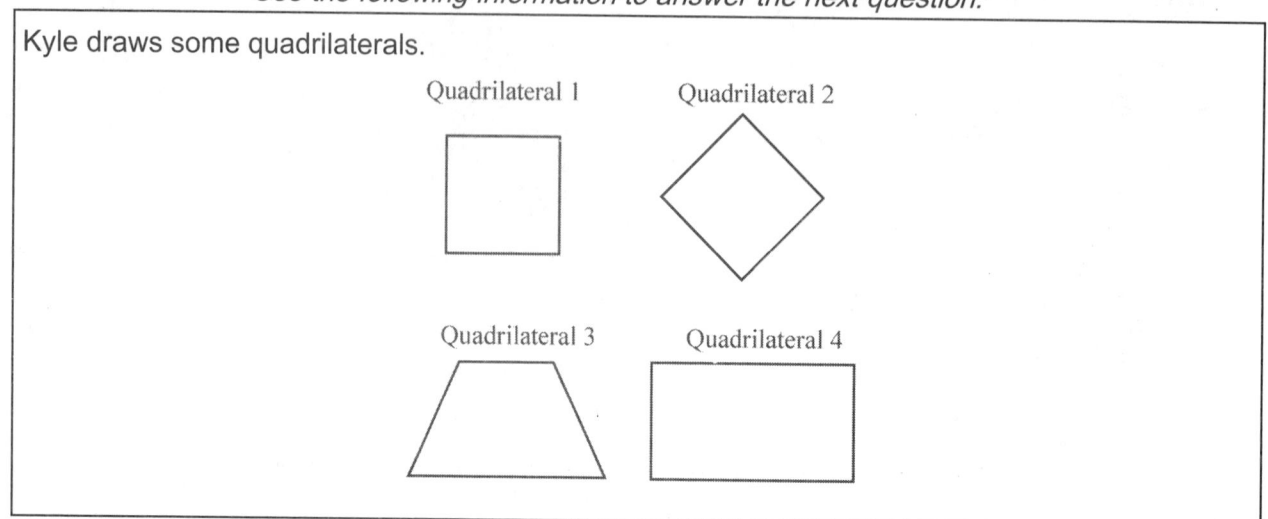

216. Which of Kyle's quadrilaterals is **not** a parallelogram?

Explain your answer using geometric words.

Use the following information to answer the next question.

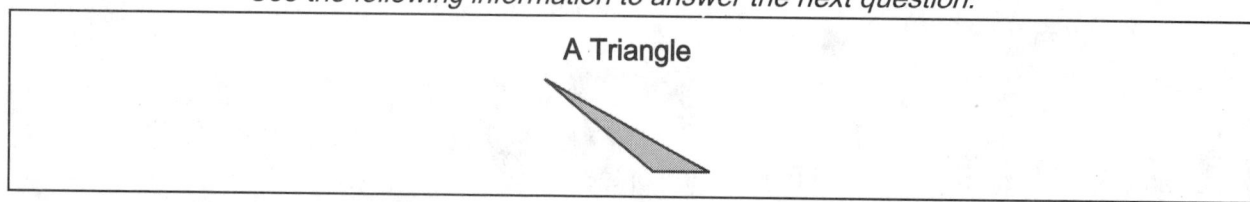

A Triangle

217. The given triangle is classified as
    A. a right triangle
    B. an acute triangle
    C. an obtuse triangle
    D. an equilateral triangle

218. Which of the following types of quadrilaterals both have opposite parallel sides and angles that measure 90°?
    A. Square and rhombus
    B. Square and rectangle
    C. Rhombus and trapezoid
    D. Parallelogram and trapezoid

219. Which of the following pictures shows a line of symmetry?

A.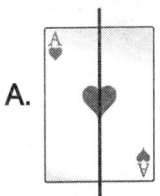

B.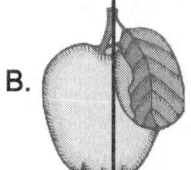

C.

D.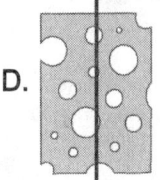

*Use the following information to answer the next question.*

On a school field trip, Sharon sees four similar paintings at an art gallery.

220. Which of the following paintings has a symmetrical shape?

A.

B.

C.

D.

# EXERCISE #2—GEOMETRY ANSWERS AND SOLUTIONS

| 207. B | 211. D | 215. C | 219. C |
| 208. 3 | 212. C | 216. See solution | 220. C |
| 209. B | 213. C | 217. C | |
| 210. D | 214. D | 218. B | |

**207. B**

Two lines that cross to form a right angle are called perpendicular lines. You can draw a perfect square in the corner where the lines meet.

Using the given street map, find which streets are perpendicular to each other.

The only two streets that form a right angle at their point of intersection are Stoneridge and Main.

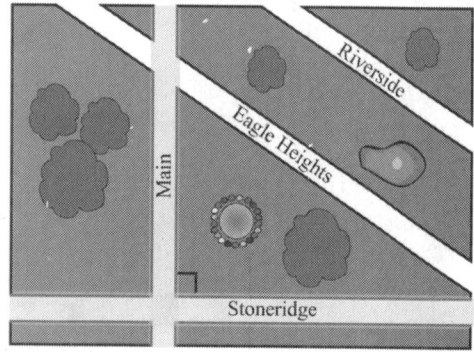

**208. 3**

**Step 1**
Determine the number of pairs of perpendicular sides.
There are 3 pairs of perpendicular sides in the given two-dimensional shapes.

**Step 2**
Verify your answer by marking the pairs of perpendicular sides.
The 3 pairs of perpendicular sides are correctly marked on the shapes.

**209. B**

Intersecting lines are lines that cross each other at a common point. The letter X is the only letter that contains a pair of intersecting lines.

**210. D**

The quadrilateral is a parallelogram.
Its opposite angles are equal.

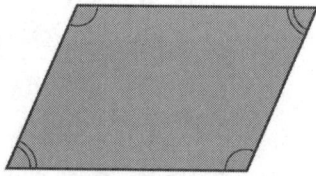

This means that a quadrilateral has two pairs of equal angles.

**211. D**

The yield sign has angles that are smaller than the carpenter's right angle. The stop sign has angles that are bigger than the carpenter's right angle. The parking sign has four angles that are the same as the carpenter's right angle.
The walk sign also has four angles that are the same as the carpenter's right angle.

The two signs that have angles equal to the carpenter's right angle are the no parking sign and the walk sign.

## 212. C

Parallel lines never intersect so the statement in alternative C is not true.

## 213. C

An acute angle has a measure that is greater than 0° and less than 90°. Acute angles are smaller than right angles.

Angle $M$ is smaller than 90°, so it is an acute angle.

## 214. D

An obtuse angle is greater than 90° (which forms a square corner) and less than 180° (which forms a straight line).

An obtuse angle is formed where the shaft of the hockey stick meets the blade.

## 215. C

To name the ray, start with the beginning point and the letter it passes through.

The highlighted ray starts at point $G$ and goes through point $I$. The name of the highlighted ray is $\vec{GI}$.

## 216.

| Points | Rationale |
|---|---|
| 4 | Applies knowledge of quadrilaterals, giving a complete and effective explanation. |
|  | **Sample Answer:** Parallelograms have two sets of opposite sides that are parallel. Quadrilateral 3 has one set of parallel sides (top and bottom), but the left and right sides are not parallel. That is why it is not a parallelogram. |
| 3 | Applies knowledge of quadrilaterals but may give an incomplete explanation. |
|  | **Sample Answer:** Number 3 is not a parallelogram because it has slanted lines that are not parallel. |
| 2 | Applies some knowledge of quadrilaterals, but may give a limited or partly incorrect explanation. |
|  | **Sample Answer:** Shape 3 is not because it does not have square corners like the others. |
| 1 | Applies some knowledge of quadrilaterals, but may not give an explanation. |
|  | **Sample Answer:** 3 |

## 217. C

**Step 1**
Classify the angles in the given triangle.
The triangle contains two angles that are less than 90° and one angle that is greater than 90°. Angles less than 90° are classified as acute angles. Angles greater than 90° are classified as obtuse angles.

**Step 2**
Classify the triangle according to its angles.
A triangle with one obtuse angle is classified as an obtuse triangle.

## 218. B

A square is a type of quadrilateral in which all four sides are equal, opposite sides are parallel, and all angles measure 90°.

A rectangle is a type of quadrilateral in which the opposite sides are equal and parallel and all the angles measure 90°.

**219. C**

An object is symmetrical when one half is a mirror image of the other half.

The snowflake is symmetrical because each half is exactly the same as the other half.

**220. C**

This painting has a symmetrical shape.

If you drew a vertical line right down the middle of the painting, the two halves would be exactly the same size and shape.

# NOTES

# NOTES

# NOTES

NOTES

# NOTES

# SOLARO Study Guides
## Ordering Information

Every SOLARO Study Guide unpacks the curriculum standards and provides an overview of all curriculum concepts, practice questions with full solutions, and assignment questions for students to fully test their knowledge.

Visit www.solaro.com/orders to buy books and learn how SOLARO can offer you an even more complete studying solution.

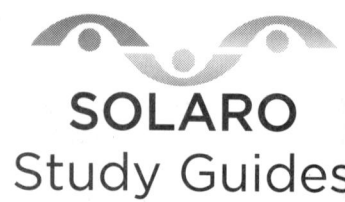

SOLARO Study Guide—$29.95 each plus applicable sales tax

| SOLARO Common Core State Standard Titles ||
|---|---|
| Mathematics 3 | Algebra I |
| Mathematics 4 | Algebra II |
| Mathematics 5 | Geometry |
| Mathematics 6 | English Language Arts 3 |
| Mathematics 7 | English Language Arts 4 |
| Accelerated Mathematics 7 (Int.) | English Language Arts 5 |
| Accelerated Mathematics 7 (Trad.) | English Language Arts 6 |
| Mathematics 8 | English Language Arts 7 |
| Accelerated Mathematics I | English Language Arts 8 |
| Mathematics I | English Language Arts 9 |
| Mathematics II | English Language Arts 10 |
| Mathematics III | English Language Arts 11 |
| Accelerated Algebra I | English Language Arts 12 |

**To order books, please visit**
www.solaro.com/orders

Volume pricing is available. Contact us at orderbooks@solaro.com